THE
NATURAL HISTORY
OF THE
POINT REYES
PENINSULA

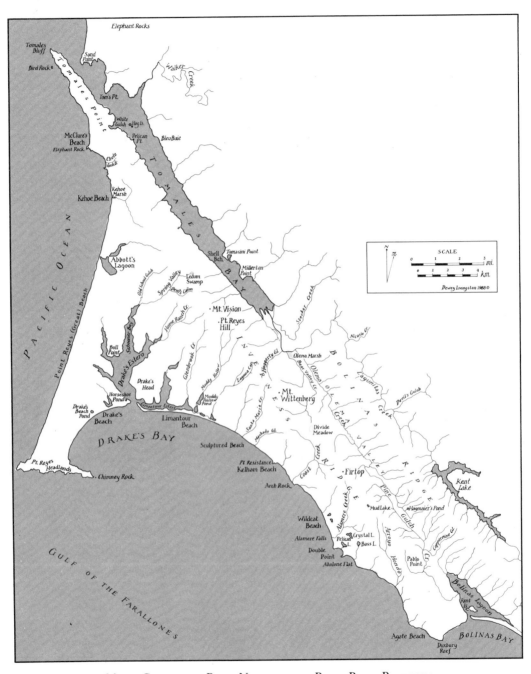

Elephant Rocks

Tomales Bluff

Bird Rock

Sand Point

Tomales Point

Tom's Pt.

White Gulch

Hog Is.

Pelican Pt.

McClure's Beach

Elephant Rock

Chole Gulch

BleuBaie

Walker Creek

Kehoe Marsh

Kehoe Beach

PACIFIC OCEAN

Point Reyes (Great) Beach

Abbott's Lagoon

Shell Bch.

Tomasini Point

Millerton Point

TOMALES BAY

Old School Gulch

Spring Valley

Ledum Swamp

Devil's Cañon

Mt. Vision

Pt. Reyes Hill

Home Ranch Cr.

Bull Point

Schooner Bay

Glenbrook Cr.

Muddy Hollow

Laguna Cañon

Haggerty Gl.

Bear Valley Cr.

Olema Marsh

RIVER

Nicasio Cr.

BOLINAS

Lagunitas Creek

Devil's Gulch

Drake's Head

Drake's Estero

Horseshoe Pond

Muddy Hollow Pond

Mt. Wittenberg

Santa Maria Cr.

OLEMA VALLEY

Drake's Beach Pond

Limantour Estero

Drake's Beach

Limantour Beach

Sculptured Beach

Machado Gl.

Divide Meadow

RIDGE

Firtop

PINE GULCH

RIDGE

Kent Lake

Pt. Reyes Headlands

Chimney Rock

DRAKE'S BAY

Pt. Resistance

Kelham Beach

Arch Rock

Coast Creek

Alamere Creek

Mud Lake

Hagmaier's Pond

Arroyo

Peppermint Cr.

Wildcat Beach

Alamere Falls

Pelican

Crystal L.

Bass L.

Double Point

Abalone Flat

Hondo

Pablo Point

Bolinas Lagoon

Kent

GULF OF THE FARALLONES

Agate Beach

Duxbury Reef

BOLINAS BAY

MAP 1. GEOGRAPHIC PLACE NAMES OF THE POINT REYES PENINSULA

THE
NATURAL HISTORY
OF THE
POINT REYES
PENINSULA

Jules G. Evens

Revised Edition

Illustrations by Keith Hansen, Laurie Fry and Rose Lewis
Maps by Dewey Livingston
Photographs by Marty Knapp

POINT REYES
NATIONAL SEASHORE ASSOCIATION

Cover photograph by Tupper Ansel Blake
Back cover photograph by Dewitt Jones
Maps and cross-sections by Dewey Livingston
Illustrations for chapter openings by Keith Hansen
Illustrations (except Chapter 3) by Laurie Fry
Illustrations for Chapter 3 (Plant Communities) by Rose Lewis
Photographs, except where noted below, by Marty Knapp
Photographs on pages 33, 37, 149, 159 courtesy of the Point Reyes National Seashore; photographs on pages 114, 117 (both), 121 and 172 (both) courtesy of the Point Reyes Bird Observatory.

Editing and Production Coordination by Nancy Adess
Book and Cover Design by Robert Cooney
Text set in Janson by Michael Sykes/Archetype West

Printed in the United States of America

Library of Congress Catalog Card Number: 92-084085
ISBN: 0-911235-05-1

This book is dedicated to those who went before —
the California Condor, the California Grizzly, the Coast Miwok —
and to those who will follow — our children.

And to the memory of my father, Jules Georges Evens, Jr.

ACKNOWLEDGMENTS

For sharing their knowledge and love of all things wild, and for their friendship and encouragement, I would like to thank William Armstrong, Tupper Blake, Bill Clow, Coyote, Dick Erickson, Michael Ellis, Meryl Evens, Laurie Fry, Keith Hansen, Ginnie Havel, Phil Henderson, Stuart Johnston, Bill Manolis, Lynn McCullough, Nancy Fiske Milne, John Milne, Al Molina, John Muir, Bonnie and Woody Nackley, Jack Nisbet, Gary Page, Michael Prokop, Armando Quintero, Ane Rovetta, Dave Shuford, Rich Stallcup, Lynne Stenzel, Bob Stewart, Walt Whitman, Jon Winter, and David Wimpfheimer.

The revision of this Second Edition was improved greatly thanks to constructive criticism and additional information generously provided by John Dell Osso, Michael Ellis, Gary Fellers, John Finger, Laurie Fry, John Kelly, Wendy Patterson, Richard Plant, Don Neubacher, Terry Sawyer, Bill Shook, Rich Stallcup, and Sylvia Thalman.

For critical review of the earlier drafts and help and encouragement in writing and editing, without whose help this book would have been less accurate and less interesting, thanks to Michael Ellis, Gary Fellers, Jim Locke, Don Neubacher, Dave Pugh, Rose Lewis, Dixie Pierson, Dave Shuford, and Rich Stallcup.

I am indebted to the staff and associates of the Point Reyes Bird Observatory. Their ongoing research, and the field work of a multitude of unnamed volunteers over the last two decades, encompasses an invaluable body of work that served as the background material for much of the text. Especially helpful were the papers, articles, reports, and journal entries by Dave Ainley, Sarah Allen, Bob Boekelheide, Harry Carter, Dave DeSante, Geoff Geupel, Phil Henderson, Burr Heneman, Harriet Huber, Stephanie Kaza, Ron LeValley, Steve Morrell, Gary Page, Susan Peaslee, Peter Pyle, Dave Shuford, and Lynne Stenzel.

The production of this book required a prodigious group effort. For their expertise and enthusiasm a special thanks to Nancy Adess (editing), Tupper Blake (cover photography), Robert Cooney (layout and graphic design), Meryl Evens (logistical support), Laurie Fry (artwork), Keith Hansen (artwork), Marty Knapp (photography), Rose Lewis (artwork), Rosalyn Miller (research), Michael Sykes (typesetting), and Dewey Livingston (mapmaking and graphics).

Access to record and specimen collections was generously provided by Barbara Stein (Museum of Vertebrate Zoology, University of California at Berkeley) and Stephen F. Bailey and Mary Marcussen (California Academy of Sciences). Ms. Marcussen further provided extensive notes on the Academy archives that were invaluable.

This book would never have been published but for the faith and the budgetary and logistical support of Don Neubacher and the Board of Directors of the Point Reyes National Seashore Association (formerly Coastal Parks Association).

Finally, I am eternally grateful to Veery and Noah Evens for their innocent spirits and bright eyes.

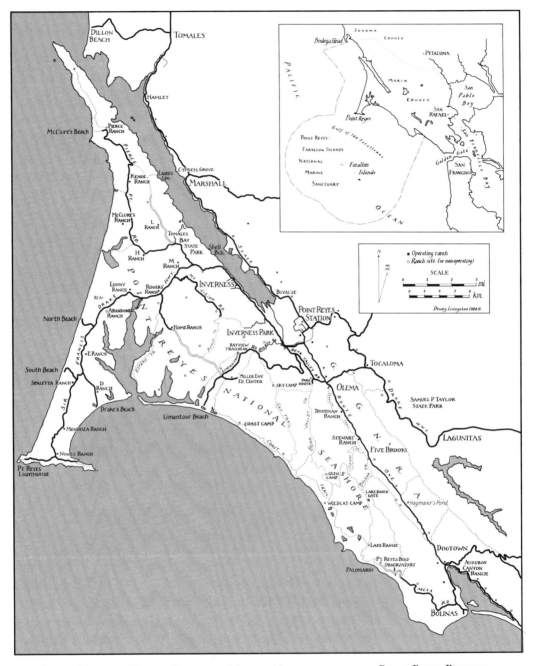

MAP 2. NAMES OF TOWNS, ROADS AND HUMAN HABITATIONS ON THE POINT REYES PENINSULA

CONTENTS

ILLUSTRATIONS

Maps

Figures

Tables

PROLOGUE

> But on the sea side of Marin is the different story; there, attached to Marin but not simply part of it, is the rival peninsula, Point Reyes . . . the coyote head, alert, breathing, listening, and facing out onto the open sea.
>
> — Arthur Quinn. *Broken Shore.* 1981.

IN THE PROLOGUE TO his lucid account of the history of the Marin Peninsula, Arthur Quinn imagines the profile of Point Reyes as the head of an alert coyote — Tomales Point a perked ear, Great Beach the forehead, Abbott's Lagoon the eye, the headlands a snout, and Drake's Estero a panting mouth. Mr. Quinn also provides a cautionary note: "If one looks too closely, he sees nothing at all, or rather all that is wrong." It is in the spirit of this warning that I have approached the natural history of Punta de los Reyes ("The Point of the Kings"), as the Spanish explorer Vizcaino baptized Point Reyes in 1603. Like a coyote, the peninsula's history is wily, and it eludes too close a look. Time, tectonics, rising and falling oceans, and an incomplete record have conspired to hide many of the origins and affinities of this peninsula, and therein lies its mystery and much of its interest.

This book is an overview of the peninsula, an attempt to explore and define its character and its haunting appeal. The natural diversity encompassed within the 100-or-so square miles of Point Reyes is vast, so I have been necessarily selective. Elk and oak, whales and ospreys, are paid more attention than mosses and mushrooms, spiders, or monarch butterflies. This is due partly to my own prejudices, partly to the limits of our knowledge, and partly to the space constraints of such a book, not to the relative importance of those neglected species.

Because of its status as a National Seashore, and thanks to its natural beauty and diversity, Point Reyes has attracted the attention of scientists, naturalists, artists, writers, and hikers alike. As a result, a substantial body of literature pertaining to the peninsula now exists in various journals, monographs, research papers, newsletters, popular magazines, and government reports. I have attempted here to distill much of that information and weave history, science, and anecdote into a coherent story and an accurate record.

*   *   *

One of the problems of considering any geographic area as a separate, self-contained province is that, as John Muir said, "everything is hitched to everything else." Compared with most places, however, the boundaries of Point Reyes are quite clear. From an altitude of 60,000 feet, through the lens of a high-altitude reconnaissance camera, Point Reyes appears distinct: a geologic "island in time," separated by time and tectonics from the North American continent. The San Andreas Fault — a massive fissure along the Pacific Rim that curves onto shore at the peninsula's southern terminus (Bolinas Lagoon), then returns to sea at its northern tip (Tomales Point) — cleaves Point Reyes from the adjoining mainland. The seemingly pastoral and tranquil Olema Valley forms a temporary suture over the powerful rift zone the fault defines. As I write and as you read these words, that geologic potential is rending Point Reyes from the rest of the continent with inexorable force.

The area discussed in this book is defined by these geographic landmarks. The San Andreas Fault provides a convenient and dramatic boundary to the east, the landward flank. Tomales Bay and Bolinas Lagoon, each bisected by the fault, are included in their entirety. On the ocean side, I include the Gulf of the Farallones, which extends from the peninsula's shoreline west to the edge of the continental shelf approximately 20 miles offshore. These waters encompass the Farallon Islands, the Cordell Banks (a submerged granitic seamount), and several shoals and submarine canyons.

The problem of connectedness, of everything being "hitched to everything else," presents itself again if we consider the evolution of the peninsula. Through the geologic processes that formed the granitic bedrock of Point Reyes, the peninsula shares a common lineage with the Monterey peninsula, and perhaps with the southern Sierra Nevada. Prior to the last glacial retreat, the coniferous forests of Inverness Ridge were continuous with the boreal woodlands of Canada; today, though isolated from one another, these forests share affinities. Though explorations of such relationships take us beyond the boundaries of the peninsula, they enrich the story, lending it continuity and texture, and I often follow the thread of these relationships. But, lest the narrative unravel, I always attempt to bring the focus back to Point Reyes, for it is the main subject of the story.

*   *   *

The peninsula's singular character and the images that contribute to it — a fog-veiled ridge, a windsculpted bishop pine, the headlands laced with phacelia and lizard tail — are the inspiration for this book. What is the source of this singularity? Certainly, geology is the underlying cause. For example, the presence of over 60 species of plants on Point Reyes that are not found elsewhere in Marin County is attributed to the different geologic histories of the two areas. Other factors also exert strong influences. The geographic position of Point Reyes at latitude 38°N. places it in a temperate climate zone, where the moist coniferous forests of the north overlap with the dry brush lands of the south. The peninsula's proximity to the Pacific Ocean moderates the climate, and the three major oceanic current systems influence the reliable periodicity of the seasons. The dovetailing of these influences creates a unique environment and accounts for the impressive diversity of life that is celebrated in the following pages.

Most natural histories focus on the present, describing the landscape and cataloging the species that inhabit it. In this book I pay close attention to the word "history," and attempt to reconstruct the landscape as it was in former times, to describe the evolution of the landscape, to sketch the character of the habitat, and to compare what is here now with what was here before. Through this perspective, the current environment manifests its history: the influences and impacts of the plants and animals of the past have shaped the present.

Landscapes of the past are invoked — salmon-swollen creeks, elk herds on the hills, canyons echoing with the cries of cougars — not because I believe they may possibly reappear, but because conjuring them into our imaginations as we wander the hills and the seashore enlivens the present landscape with the shadows of our ancestors.

I only went out for a walk, and finally concluded to stay out
till sundown, for going out, I found was really going in.
—John Muir. Unpublished Journals. 1900.

At first there is no discrimination in the eye, nothing but the land itself, whole and impenetrable. But then smallest things begin to stand out of the depths — herds and rivers and groves — and each of these has perfect being in terms of distance and of silence and of age. Yes, I thought, now I see the earth as it really is; never again will I see things as I saw them yesterday or the day before.
—N. Scott Momaday. The Way to Rainy Mountain. 1969.

We need to keep some of our vanishing shoreline an unspoiled place, where all men, a few at a time, can discover what really belongs there — can find their own Island in Time.
—Harold Gilliam. Island in Time. 1962.

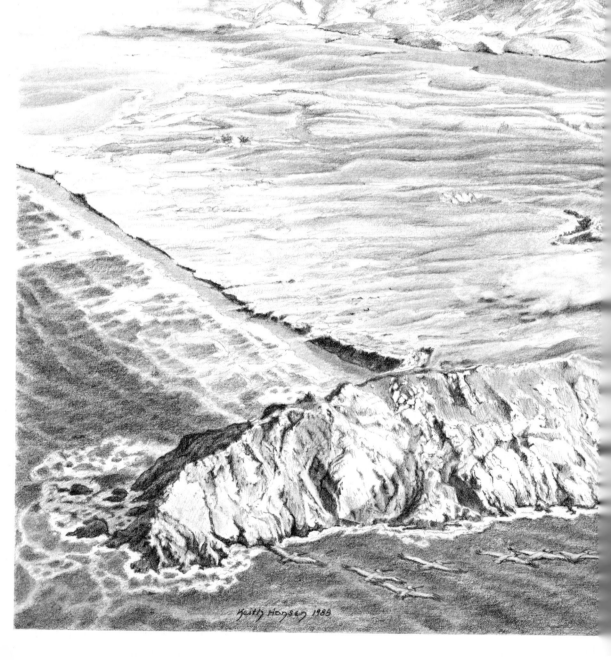

CHAPTER ONE

THE CYCLE
OF THE SEASONS

Keith Hansen 1988

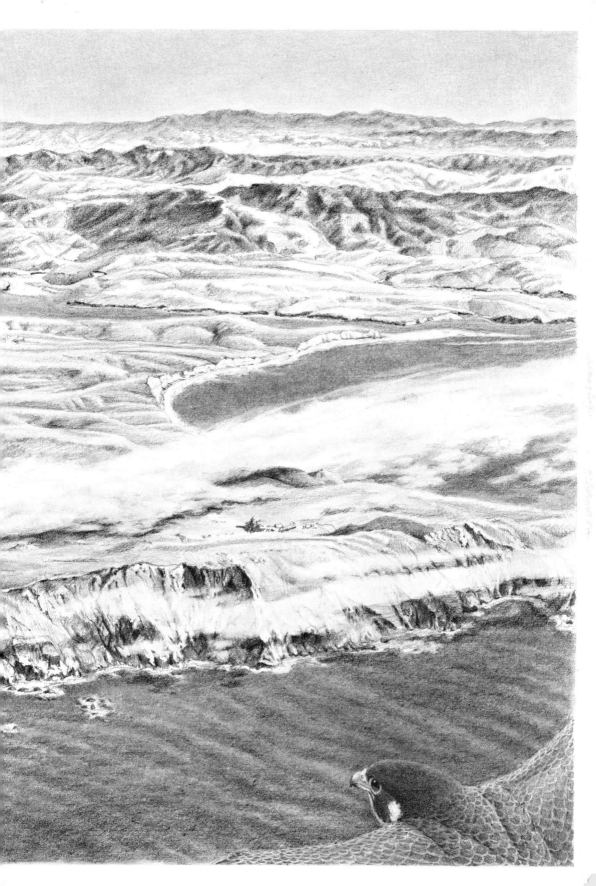

In solitude I find myself inordinately affected by the weather. It is as though meteorology takes the place of intimate company, and the distinction between outer weather
and inner mood is gradually obliterated. In such situations it is not so much a question
of trying to give myself over to nature as trying to hold something back, some bit of perspective and self-evaluation. This is what fog loves to steal from you.

                                         – Robert Finch. *"North Beach Journal."* 1986.

THE COAST MIWOK AND THE POMO, who inhabited these shores for at least 5,000
years, were tideland collectors, acorn gatherers, and game hunters who survived
and measured time by the seasonal abundance of food. For those early people each season, counted by phases of the moon, brought its own sustenance. On some moons
acorns were abundant, on others the salmon were running. One moon was for collecting clams, one was for gathering herbs; one marked the return of the ducks, another
marked their departure. On the bright full moon of mid-winter, "hunting could be difficult."[10, 20]

    Though we latecomers have largely lost our awareness of the relationship between
the moon and the availability of food, we are still aware of the seasons. Under the influence of Point Reyes's temperate climate we notice the gradual greening of the coastal
slope, the changing contours of the sand dunes at Limantour; we hear the dawn chorus
of birds herald the lengthening days of spring. It could be argued that there are only two
seasons, the rainy and the dry, or that there are 13, as defined by the native people. But in
the pages that follow, we winnow the year into four seasons – winter, spring, summer,
and fall – because it seems to fit our current understanding of the world. Yet as you read
the narrative below, it may become apparent that the seasons are infinite, a tapestry of
endless cycles, each overlapping and intertwining others. As we notice that the young
red-tailed hawks fledge when the buckeyes bloom, that the silk moths fly when the ceonothus flowers, that the song of the orange-crowned warbler accompanies the leafing
out of the willows, the awakening of the natural world becomes part of our daily lives.
Through our participation in the cycles of nature we recognize our influence on the environment, and come to accept and welcome its influence on us.

    Like the rest of the central coast of California, Point Reyes is a land of winter rain
and summer drought. Yet despite the clear definition between seasons, the monthly
temperature is remarkably constant, with a mid-winter average of about 50°F and a
mid-summer average of about 55°F. Indeed, this narrow range of variation makes this
one of the most equitable climates on the continent. The moisture-laden air insulates the
climate from extremes; ice is very rare, snow is a once-in-a-lifetime event. Point Reyes'

weather, though equitable, is by no means fair.

> For pure, unadulterated sea air, full of fog and oxygen, charged with ozone, salubrious and salsuginous, invigorating and life-giving air, that will make the pulses leap and bring the roses to the cheek, one should go to Point Reyes, where it can be had at first hand, bereft of nothing.
>
> —J. P. Munro-Fraser. *History of Marin County.* 1880.

In the spirit of a Victorian real estate advertisement, Munro-Fraser glorifies the two elements that lend Point Reyes its most characteristic weather: wind and fog. To explain these dominating influences and to understand the reasons for their persistence here, we must first understand the movements of the Pacific High pressure system and its effect on the circulation patterns of the North Pacific Ocean, for the influences of the Pacific High dominate the climate of Point Reyes as strongly as the influences of the San Andreas Fault dominate its geology.

MARITIME INFLUENCES

> At Point Reyes the amplitude of mean monthly temperatures is only 3.8 C, only 0.5 more than the amplitude over the open ocean.
>
> —Jack Major. *Terrestrial Vegetation of California.* 1977.

THE NORTH PACIFIC HIGH is a mass of cool air that sits on the ocean about 1,000 miles off the coast of California and migrates north and south seasonally with the apparent movement of the sun. The movement of this pressure system directly affects the local weather patterns. During the northern hemisphere winter, when the sun is positioned over the Tropic of Capricorn, the Pacific High settles off the coast of central Mexico at about the Tropic of Cancer. As the days lengthen and the earth begins to tilt its North Pole toward the sun, the High migrates northward, gaining size and pressure, finally positioning itself at about 38°N, the latitude of Point Reyes. Its movement northward generates the spring winds. Once in place, the strengthened high-pressure system stabilizes the weather, protecting the central California coast, dissipating Pacific storms or deflecting them to the north or south. Later in the year, as the days shorten, the Pacific High weakens and migrates south, leaving Point Reyes vulnerable to the onslaught of the coming winter storms. This migratory pattern, and the strengthening and weakening pulse of the system, affect the circulation patterns and temperatures of the surface waters of the Pacific Ocean.

Air masses move from areas of high pressure toward areas of low pressure. Therefore, air moves outward from the center of the North Pacific High pressure system, something like a huge fan, which, spinning clockwise (because of the earth's rotation), sends massive currents clockwise around the Pacific Ocean. These massive movements of air associated with the Pacific High in turn drive the surface waters of the ocean.

The North Pacific Gyre consists of several oceanic currents that, generated by the Pacific High, circulate clockwise around the margin of the Pacific Ocean. One of these is the California Current, the eastern arm of the warm Kuroshio Current that flows northward near Japan then veers northeastward across the North Pacific. The waters of the Kuroshio gradually cool as they reach into the northerly latitudes. They retain their coolness as they follow their clockwise path toward the eastern Pacific and converge into the California Current. The California Current is wide, extending out from shore nearly 400 miles, and relatively slow as ocean currents go, traveling from one-half to seven and one-half miles a day.

The surface seawater temperatures of the California Current play an important role in regulating the climate at Point Reyes and the rest of central California. The annual temperatures vary within a narrow range from about 48°F to about 61°F with an average of about 54°F. (See Figure 1.) Changes of only a few degrees in the surface water temperatures have significant physical and biological consequences. The annual hydrographic cycle of the California Current encompasses three distinct phases: (1) the Upwelling Period, (2) the Oceanic Period, and (3) the Davidson Countercurrent Period. Although variable in timing and duration, each is predictable and affects the local climate.

(1) The **Upwelling Period** usually occurs during spring and summer, but sometimes begins as early as February and extends into September. This period has the longest duration and the greatest influence of the three phases. The term "upwelling" refers to the movement of cold, nutrient-rich, deep sea water to the nearshore surface. This occurs as spring winds drive the

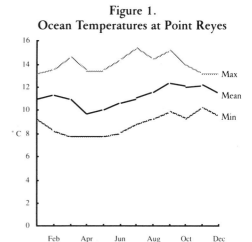

Figure 1.
Ocean Temperatures at Point Reyes

Figure 1. Average monthly ocean surface temperatures (degrees Celsius) at Point Reyes. The pattern of the mean shows the typical seasonal pattern, with temperatures decreasing gradually through winter to a spring low, then increasing gradually through summer to an autumn high.

warmer surface water offshore, inducing cold waters from a depth of 600 to 1,000 feet to rise up to the surface. When upwelling reaches a peak in June and July, the surface waters of central California are the coldest along the west coast. Water temperatures

Looking south from McClure's Beach toward Elephant Rock.

range from about 48°F to 56°F during this period. There is much mixing of waters from different depths, and because the water is cold and the days are long, plankton production is at a maximum.

(2) The **Oceanic Period**, occurring primarily in September and October but often extending a month earlier or later, sets in as the winds cease and the southward water flow slackens to allow inshore and northward flows of warm, subtropical waters. At other times of the year these warmer waters are forced farther offshore by cold upwelling waters. Water temperatures reach an annual high, salinity remains high, and plankton production is at the lowest level for the year. Water temperatures range up to about 61°F during this period.

(3) The **Davidson Countercurrent**, a back eddy of the dominant California Current, occurs during winter when strong southerly winds that accompany winter storms prevail. The Davidson Countercurrent moves nearshore opposite the main body of the California Current, which is now farther offshore. Plankton production is low, surface salinities reach the annual low because of runoff from winter storms, and decreasing temperatures lessen evaporation.

The three oceanic phases outlined above are generalizations of large-scale patterns. Many local gyres and currents overlay these larger oceanic events. For example, the Gulf of the Farallones Current generates a clockwise gyre off the Golden Gate that

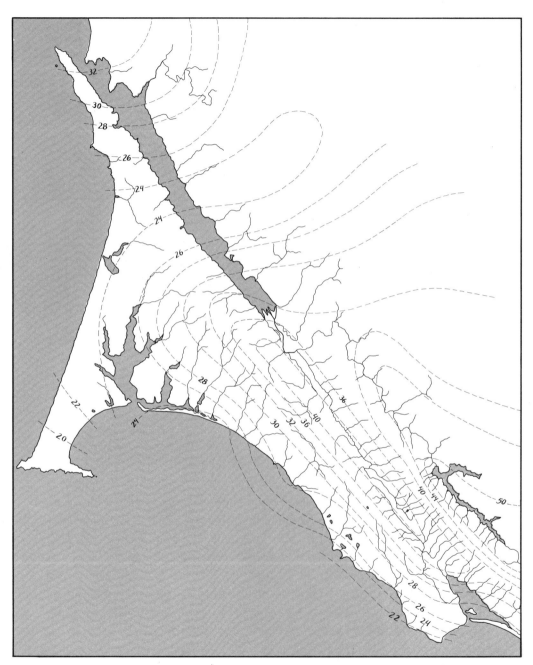

Map 3. Annual precipitation at Point Reyes peninsula. Note the twofold increase in rainfall between outer Point Reyes and the Olema Valley, a distance of about 10 miles. (Based on rainfall data from Marin Municipal Water District.)

reaches northward to Duxbury Point. The entrance to San Francisco Bay is the focal point of some of the most complex inshore currents along the California coast, but these have only secondary impacts on the local climate.[1, 3, 4, 8]

WINTER: The Rainy Season

So, the Davidson Countercurrent accompanies the amelioration of the Pacific High, which protects Point Reyes from storm fronts. The result is a short, wet winter and a long, dry summer — a Mediterranean climate similar to the weather pattern that occurs in southern Europe and northern Africa, as well as central Chile and southwest Australia. (It is interesting to note that it was the hospitable Mediterranean climate that fostered the birth of civilization.) However, the cold water of the upwelling cycle and the resultant coastal fog serve to moderate the climate at Point Reyes so that the annual range of average temperatures is much less than in other "Mediterranean" regions.

Sanderlings and sand verbena

Although the timing of the rainy season is fairly constant, usually beginning in November and dissipating in March, there is vast annual variation in the amount of rainfall due to water temperature anomalies in the North Pacific Gyre. Years of high rainfall tend to correspond with high water temperatures. This phenomenon has been especially evident over the last two decades. The winters of 1969–70, 1982–83, and 1983–84 were exceptionally wet, receiving about 150 percent of the average rainfall. The winters of 1971–72, 1975–77, and 1986–91 were drought years, receiving only about 60 percent of the average rainfall. Whether this extreme variability is a new pattern, or simply falls within the normal variation of the long-term pattern, is difficult to assess. There is some indication of alternating pulses in the upwelling and downwelling cycles that produce these weather patterns (see *Seabirds of the Farallon Islands*, Ainley and Boekelheide, eds., 1990).

The average annual rainfall at Inverness (Figure 2, pg. 10) was approximately 37 inches, nearly identical to the 15-year mean at Bear Valley Headquarters, but about twice the 18 inches per year measured at the Point Reyes Lighthouse or the Farallon Islands (see Map 3).

Occasionally the Pacific High is so strong that it remains in place through the winter and the rainy season never materializes. A look at the historic record indicates that every decade since the 1840s, when records were first kept, has hosted a drought winter, with the exception of the relatively wet 1880s. If we define drought as those years in which the total annual rainfall was less than one-half the annual mean, droughts occur on the average of once every 12 years.

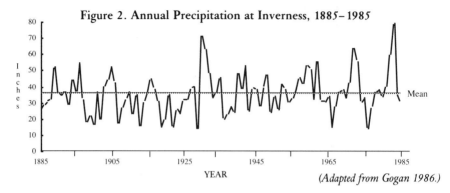

Figure 2. Annual Precipitation at Inverness, 1885–1985

YEAR

(Adapted from Gogan 1986.)

When the first gentle rain of late autumn gives way to a full-blown December gale, and the Gulf of the Farallones is churned by the collision of a cold arctic front with a warm tropical air mass, winter has arrived at Point Reyes full-bore, loaded for bear. The winter sea is full of froth – roily and gray. When Pacific swells combine with new-moon tides and arctic storms, the beaches are sculpted by the unrelenting surge. In mid-winter, the sand spit at Abbott's Lagoon is breached by the swollen surf. At Drake's Beach the sublittoral geology, Miocene Monterey chert, covered by sand during most months, is exposed to the elements to be pounded and rounded by the surf. At Duxbury Reef, the shale is pitted and pocked by shorecast spray.

During a brief break in the December storm track, when weather fronts line-up "from here to Hawaii," as the forecasters are fond of saying – that is the time to walk the beach. The surf spews its foam upon the driftwood-laden shore, strewn with the ocean's debris: bloated stalks of bull kelp, flotation bulbs from Japanese fishing nets, rockfish carcasses, shells, shoes, crab carapaces, dead murres and scoters, bottles, rope, and barnacle-encrusted trunks of trees. Occasionally some large marine mammal – a whale, sea lion, or porpoise – washes ashore, providing scavengers with a bountiful feast. Gulls, ravens, and sometimes fulmars, converge. Turkey vultures seem to scan the shore continually, "tippy gliding" back and forth. Raccoons and striped skunks, too, venture out at night to search the tideline. At Limantour one can often see tracks of gray fox in the damp sand left by the morning ebb.

The gray whale is the symbol of winter at Point Reyes. A pregnant female rolls through the swells off Great Beach, rounding the headland as she migrates south to her breeding grounds in Magdalena Bay. Perhaps every individual in the eastern Pacific population has passed these shores — traveling southward in winter, northward in spring — though some move far offshore. Migration peaks between the winter solstice and New Year's Day; when the sea is calm enough, whales spout across the seascape.

Seals use the winter beaches for resting. In recent years, bull elephant seals have taken to basking on some remote beaches, especially in January. Viewed from above, as we stand on the headland looking down through binoculars, the pale sausage-shaped body is mistaken for a driftwood log until it raises an odd trunk, bellows, and flips sand onto his back.

Near the mouth of Drake's Estero, the sandy bars exposed at low tide provide a haul out site for hundreds of harbor seals, waiting for the next flood tide and the fish it will bring. Here, too, roosted alongside the seals, scores of white pelicans spend the winter preening and yawning. By mid-winter most brown pelicans have returned to their coastal breeding grounds farther to the south, but the white pelicans wait out the winter before flying back to the inland lakes where they will nest and raise their young.

On a calm January morning, a hiker at Limantour Spit, Drake's Estero, Abbott's Lagoon, or the inner reaches of Tomales Bay may see a falcon perched on a low driftwood branch surveying the surrounding tidal flats. The bird is slender-bodied with a large head and swept-back wings — a merlin. It jumps from its perch and, flying within two feet of the ground, strafes the flats for several hundred feet before it scatters a surprised flock of dunlin, deftly grasping one in its oversized talons. The flock, its ranks lessened by one, regains its composure, regroups, and wheels over the estuary in alternating flashes of light and dark as the merlin returns to its driftwood perch to pluck its quarry. Peregrines also winter here; larger than merlins, their low-flying approach tends to flush every bird in sight.

The year's highest tides occur in January, flooding the salt marshes, forcing voles, shrews, and marsh birds out of their preferred habitat to take refuge in the upland vegetation. Predators — hawks, gulls, egrets, and herons — stalk the fringe in search of marshland refugees.

*   *   *

On the flood tide of a dark moon night in February, herring swarm into Tomales Bay, spawning amidst the eelgrass beds that line the calm shallows. The birds are waiting, mysteriously cued into the bounteous spawn. Scoters gather by the tens of thousands; bufflehead, ruddy duck, scaups, and grebes by the thousands; loons, brant, cormorants, pintail by the hundreds. At sunrise, the turbulent sky is shaded albacore and salmon, the clouds are amorphous stratus, fractured after yesterday's storm. We glide through the flocks in our silent canoe. Having gorged on fish and eggs, the birds are heavy and wait until our close approach before rising to fly the minimum distance to safety, landing, and swimming away — a wake of nervous birds. Leaning over the gunnel, we look down into the eelgrass, the narrow green blades now shredded and tattered by the hungry attention of so many bills and beaks. A bat ray, with a disturbingly human face, broad and oriental, banks gracefully and disappears in the underwater pasture. Leopard sharks too, sleek and tiger-striped, have been attracted by the spawn; several pass to starboard. The herring run is an animal mega-event: its cycles are incorporated into distributional patterns of the species present. Through their genes, or some other occult heritage, each species is in the neighborhood, ready to feast when the herring arrive.

*　　　　*　　　　*

The early bloom begins in February, a welcome sign of renewal after months of rain and short, chilling days. The flowers are most profuse on the coastal headlands, where yellow and purple rock gardens of phacelia, sun cups, blue dicks, begin to appear; but each habitat has its winter flowers: sand verbena on coastal strand and dunes, blue-eyed grass on the coastal prairie, red maids and milk maids in the oak woodlands.

In the shade of the dampest lowlands of the fir forest the trillium (also called "wake robin") first blooms in February, a trinity of deep green leaves framing the immaculate white tri-petaled flower. As they age through spring, the petals turn pink to lavender. There are two species on the peninsula, the uncommon coast trillium and the rather rare giant trillium. Look for the latter, with purple mottling on its leaves, in Arroyo Hondo, along the Bolema Trail, or in the canyons around Inverness.

The first flowers of the rare, fragrant fritillary can be found in open fields amidst early blooming Douglas iris in the coastal scrub. Look for it especially around ungrazed areas of the hills around Limantour.

SPRING: The Windy Season

As the days increase in length and the sun climbs higher in the sky, the North Pacific High pressure system migrates northward and farther offshore. As it moves it swells in size and strengthens in pressure. At the same time, the increasing day length and higher temperatures are creating a low-pressure system over California's Great Central Valley. The movement and growth of the North Pacific High and the gradient between the two systems account for the persistent northwest winds that buffet Point Reyes during the spring months. Although maximum speeds exceed 80 miles per hour, on an average spring day, velocities peak at about 35 miles per hour. These winds are consistent enough in direction and powerful enough in intensity to drive the nearshore surface waters southeasterly, parallel to the shoreline of central California. As the water moves, the additional influence of the earth's rotation (the Coriolis Effect) deflects these surface waters several hundred kilometers offshore. The relatively warm surface water is then displaced by colder subsurface water and the process of "upwelling" is underway.

As a result of the upwelling process, the coastal "fog belt" is a well-defined area that receives more moisture and experiences less daily temperature fluctuation than adjacent habitat. This, in turn, affects the distribution of several species of plants and animals. (See "Coastal Scrub," p.59, and "White-crowned Sparrow," p.122.) The salinity of the fog may also have an effect on plant distribution.[3, 19]

Spring trillium and tree frog

As the winter rains diminish, the spring winds develop. Persistent and predictable, over time they have sculpted the coastal bluffs and ridgetop forests. The cypress trees at the Lighthouse strain against the northwesterlies, their leeward trunks protecting colonies of leather ferns from the onslaught.

Don't believe the locals who tell you winds only last three days then abate. Under proper conditions they will blow unrelentingly through April and May, finally surrendering to the immutable fog.

Often, in summer, while the Olema Valley basks in warm sunshine, the outer Point is blanketed in a dense fog. The fog is so persistent that it prompted local historian Jack Mason to claim that Point Reyes is "the foggiest place on the coast." Indeed, in the "Synoptic and Aeronautic Meteorological Book," Dr. Horace Byers ranks Point Reyes second only to Nantucket Island off Massachusetts for its dense fogs.

Perhaps no other season is as long and drawn-out as spring at Point Reyes. Spring extends backward even to January, first glimmering on the iridescent throat of Anna's hummingbirds as they perform aerial breeding displays above the coastal scrub, or forward even into October when the marsh rosemary blooms. But spring becomes emboldened in March when the willows and buckeyes are in full leaf and the ascending trill of orange-crowned warblers sweetens the air, which is sometimes imbued with an unfamiliar warmth. On the fairest days, some bold and hardy human souls dive into the surf at Limantour for a springtime baptism.

March is a month of change — November's alter ego. Winter storms dissipate as the North Pacific High shifts into place. March may host a calm respite between the last tropical storm and the reliable winds of April, but most afternoons are breezy, especially at headlands and hilltops. The headlands and fields along the immediate coast are places to find the best blooms.

Out toward Point Reyes, pink flowering currants — nodding in the breeze — trim

California bay trees on Olema Hill, wind sculpted by the prevailing northwesterlies. The eastern slope of Inverness Ridge, heavily forested with Douglas fir, is visible in the background.

the roadsides. The creamy white, spiked inflorescences of red elderberry shrubs are blooming on damp north-facing slopes or beneath the alders at the base of Mount Vision. Further out, on the shores of Abbott's Lagoon or on the eastern headlands at Chimney Rock, the wildflowers command attention. Owl's clovers, tidy tips, and sun cups wrap the promontories in a chaos of color and fragrance. Some specialties to look for include pussy's ears, a delicate, pale star tulip with a short stem, often hidden amidst the taller grasses. Baby-blue-eyes and wallflowers abound. California phacelia (meaning "clustered" in Latin) is beginning to unfurl violet-blue blossoms on the south faces of leeward headlands.

In March, gray whales are migrating northward, back toward the feeding grounds in the Alaskan Gulf. Most often, the whales seen from shore are females accompanied by calves; the newborns apparently prefer shallow waters. However, sometimes courting adults can be seen frolicking and even mating on the water's surface. Chimney Rock, the Lighthouse, or any headland promontory provides a good vantage point for observing this behavior.

Frogs and salamanders are also breeding now. Still, freshwater ponds (Hagmaier's Pond, Five Brooks, Mud Lake, Bass Lake, etc.) harbor California newts, often clutched in sexual union. Rough-skinned newts prefer faster-flowing streams, as at Bear Valley or Olema Creek. Freshwater marshes (Olema Marsh, Dogtown Marsh, etc.) are alive with a chorus of tree frogs, especially at night following recent rain. Sometimes red-legged frogs can be found (Laguna Ranch Pond or the ponds above Limantour Estero, just northeast of Muddy Hollow, are likely spots); however, many have been displaced by the introduced bullfrog.

Resident birds are breeding by now. Red-tailed hawks are paired, song sparrows and marsh wrens are singing, woodpeckers are busy excavating nesting holes. Tree swallows have returned from Mexico en force and are frequenting last year's abandoned downy woodpecker cavities. In Haggerty Gulch or atop Inverness Ridge, ospreys circle snags, repairing the winter damage to last year's nest or building anew.

April may have been the cruelest month in T. S. Eliot's environment, but at Point Reyes it is the least predictable. Rains can linger through mid-month, but most storms have lost the ferocity of winter. A day can be balmy and calm, suddenly interrupted by the formation of a chilling fog that dampens the bones. Most years, northwest winds assault the coast with unrelenting persistence, but other years April is graced by an uncharacteristic stillness. In recent times, the drought years (1977 and 1978) and the El Niño year (1982–83) stand out as examples of relatively windless springs.

For all its flirtatiousness, April offers excitement and unexpected surprises. On a recent April morning I stood with my daughter at Indian Beach. The air was almost tropical; a faint fog hung low over the still waters of Tomales Bay, yet to be burned off by the just-rising sun. The haunting cry of a common loon, somehow embodying both mournfulness and joy, filled the small cove at Indian Beach—a wide-eyed harbor seal rose slowly above the surface, then seeing us nearby on shore, splashed suddenly and disappeared.

Most species of wildflowers bloom in April and some fields are now alive with a chaos of color. Perhaps the most representative mix of color is the blend of the deep orange California poppy and the royal blue sky lupine growing side by side. Later, these patches of sky lupine add a reddish hue to the scene as their banners change color with pollination.

Passing through the coastal scrub and along the forest's edge, one cannot help but notice the blue blossom (*Ceonothus*), brilliant against the new green growth of the surrounding coyote bush. Also obvious are the large, white, umbrella-like flowers of cow parsnip raising their heads above the green hillsides.

By mid-month many of the wintering birds have left the ponds and tidal flats, and other migrant flocks are passing through. At dusk at Limantour or Drake's Estero, large flocks of short-billed dowitchers whistle as they ascend toward the sunset. Caspian terns, squawking harshly, fly northward along the shore, peering down into the surf. Now is an opportunity to see some birds molting into breeding plumage, changing from the drab hues of winter into the startling patterns of courtship. By late April, many loons are in full breeding dress and are easily seen close to shore. Look for common loons anywhere along the shores of Tomales Bay. On the outer coast in calm embayments, as at the Fish Docks or from Drake's Beach, one can also find red-throated and arctic loons. On tidal flats look for black-bellied plovers. These large, plump, short-billed shorebirds often confound people in the winter "nonbreeding" plumage when they are "white-bellied." However, by April, many live up to their name and achieve the splendor of their breeding dress.

SUMMER: The Foggy Season

. . . it was in the height of summer, and so neere the sunne, yet were wee continually visited with life nipping colds as we had never felt before . . . those thicke mists and most stinking fogges.

— Chaplain F. Fletcher. *The World Encompassed.* Upon visiting Point Reyes aboard the *Golden Hinde* in June 1579.

As winds sail toward shore across the Pacific, hugging the boundary of the North Pacific High that drives them, they absorb considerable moisture from the surface of the ocean. During the Upwelling Period, the surface temperatures offshore are warmer than those nearshore and the winds have become saturated with warm water vapor. Onshore winds transport the warmer, moisture-laden air over the colder coastal waters; as the air cools it reaches "dewpoint" and becomes fog. Meteorologists define fog as condensed atmospheric water vapor in sufficient concentration to reduce visibility to 3,280 feet (1,000 meters). Visibility at the Point Reyes Lighthouse on a foggy summer day is reduced to as low as 150 feet. These summer fogs are defined as "advection

White-crowned sparrow with sticky monkey flower

fogs" because they are generated by horizontal movement of air. Such conditions exist only in regions where the sea surface is much colder than the air traveling over it; the Oyashio Current in the Bering Sea, the Labrador Current off the Grand Banks of Newfoundland, and the coast at central California are the regions of maximum annual fog frequency in the Northern Hemisphere.[4]

*　　　　*　　　　*

At the summer solstice atop Mount Vision, the June sky is lazuli bunting blue and the cones of gently contorted bishop pines crackle quietly in the hot noonday sun. Looking west toward the Lighthouse, we see a snowdrift of fog cloaking the outer Point, blanketing Drake's Bay and the ocean out toward the Farallones. Thick fingers of opaque whiteness cling to the estuaries and watercourses. As we walk downslope, through golden fields of dried grasses, into a maze of evergreen coyote bush and the pale orange blooms of sticky monkeyflower, the air cools considerably. Soon we hear the clear song of a white-crowned sparrow; we are in the fog belt, being chilled by the moist air so characteristic of a Point Reyes summer.

*   *   *

The fog provides Point Reyes with one of the country's most dramatic and haunting landscapes. From the Olema Valley, especially in the early morning or late afternoon, we see the white cumulus hugging the east-facing slopes, densely forested with Douglas fir, unshaded. Approaching mid-day, as the land warms, the fog retreats to the

Figure 3. Monthly Patterns of Rainfall and Fog, Outer Point Reyes

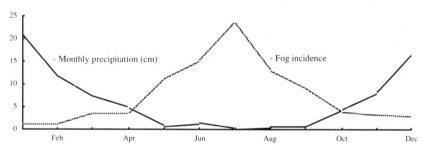

The values on the vertical axis represent centimeters of rainfall or the number of foggy days per month. (Adapted from Barbour et al 1973.)

shoreline or sometimes just offshore, allowing the coast a mid-day bath of warm sunshine. By early evening the bank again advances, reclaiming its territory up the coastal slope to the ridge top, where it usually halts. After sunset, as the land cools, the fog rolls over the ridge, sometimes lifting to a higher inversion layer. Again at dawn the fog reforms, then retreats seaward as the land reheats. This ebb-and-flow cycle may repeat itself week after week through summer if the conditions remain stable.

When the water temperature is not cold enough to generate advection fog, the moist air rises vertically as it meets the coastal hills, cools, and condenses into a gray overcast. The dampening effect of the maritime air makes Point Reyes one of the coolest summer environments on the continent.

The advective fogs that can blanket Point Reyes from May through August provide fog drip for many of the drought-tolerant plants that carpet the headlands and pastures. Indeed, during summer, the outer Point may have more available moisture than the leeward side of the Inverness Ridge. Although long-term measurements have not been made at Point Reyes, studies in similar climates in Humboldt County and Berkeley indicate that 10 to 12 inches of fog drip may be available in summer.[3, 13, 16]

FALL: The Sub-tropical Season

As the autumnal equinox approaches, the Central Valley low-pressure system dissipates and the pressure gradient between it and the Pacific High weakens. The northwesterlies are now blocked by a stable Pacific High and the movement of the surface waters of the ocean ceases. The cessation of upwelling and the beginning of the Oceanic Period coincide with the warmest coastal temperatures in central California. Point Reyes shares in this blessed season, and the temperatures at the Lighthouse can soar into the eighties beginning in August and sometimes lasting into early November. This is fall, when sub-tropical weather, held at bay by arctic currents the rest of the year, is allowed to intrude northward and bathe Point Reyes in California's equivalent of Indian Summer. Fall at Point Reyes is remarkable for its lack of tangible weather, its extreme hospitality. Wind and fog, our usual companions, are in short supply; the abundance of sunshine and warm southerly breezes is almost disconcerting.

By mid-August the fog lessens, burning off earlier and rolling in later each day. It has been six months since the last drenching rains and the landscape begins to show the effects of drought. With the protective blanket of fog rolled back the increase in solar radiation becomes obvious, especially on the grazed hills — parched and crisp. The contrast between the dry hills and the

Gray squirrel

conifer forests is greatest in the fall — seasonally brown fields against evergreen woods. On the agricultural fields blackbird flocks gather, increasing in size through fall as more birds arrive from their wetland breeding grounds. (At dusk, the flocks return to roost in the cattail and tule marshes of Abbott's Lagoon or Olema and Kehoe marshes.) In the coastal scrub the dried stalks of parsnip, hemlock, and other forbs are laden with seeds, and siskins and sparrows forage on the umbels.

Most wildflowers have withered, except in the swales where a few marsh monkeyflowers still bloom, or in the salt marsh where marsh rosemary is in full flower. On the oceanfront bluffs, too, some flowers continue to flourish, apparently oblivious to the shortening days and the promise of winter. In August acorns are still green on the oaks, but the gray squirrels, acorn woodpeckers, and jays are already reaping the harvest and storing mast for the coming winter. If the Coast Miwok were still here, they would be preparing for the gathering.

By early September the signs of autumn are everywhere. Swallows are absent some days, present on others – large migrant flocks muster above ponds and marshes where emergent insects are on the wing. Perhaps the warmer temperatures account for the abundance of insects now; notice the dragonflies and darning needles around the ponds and marshes, or the monarch and checkerspot butterflies over the prairie and dune. Young gopher snakes are dispersing above ground, ever cautious of the fledgling kestrels and red-tailed hawks overhead. Evidence of warming water temperatures is the reddish cast to the breakers at Bolinas, Limantour, and Drake's beaches; this is the "red tide" caused by an abundance of minute organisms – dinoflagellates of the genus *Gonyaulax.* Just beyond the breakers flocks of brown pelicans, Heermann's gulls, and elegant terns are flying northward or wheeling and diving into the ocean. Offshore, humpback and blue whales have arrived to feed on euphausid shrimps, and shearwaters are passing by on their great migratory gyre around the Pacific rim.

Mid-October, a Scottish bagpiper and the residents of Inverness gather on Mount Vision to welcome the swollen hunter's moon rising over the barren hills. To runic tunes, the fallow moonbeams reflect across a silver finger of night fog pointing up Tomales Bay and backlight the bishop pines, like a Japanese woodcut. The constellations – Orion, Aquila, Andromeda – are vivid against the eastern sky, but they will fade as the big moon rises, commanding attention. As the last celebrants leave, the deepest notes of a great horned owl echo from a distant hollow.

On the hillside by daylight, the grasses are dry and golden. Even the tips of the perennial rushes are brown and brittle. Most of the breeding warblers and vireos have left for the tropics. Now flocks of Oregon juncos and white-crowned and golden-crowned sparrows forage beneath the coyotebush; kestrels and flickers perch atop the pines. The winter birds are back.

Down on the tidal flats of Drake's Estero numbers of arctic breeding shorebirds are increasing, but on the open water of Tomales and Drake's bays, few diving ducks have arrived. As the waters at more northerly latitudes freeze, maybe by the end of the month, flocks of canvasback, scaup, and bufflehead will begin arriving, congregating in vast rafts in leeward coves.

As All Hallow's Eve approaches, the shorter days bear unmistakable signs of winter – willows and alders are losing their leaves, there is a certain slant to the gray afternoon light, the loon's haunting call is heard occasionally across the misty water. Though the fair weather may continue well into November, the Oceanic Period is coming to an end. As the Pacific High weakens and again migrates southward with the apparent movement of the sun, the Davidson Countercurrent will again move inshore and surface temperatures of the ocean's waters will begin to drop. The last migrant landbirds leave the peninsula. Humpback and blue whales disappear from the Gulf of the Farallones and the first migrant gray whales are sighted from the Lighthouse. At Bear Valley there is a restlessness in the oaks as the woodpeckers and squirrels quarrel over the last acorns. The robins in the blackberry bramble and the deer at Divide Meadow stretch their necks and glance skyward every few minutes as the storm clouds gather for the first winter storms.

ANOMALOUS PATTERNS

T HE PRECEDING DISCUSSION of ocean currents and weather patterns is an idealized account of "normal" weather at Point Reyes. In fact, with its winter storms, spring winds, summer fog, and dry sub-tropical autumn, Point Reyes has as predictable a weather regime as just about any place in North America. Yet even this dependable pattern gets disrupted by large-scale phenomena with global ramifications. These disruptions also may have patterns; however, none of these is perfectly understood.

El Niño

Let us start with El Niño, a warm water countercurrent that appears periodically on the west coast of South America. (It often occurs at Christmastime, giving rise to the name El Niño, a Spanish allusion to the Christ Child.) El Niño is poorly understood, but we know that it occurs every decade at three- to ten-year intervals and is accompanied by a reversal in direction of the southeasterly trade winds in the South Pacific. This reversal may occur after the prevailing trades have blown particularly strongly for a long time, pushing surface water to the west side of the equatorial Pacific and causing an east-to-west uphill slope in sea level. When the trades finally recede, or reverse, this hill of warm equatorial water washes eastward, back toward the west coasts of the Americas. In some years it apparently reaches California, causing abnormally high ocean temperatures.

The anomalous warm water that accompanies particularly strong El Niño events can engender especially wet winters along the central California coast. A recent example was the winter of 1984, a year of record rainfall that followed an El Niño of extraordinary magnitude. That El Niño event had warmed coastal waters on average more than 5°F from May 1982 through December 1983. Other recent years of exceptionally warm water temperatures include 1972–73, 1976, 1990 and 1992.[2, 3, 11, 18]

Because cold water is more productive than warm water, the biological effects of El Niño-like events can be far-reaching. The 1956 El Niño probably dealt the final blow to

California's already depleted sardine industry. Warm water lowers production of phytoplankton and zooplankton, foundations on which food pyramids are built. As a result there is lower recruitment of fish larvae by rockfish and other inshore species. In turn, there is less food available for breeding seabirds and marine mammals. At the Farallon Islands and along Point Reyes' rocky coast, cormorants, puffins, and guillemots failed to breed in 1983 and less than half of the murres laid eggs. Not only were few young produced, but adult seabirds suffered high mortality. A similar disturbance occurred again in 1990. Warm currents also attract normally tropical species into these waters. In 1982 and 1983, barracuda were caught in the Gulf of the Farallones and rough-toothed dolphin and striped dolphin, both southern species, were found stranded on central California beaches. Pelagic red crabs, pelagic purple snails, and loggerhead turtles, normally rare north of Mexico, became fairly common here.

Many wide-ranging phenomena have been attributed to El Niño: fires in Australia, drought in Japan, rain in the Galapagos Islands, record rainfall in California. Undoubtedly, many other phenomena associated with El Niño, both physical and biological, go unrecognized.

Drought and Flood

Variations in local rainfall patterns are related to global variations in the movement of air masses, ocean currents, and water temperatures. These relationships are complex and not easily understood. We are left to examine the local measurements and to gauge and ponder the seeming vagaries of drought or flood. Perhaps "anomaly," a word that connotes irregularity, does not accurately describe these phenomena. If we look at the annual rainfall patterns for the last 100 or more years (See Figure 3), there seems to be a regular pattern of dry and wet years with one drought and one flood every decade or so. Some years, an extremely dry year is followed by an extremely wet year (or vice versa), or there are two wet years in succession. Lately, droughts seems to be occurring with increasing regularity.

The weather pattern that produced the near-record rainfalls of the winters of 1982–84, with two wet winters in succession, was illustrative of the effect of large-scale phenomena on local events. The most impressive storm in those impressive winters drowned Point Reyes in over 12 inches of rain in 24 hours. On January 4, 1982 the skies opened when a warm, moisture-laden, tropical air mass collided with a cold arctic front. The warm air was related to some anomalous dynamics in the Southern Oscillation – a pressure differential between the south Pacific High and the Indian Ocean low – which caused the unusually warm ocean waters on these shores (explained earlier under "El Niño"). The migration of arctic air was probably indirectly related to the distant disturbance as well. This collision of north and south happened to coincide with the perigean moon and the highest tides of the year. The result was landslides, flooding, and severe sedimentation of Tomales Bay, the effects of which are still visible, especially along Sir Francis Drake Highway from Olema Marsh northward through Inverness.

THE MICROCLIMATE

In the coolest moistest canyons . . . can occasionally be found a variety of fern whose typical locale is the Aleutian Islands; in the hottest driest canyons, only a few miles away, can be found small blackish fern which also survives in the Sonoran desert.
— Arthur Quinn. *Broken Shore.* 1981.

A LTHOUGH THE OVERALL CLIMATE is moderate, with a narrow range in annual temperatures and a rather strict seasonality to the weather patterns, the microclimates of the Point Reyes peninsula can vary in the extreme between sites. Perhaps the most striking example is the twofold increase in annual rainfall at Bear Valley compared to that at the Lighthouse. (See Map 3.) The effect of this difference is also obvious in the distribution of the vegetation, contrasting the densely forested eastern slope of Inverness Ridge above Bear Valley with the sparse coastal scrub and grassland of the western slope and outer Point. (See Map 5, Chapter 3.) At any time of year temperatures in east- or south-facing canyons may be 12° to 14°F warmer than on ocean bluffs because of differences in exposure to sun, wind, and fog.[3, 4, 8]

Upon close scrutiny, we also notice distinct communities on opposite slopes of the same canyon. This is especially true of the east-west running canyons where south-facing slopes are exposed to maximum solar radiation. These south-facing slopes, with small-leaved shrubs and trees — manzanita, huckleberry, sage, scrub oak, ceonothus — resemble a Mexican hillside. (Indeed, many of these species belong to the "madro-tertiary geoflora," which migrated here from the Sierra Madre of northwestern Mexico during the Miocene epoch.) The opposite north-facing slope, with its dense cover of ferns, salal, Douglas fir, and broad-leaved shrubs like thimbleberry, elderberry, and hazelnut might as well be in British Columbia.

The eastern extent of the summer fog is another determinant of microclimate at Point Reyes. Fog provides moisture to soil and plants in two ways: (1) fog drip and (2) reduced evapo-transpiration. Precipitation from fog drip varies depending on the type of vegetation present to capture the moisture, but the amount can be substantial, as anyone knows who has walked beneath the cypress trees on the outer Point in summer. A study on the San Francisco peninsula measured nearly 60 inches of fog drip in one year beneath an exposed tanoak tree, and another in Berkeley measured nearly 10 inches beneath a Monterey pine. Furthermore, fog shades the land from the drying effects of the summer sun, reducing the amount of water that evaporates and the amount of moisture that is lost through transpiration by the plants, thereby lessening the liability of life in an environment of summer drought. But fog may carry its own liability, especially on the immediate coast. Studies have shown that oceanic fog contains sea water, and this brackish moisture must be stressful to many species.[4, 14, 16]

REFERENCES

1. Ainley, D. 1976. The occurrence of seabirds in the coastal region of California. *Western Birds* 7:33–68.

2. Ainley, D. 1983. El Niño in California. Point Reyes Bird Observatory Newsletter 62 (Summer 1983).

3. Ainley, D. G. and R. J. Boekelheide, eds. 1990. *Seabirds of the Farallon Islands: Ecology, Dynamics, and Structure of an Upwelling Community.* Palo Alto: Stanford University Press.

4. Barbour, M. G., R. B. Craig, F. R. Drysdale, and M. T. Ghiselin. 1973. *Coastal Ecology: Bodega Head.* Berkeley: University of California Press.

5. Berry, F. A., E. Bollay, and N. R. Beers, eds. 1945. *Handbook of Meteorology.* New York: McGraw-Hill.

6. Conomos, T. J. 1979. Properties and circulation of San Francisco Bay waters. in *San Francisco Bay: The Urbanized Estuary*, edited by T. J. Conomos. Pacific Division of the American Association for the Advancement of Science.

7. Finch, R. 1986. North beach journal. In *On Nature*, edited by D. Halpern. Berkeley: North Point Press.

8. Gilliam, H. 1966. *Weather of the San Francisco Bay Region.* Berkeley: University of California Press.

9. Gogan, P. 1986. *Ecology of the Tule Elk Range, Point Reyes National Seashore.* Ph.D. dissertation. University of California, Berkeley.

10. Heizer, R. F., and A. B. Elsasser. 1980. *The Natural World of the California Indians.* Berkeley: University of California Press.

11. Kaza, S., and R. Boekelheide. 1984. Measuring the pulse of life. *Pacific Discovery* 37 (1).

12. Major, J. 1977. California climate in relation to vegetation. In *Terrestrial Vegetation of California*, edited by M. G. Barbour and J. Major. New York: John Wiley & Sons.

13. Mason, J. 1970. *Point Reyes: The Solemn Land.* Inverness, Calif.: North Shore Books.

14. Oberlander, G. T. 1956. Summer fog precipitation in San Francisco peninsula. *Ecology* 37:851.

15. Ornduff, R. 1974. *Introduction to California Plant Life.* Berkeley: University of California Press.

16. Parsons, J. J. 1960. Fog drip from coastal stratus, with special reference to California. *Weather* (London) 15:58–62.

17. Patton, C. P. 1956. *Climatology of Summer Fogs in the San Francisco Bay Area.* Berkeley: University of California Press.

18. Peaslee, S. 1983. El Niño stirs up the weather. *The New Weather Observer*, (7).

19. Quinn, A. 1981. *Broken Shore: The Marin Peninsula.* Salt Lake City: Peregrine Smith.

20. Thalman, S. 1990. Personal comments regarding Miwok history.

21. Walter, H. 1973. *Vegetation of the Earth in Relation to Climate and Eco-physiological Conditions.* London: English Universities Press Ltd.

22. Weber, G. E. 1981 Physical environment. In *The Natural History of Año Nuevo*, edited by Le Boeuf and Kaza. Pacific Grove, Calif.: Boxwood Press.

CHAPTER TWO

GEOLOGY
Substrate and Soils

Keith Hansen 1988

If geologic time could somehow be seen in the perspective of human time . . . sea level
would be rising and falling hundreds of feet, ice would come pouring over continents
and as quickly go away . . . oceans would swing open like doors, mountains would grow
like clouds and come down like melting sherbet, continents would crawl like amoebae . . .
volcanoes would light the earth as if it were a garden full of fireflies.

—John McPhee. *In Suspect Terrain*. 1985.

IF WE COULD SOMEHOW see Point Reyes in the perspective of geologic time, it might
appear as a gray whale, migrating northwesterly along the continent's edge, its backbone (Inverness Ridge) emerging periodically from the sea, its granitic head rising above
the surface, then, lifting its flukes (Duxbury Reef and Bolinas Lagoon) and diving. Again
submerged, it continues its northward passage along the western edge of the continent.
As we look down from above, the whale's body is partially submerged, its right flank
tucked into the San Andreas Fault, half of its snout emerging as Tomales Point, a pectoral fin stretching westward to the headlands; Duxbury Reef forms its left fluke, Bolinas
Lagoon its right.

We are not sure where it has been, but it seems to be moving inexorably forward,
driven by some deeply rooted impulse, beyond the grasp of our dawning comprehen-
sion. Time, tectonics, wind, and a rising and falling ocean have conspired to hide from
us many of the origins and affinities of this peninsula, and therein lies its mystery.

The origin of the Point Reyes peninsula is obscure. Perhaps it began in some shallow lagoon along the Mexican coast, where fine sediments of sand, clay, and lime were
deposited in a pre-Cretaceous period more than 140 million years ago, or even as early
as the great Paleozoic era (at least 225 million years ago) before the ascendancy of birds
and mammals. These initial ingredients accumulated through millions of years, then
emerged from the amniotic sea and were kneaded and rolled into fine-grained rocks —
sandstones, shales, limestones — by some massive movement in the earth's mantle.
Exposed to weather above sea level, some of the soft sedimentary strata eroded,
obscuring the natal symmetry, sculpting chaos where order had reigned. Then, toward
the end of the Mesozoic era, in the middle Upper Cretaceous period, about the time
that snakes slithered onto the scene and oaks, buckeyes, and sweetgums began to
bloom, 83.9 million years ago to be precise, molten granite from deep in the earth engulfed the sedimentary rock. The heat and pressure of this granitic "intrusion" solidified
the sedimentaries into crystalline schists (finely laminated metamorphic rock in which
the minerals are arranged in thin layers) and limestones — metamorphic rocks. Continued erosion probably accounts for the fact that these metamorphic rocks are rare today

The Northwesterly Migration of a Granitic Whale

The direction of the movement of the peninsula along the San Andreas Fault is an unambiguous northwest. The rate (crustal deformation), however, is more difficult to determine. The rate of movement of the Pacific Plate relative to the North American Plate was recently estimated at 1.29 inches (33 mm) per year; however, estimates as high as 2.15 inches per year have been reported. Occasionally, a major slip along the fault will take place, as in 1906 when the peninsula jumped about 13 feet (4 meters) instantly.[14]

Using the conservative rate of movement of 1.29 inches per year, we can calcu-late that at the time of the granitic intrusion, the sediments that now compose the oldest rocks of Point Reyes may have been about 1,700 miles south of their present location, somewhere off the coast of central Mexico, south of the Baja peninsula, at about the same latitude as Las Tres Islas Marias or Puerto Vallarta. However, such a pat formula probably oversimplifies the complexities of crustal deformation. The origins of the granitic whale remain obscure and will be the subject of debate for years to come.

on Point Reyes, having become dominated by the now-abundant granite of Inverness Ridge, but a few small outcrops (roof pendants) remain to hint at their origins.[1,4,7]

As the earth continued to pulse, the granitic whale rose above the sea, then breached, then surfaced again. The ebbing and flowing sea deposited layers on the granite — sandstone, then shale, greensand, siltstone, and mudstone. Today, as the whale has again surfaced, in the flickering moment that we ride its back we identify the sediments remaining on the western flank — Laird's sandstone, Monterey shale, Drake's Bay formation — the granite body only visible along the northern ridge (from Mount Wittenberg north to Tomales Point) and at the tip of the left pectoral fin (Point Reyes Headlands).

Perhaps our cetacean metaphor will provide us with a living, breathing image that will help us keep in mind, as we learn the specifics of the geology, that the very bedrock is constantly changing, traveling on a tectonic course, driven by the inexorable forces of two crustal plates in constant conflict. Point Reyes is a vanguard on the edge of the ever-growing Pacific Plate, as it collides with the North American continent, and is deflected northwesterly along the continent's intransigent shore.

In few places is the drama of this confrontation more evident than along the Olema Valley, a temporary suture over the San Andreas Fault. Here, at Bear Valley, or at the base of Tomales Bay, one can stand on the fault and actually see the result of the tectonic tension underfoot. The area now known as the Earthquake Trail near Bear Valley headquarters became well known to geologists after the 1906 earthquake because of the

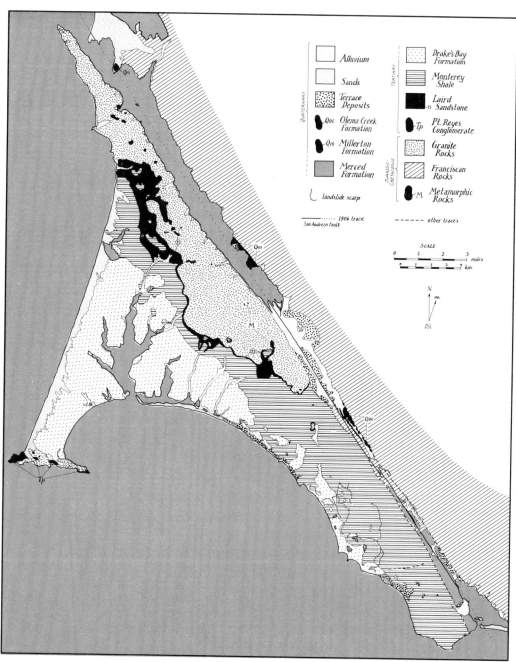

Map 4. Geologic map of the Point Reyes peninsula showing the areal
extent of the major geologic formations. (Adapted from Galloway 1977.)

obvious 14- to 18-foot offsets created on the surface by the sudden movement of the underlying fault. The self-guided Earthquake Trail explains the geology of the San Andreas at Point Reyes according to plate tectonic theory, and provides a vivid example of the surface displacement that results at an earthquake epicenter. Interestingly, the only local fatality attributed to the quake was "a cow . . . swallowed by the crack, disappearing all but the tail . . . the testimony on this point is beyond question." Apparently, the victim was a Holstein named Matilda, though the veracity of the report has been questioned by a few cynics.[20]

THE SAN ANDREAS PROVINCE

THE SAN ANDREAS FAULT is described by geologists as a "northwest-trending transform fault" that separates the North American Plate on the east from the Pacific Plate on the west.[1]

Point Reyes has many affinities with the Northern Coast Ranges of California — geography, climate, flora and fauna. Yet geologically, Point Reyes (with the Farallon Islands, the Cordell Banks, and Bodega Head) is a distinct province, separated from the Coast Ranges by the San Andreas Fault. Perhaps the most distinctive feature of this San Andreas Province is the presence of granite, which is conspicuously absent from the rest of the Northern Coast Ranges. (See Map 4.)

The typical geology of the Northern Coast Ranges is well represented along the "mainland" — from the eastern shore of Tomales Bay to the south end of Bolinas Lagoon. This Franciscan formation, primarily undifferentiated sedimentary rock — graywacke, shale, conglomerate, chert — is of late Jurassic and Cretaceous age, about 136 million years old. Most of the outcrops seen on the east shore of Tomales Bay or the Olema Valley are graywacke, formed deep under oceanic waters. According to the theory of plate tectonics, this Franciscan rock was lifted above the surface by the folding of the earth's crust as the old Pacific Ocean floor collided with the westward-moving North American continent. Franciscan rocks are not found west of the San Andreas Fault.[16]

Most of the rocks west of the fault, in the San Andreas Province, are from the Tertiary period and are therefore somewhat younger than those to the east of the fault. At Point Reyes, the oldest formations are limited to the granite of Inverness Ridge, which forms the western boundary of the fault zone. The age of the granite is not well known, but it is thought to have formed at about the same time as the adjacent Franciscan rock, though in a different place and by different processes. Small pockets of metamorphic schist and limestone are found in and upon the granite. Otherwise, the peninsula is dominated by relatively young marine sedimentary rocks — Monterey shale and Laird sandstone of Miocene age (12 to 26 million years old), and the younger Drake's Bay formation of Pliocene age (4 to 12 million years old). Each of these rock types receives further explanation below.

Thinking of the peninsula as a whole, then, three primary geologic regions stand out: (1) Inverness Ridge, extending nearly the length of the peninsula, on a northwest-southeast axis, formed by the eastern edge of the Salinian Block, a massive granitic body; (2) Point Reyes Promontory (Headlands), the westernmost flank, a granite outcrop overlain by conglomerate; and (3) the area in between, a basin of sediments with some structural elements underlain by granite. We will discuss these provinces chronologically, from oldest to youngest.

METAMORPHIC ROCKS: Roof Pendants – Barnacles on the Whale's Back

THE OLDEST ROCKS on the peninsula are remnant outcrops (roof pendants) of metamorphic material – schist, quartzite, limestone (marble) – that now nest amidst granite. They occur in small patches along Inverness Ridge, little incrustations, like the barnacles on a gray whale's skin (although some are imbedded in the granite). These metamorphic remnants were parented by sediments of lime, sand, and clays that were deposited as in a shallow sea. The date of sedimentation is unknown and no fossils that would aid in aging the rock have yet been found in them. But we do know that these remnants are older than the molten granite that engulfed the sediments no less than 84 million years ago and metamorphosed them into mica schists and limestone. Recent evidence pushes the age of these rocks back to 110 to 120 million years.[4, 6, 17]

The few outcrops of metamorphosed rock, representing the precursive geology of the Point Reyes peninsula, are associated exclusively with the granitic shield that stretches almost 20 miles from Tomales Point south to Mount Wittenberg. Outcroppings of schists, which look like laminated porcelain, are rather rare, but are best viewed at the south end of McClure's Beach (just north of Elephant Rock), in the cliffs along Heart's Desire and Shell beaches, or at the north end of Marshall Beach on Tomales Bay. At the base of Drake's View Road (six-tenths of a mile north of Inverness Park) mica schist in quartz diorite is also well exposed. Limestone pendants are exposed on the southeast slope of Mount Wittenberg, along Haggerty Gulch (where they occur with schists), and at Lockhart Ranch, one-half to one mile up Balboa Road, where the largest outcropping occurs. The most visible examples of crystalline limestone roof pendants are: (1) in Silver Hills, the canyon that runs west from the junction of Bear Valley Road and Sir Francis Drake Boulevard (enclosed in quartz diorite); (2) at the road cut on

Lime Kilns and Copper Mines

On the east bank of Olema Creek, in an outcrop of Franciscan limestone, are some mysterious caves with huge Douglas firs growing out of their ceilings, roots winding through the moss and lichen-covered walls. These are not natural caves, but man-made lime kilns, about 70 feet long and 18 feet wide, built of handcut rock with skillful masonry. Three arched entryways lead to three domed kilns, each about 10 feet in diameter. The kilns were used for the ancient practice of burning limestone to obtain lime. The first historical document that mentions these lime kilns is dated July 13, 1850. The builders apparently had planned to haul lime to San Francisco using ox carts and Indian labor. However, all the evidence indicates that the kilns were not very productive and the operation folded after a few years.

In 1863, shortly after the lime kilns were abandoned, commercial copper mines were opened in the Olema Valley, four miles south of the kilns and about a mile east of Dogtown, in Coppermine Canyon. They were mined in the 1860s and again in 1918 when about 11 tons of copper ore (primarily chalopyrite) were produced. Today these mines are abandoned, their shafts and chambers visited only by curious geologists, bats, and mole crickets.[2, 6, 20]

Balboa Road; and (3) in Redwood Canyon, west of Sir Francis Drake Boulevard from Willow Point (Bender scheelite).

Some similarities between the remnant metamorphics and similar strata in other California ranges (Santa Cruz, Santa Lucia, and Gabilan) suggest a Paleozoic origin; however, fossils of cup corals (crinoids), present in those other formations, have yet to be found on Point Reyes. It is curious that some of the metamorphic strata are folded and twisted within the granite, showing that the rock must have been deformed after intrusion, while other outcrops nearby show metamorphics in neat undeformed layers, as if all had been calm since the two bodies merged. There are mysteries hidden still in the bedrock of Point Reyes; origin and age are two of them.

GRANITIC BEDROCK:
The Spine of the Whale

The foundation of Point Reyes was laid in granite — grey granite, speckled black on white, crystalline, solid as a rock should be, refined deep inside the earth, risen somehow in its purity to the surface, a thing from which monuments more lasting than human memory can be wrought.

— Arthur Quinn. *The Broken Shore.* 1981.

INVERNESS RIDGE is the exposed eastern edge of the Salinian Block, a large granitic basement between the San Andreas and the Sur-Nacimiento fault zones from Bodega Head south to Ben Lomond in Santa Cruz County or even all the way to the Tehatchapi Mountains in Southern California. A geologist's reference to this massive block as "a comagmatic suite of rocks" describes its uniformity of character and its common parentage. The granite of Point Reyes is commonly called "granodiorite." Granite of very similar composition has been identified at the Farallon Islands, the Cordell Banks, Bodega Head, Montara Mountain (San Mateo County), Ben Lomond (Santa Cruz County), and the Santa Lucia Mountains (Monterey and San Luis Obispo counties), suggesting that each area, though geographically separated, had similar origins and that each is an exposed portion of the Salinian Block. Many of these sites also contain remnants of metamorphosed schists and crystalline limestone analagous to those at Point Reyes.[9, 17, 18, 19]

Granitic outcrop

The considerable variation in the composition of the granite, from quartz diorite to quartz monzonite, seems to follow a pattern: the rock at Tomales Point and Point Reyes has less feldspar and silica and more dark minerals than the lighter rock near Mount Wittenberg. In general, the granite of Point Reyes is coarse-grained, abundant with quartz, light-colored, but mottled with black biotite (a mica-like mineral) and hornblende.[17]

Until recently, geologists aged the granitic bedrock as Late Cretaceous (84 million years old) and therefore younger than the neighboring Franciscan formation across the fault. This age discrepancy, along with the absence of granitic intrusion and associated metamorphic pendants within the Franciscan rock, was some of the first evidence for large-scale movement along the San Andreas Fault. Recently, however, it has been estimated that the granite is as old, or perhaps older than the Franciscan formation. This revision in thought has not altered the theory that when the molten granite that now forms Inverness Ridge was emplaced, it was probably several hundred miles south of the present location at 38°N and deeper in the earth, for, as well as moving northwesterly along the continent's edge, the mass has been uplifted, resubmerged, and uplifted again. The contrary forces of weather eroded the block as it rose and sank and rose again.[13]

By the Paleocene epoch, in the early Tertiary period, about 65 million years ago, the earth's vegetation was well developed and diverse. Insects, reptiles, and bony fishes had established themselves as successful earthlings, birds had mastered the air, but the great radiation of mammals had not yet begun. The underlayer of granite now beneath

Point Reyes had cooled and solidified; an overlaying blanket of metamorphics had eroded considerably. During this period the body of Point Reyes was forced below the sea again, where it gathered the Paleozoic conglomerate that now covers the Point Reyes Headlands. We might imagine this gathering of sediment as a bulldozer plowing up the soil or a gray whale furrowing the ocean floor with its snout or fin as it forages along the bottom.

Today, the granitic mass of Inverness Ridge, north of Mount Wittenberg, is exposed over a vertical elevation of 1,300 feet from the top of Point Reyes Hill to sea level on Tomales Bay; however, this is a diagonal cross-section of a block that has been tilted in a southwesterly direction; the true vertical thickness is approximately 1,000 feet.[6]

Again, if we think of this granitic basement as a whale migrating north, we can imagine its brow and back breaking through the surface from Tomales Point to Mount Wittenberg; the posterior half of the mass is submerged, sinking progressively deeper below the surface south of Mount Wittenberg. Marine sediments of Tertiary age (2 to 65 million years old) overlay the basement, to a shallow depth toward the north, deeper to the south.

The southern extent of Double Point, just south of Pelican Lake. The geology of this area is called Drake's Bay formation, a mixture of siltstone, mudstone, and greensand. The cliffs to the left of the picture are the western edge of a large landslide that extends from Palomarin north to Wildcat Beach. (Photo taken June 7, 1957, courtesy of Point Reyes National Seashore.)

TERTIARY ROCKS

The Point Reyes conglomerate, which outcrops only along the westernmost cliffs of the Point Reyes Headlands, is dated from the earliest epoch of the Tertiary period – the Paleocene, about 65 million years ago. The maximum thickness of the layer is about 700 feet, though it has probably eroded. Pink feldspars from this formation can be found in the sand along Drake's Beach. This conglomerate is the oldest marine sediment yet found atop the granite bedrock of Point Reyes. This formation has also been reported from the Cordell Banks (a submarine ridge 20 miles west of Point Reyes), but none has been found elsewhere on the peninsula.

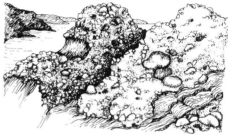

Point Reyes conglomerate

The conglomerate is composed mostly of angular granitic rocks embedded in a loose granite sand, but rounded cobbles of andesitic porphyry (a fine-grained volcanic rock with large feldspar crystals) and chert are also embedded. The granite is derived from the local bedrock, but the origin of the volcanic andesite is uncertain. Its similarity to the cobbles found in the Carmelo formation on the Monterey Peninsula at Point Lobos suggests strongly that there is a relationship between the two sites. The two formations also contain the same fossil evidence. The rocks and pebbles in the outcrop are graded by size; these and other geologic features suggest that it was formed in a submarine landslide, where surging water helped settle the debris according to size and weight.[13, 17]

Figure 4. Geologic cross section of Point Reyes peninsula showing the basement of granite overlain by marine deposits. (Adapted from Galloway 1977.)

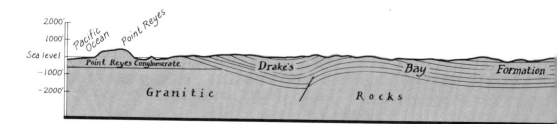

MIOCENE ROCKS

Laird Sandstone

The granite bedrock of Inverness Ridge is overlain along its western flank by Laird sandstone, a medium- to coarse-grained rock of younger origin (Miocene epoch — 12 to 26 million years ago). Outcrops are light brown, but in White Gulch, just north of Pierce Point Ranch, they are a creamy white. Wherever it occurs, it is in association with granite, was derived from a weathering of the granitic basement, and was probably deposited by an advancing sea.

Its extent is restricted mostly to the western flank of the granitic backbone of Inverness Ridge, except for a small island above Divide Meadow on the Bear Valley Trail. Sandwiched between granite and Monterey shale, it occurs in a narrow ribbon that stretches from Bear Valley northward to Kehoe Beach. Exposures of Laird's sandstone are visible in the road cuts on the Limantour Road (three miles from the entrance), in the cliffs at Kehoe Beach, and above White Gulch.

Monterey Shale

The most extensive of the Tertiary marine sediments, the gray to brown, organic Monterey shale overlays the granite basement from the Bolinas Mesa north to Kehoe Beach. At the southern end of the peninsula, this formation is about one and one-half miles thick; northward it becomes shallower, feathering out over the granite, merging with the Laird sandstone, and overlain by the Drake's Bay formation.

Cliffs at Bolinas Point and Duxbury Point . . . are retreating under the impact of wave attack at a rate of 1 foot to 3 feet per year.

—John J. Clague. *Landslides of Southern Point Reyes National Seashore.* 1969.

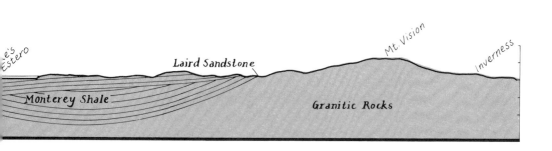

The Monterey shale is made up of cherts, sandstone, and organic shales containing the remains of many single-celled organisms (foraminifera and diatoms) as well as fish scales and plant material. The silica from the shells (tests) of the diatoms causes the chert to be hard and shiny, resembling porcelain. Most outcrops bleach white when exposed to the weather. At the north end of its distribution, between Abbott's Lagoon and Kehoe Beach, or near the Estero Trailhead, the outcrops look like layered flagstones.

The shale is well exposed on a southwesterly facing slope along the coastal cliffs from Duxbury Point north to Bolinas Point. Duxbury Reef, the whale's port fluke, is a particularly erosion-resistant outcrop of thin, often rhythmically layered shale. In the road cut midway between the Laguna Ranch Hostel and the Clem Miller Environmental Education Center, an exposure of Monterey shale displays the contortion more characteristic of the formation. Indeed, most of the hogbacks (ridges formed by the outcropping edges of tilted strata) pointing southwestwardly toward Drake's Bay, along the road to Limantour on the coastal slope of Inverness Ridge, are formed by contorted Monterey shale.

It should be pointed out that in his exhaustive description of Point Reyes geology, Galloway identified the shales at the south end of the peninsula (Bolinas Mesa and Duxbury Reef) as belonging to the Monterey formation. Subsequent fossil evidence has shown that these sediments are in fact younger, the same age as those Galloway classifies as Drake's Bay formation.

PLIOCENE ROCKS

Drake's Bay Formation

This marine sediment filled the basin between Inverness Ridge and the Point Reyes Headlands toward the end of the Tertiary age, in the early Pliocene epoch (about eight million years ago) at a time when the sea was again rising over the land (transgression). To explain the effects of this transgression we will again invoke the image of Point Reyes as a whale. The Drake's Bay formation is underlain by greensand that accumulated on the whale as it dove in a shallow sea. We know this because the sand is fine and uniform, not layered like the siltstones of the Monterey formation. This essential difference provides a clue to the different environments that prevailed over the Monterey formation and the Drake's Bay formation. The Monterey sediment is thinly layered, indicating that there were few benthic organisms (burrowing worms, amphipods) around to mix the mud and sand; as a result it settled out in differentiated layers (rhythmic bedding). The scant evidence of benthic organisms in the Monterey sediments suggests that it was deposited in very deep water where little oxygen was available to support animal life.

The undulating cliffs at Drake's Beach reveal the siltstone and sandstone of the Drake's Bay formation. This is an aerial view looking northwesterly toward the Mendoza syncline. (Photo by William Rosenberg, June 26, 1959, courtesy of Point Reyes National Seashore.)

The greensand of the younger Drake's Bay formation is not layered and is riddled with the burrows of invertebrates, indicating an oxygen-rich environment that supported an abundant community of animals. The greensand is fossil-rich. Fossils not only of invertebrates, but also of fish, seals, and whales are abundant in wave-cut cliff faces. (For a discussion of whale fossils, see Chapter 7.)

The greensand basement of the Drake's Bay formation is overlain by shale, which intermixes with sand and grades into siltstone and mudstone. The softness of these overlying sediments accounts for the rounded shapes of the treeless hills that reach westward across the outer peninsula. The overlying sediments become lighter colored toward the surface and contain abundant fossils of single-celled algae (diatoms) and animals (radiolarians). The light color of these sediments is caused, in part, by the abundance of silica from the shells of these single-celled organisms.

The Drake's Bay formation is more extensively exposed than any other formation on the peninsula. The cream-colored cliffs at Drake's Beach, which may have reminded Sir Francis Drake of the white cliffs of Dover, are the most visible exposure of this formation.

SOILS

L IKE THE BEDROCK, the soil types of Point Reyes are distinct from those of the adjacent mainland on the eastern shore of Tomales Bay or the east side of the Olema
Valley. The soil types reflect the underlying geology and, through the resulting physical
properties (ability to hold water, acidity, etc.), determine the plant communities that
colonize them. The soils of the peninsula are broadly classified into six major soil types
(See Map 4, page 28); the characteristics of each are summarized below.[11]

The **Kehoe-Sheridan** soils cover the north flank of Inverness Ridge from Tomales
Point south to Tomales Bay State Park. This is the type of soil in which the bishop pine
forest grows. These soils are derived from sandstone and quartz diorite. They are
moderately deep (about three feet), well drained, and loamy.

The **Palomarin-Wittenberg** complex covers the southern half of Inverness Ridge,
occurring almost entirely within the Douglas fir forest. These loamy soils are derived
from silica-laden sandstone and shale. They are deep (to five feet or more), well drained,
and strongly acid.

The **Tomales-Steinbeck** soils extend from outer Point Reyes, surrounding Drake's
and Limantour esteros, south to Point Resistance, overlaying the extent of the Merced
and Drake's Bay formations of the bedrock. Most of the area is covered by pasture and
coastal scrub. These soils, derived from the soft sandstone of the underlying Drakes's
Bay formation, are deep (to about four feet) and moderately well drained. The Tomales
soils comprise about 55 percent of this area, Steinbeck only about 20 percent; the rest are
a mixture of soils of minor extent. The Tomales series is fine, clayey, and strongly acidic.
The Steinbeck series is fine-loamy and only medium or slightly acidic.

The **Pablo-Bayview** soils occur in a long, narrow strip at the base of the western
slope of Inverness Ridge and are bound on the west by the Tomales-Steinbeck soils and
the Pacific Ocean. These loamy soils are derived from the weathered products of the
shale and sandstone higher upslope. They are well drained and shallow, covering the
bedrock to a depth of about 10 to 20 inches.

The **Dune-Sirdrak** soils are wind-blown deposits that occur in a narrow strip on
the windward shore, along the extent of Great Beach from near the outer Point north to
about Kehoe Beach and including Abbott's Lagoon. The soils are sandy and can be quite
deep, to about six feet. These dunes have very little ability to hold water, and are therefore sparsely vegetated with drought-tolerant plants (see "Coastal Strand" in Chapter 3).

At the southern end of the peninsula, the area known as the Bolinas Mesa is composed of moderately or well-drained soils classified as **Cronkhite-Dipsea-Centissima**,
each of the three types in roughly equal proportions. These soils, derived from sandstone and shale, are relatively deep (about five feet to bedrock).

Watercourses

The effects of faulting and surface movement are apparent in the complex drainages in the vicinity of Five Brooks in the center of the Olema Valley. Most noticeable are Olema Creek and Pine Gulch Creek, which run parallel to one another only 1,500 feet apart but in opposite directions — Olema Creek running north to Tomales Bay, Pine Gulch Creek running south to Bolinas Lagoon.

LANDFORMS

The only certainty is that this exceedingly mobile section of the earth's crust will continue to change in unpredictable ways. Man can only stand on this threshold and peer with wonder a short distance into spans of time inconceivably greater than the span of his own life and, very probably, that of his species.

— Harold Gilliam. *Island in Time.* 1962.

T HE POINT REYES PENINSULA is a geomorphologist's treasure chest, with a plethora of examples of landforms. Volcanoes and glaciers have not contributed to the lay of the land at Point Reyes, but these shortcomings have been compensated for by the effects of wind, water, and tectonics. In her book *The California Landscape*, Mary Hill uses Point Reyes as an example of the following landforms:

Concretion (a hard, rounded mass in sedimentary rock) — exposed in the Bolinas cliff at the high tide line and in the cliffs at Drake's Beach about one mile southwest of the Visitor Center.

Drowned river valley — Drake's Estero and Bolinas Lagoon.

Fault — A "textbook" example of a vertical fault is visible in the sea cliffs at the north end of Kehoe Beach; other small faults are visible in the white cliffs at Drake's Beach and along the headlands at outer Point Reyes.

Fault line — Tomales Bay, Olema Valley, Bolinas Bay.

Offset stream — Olema Creek.

Sag pond — Olema Valley (2.1 miles south of the village of Olema, east side of Highway 1.

Fault-controlled valley — Tomales Bay and the Olema Valley.

Bay mouth bar — Bolinas Lagoon.

Lagoon and estuary — Abbott's Lagoon, Bolinas Lagoon, Drake's Estero, Limantour Estero.

Landslide – The coastline between Wildcat Beach and Palomarin is characterized by a large number of ancient landslides; the seven lakes at Lake Ranch are all associated with an ancient slide. Another example is at the southwest end of Drake's Beach, near the Coast Guard boathouse. (See reference 3 for further discussion.)

Marine terrace – Extending from the Bolinas Mesa to Limantour Estero is a marine terrace that is one of the most striking features of the peninsula. Landslides obscure the terrace at Lake Ranch, but it originally extended from Coast Creek south to Palomarin.

Marsh – Although small in extent, the area supports a diversity of marshlands: freshwater marsh at Ledum Swamp, upper Olema Marsh, Laguna Ranch Marsh, Kehoe Marsh, and upper Abbott's Lagoon; brackish marsh at lower Olema Marsh and Pine Gulch Creek; salt marsh at the south end of Tomales Bay, around Bolinas Lagoon, and at Drake's and Limantour esteros.

Sea stacks

Sandspit – Stinson Beach, Limantour Spit.

Sea arch – Arch Rock.

Sea cave – Several inaccessible sites at the tide line below the headlands.

Sea cliffs – Tomales Point, Point Reyes Headlands, Double Point.

Sea stack – Numerous examples at Double Point, Miller's Point, Chimney Rock, Elephant Rocks, Bird Rock.

Tafone (a honeycombed weathering pattern caused by wind or rain) – Rare in the cliffs and dunes, but excellent examples are at Elephant Rock above the mouth of Tomales Bay at Dillon Beach.

Waterfall beach – Alamere Falls, near Double Point.

Underwater reef – Duxbury Reef, the largest shale reef in North America.

REFERENCES

1. Atwater, T. 1970. *Implications of Plate Tectonics for the Cenozoic Tectonic Evolution of Western North America*. Geologic Society of America Bulletin 81.

2. Bowen, Oliver E., Jr. 1951. Highways and byways of particular geologic interest. In *Geologic Guidebook of the San Francisco Bay Counties*. California Division of Mines Bulletin 154.

3. Clague, J. J. 1969. *Landslides of Southern Point Reyes National Seashore*. California Division of Mines and Geology, Mineral Information Service 22 (7).

4. Curtis, G. H., Evernden, J. F., and Lipson, J. 1958. *Age Determination of Some Granitic Rocks in California by the Potassium-Argon Method*. California Division of Mines Special Report 54.

5. Galloway, A. J. 1962. *Field Trip 3: Point Reyes Peninsula and the San Andreas Fault Zone*. California Division of Mines and Geology Bulletin 181.

6. Galloway, A. J. 1977. *Geology of the Point Reyes Peninsula, Marin County, California*. California Division of Mines and Geology Bulletin 202.

7. Gluskoter, H. J. 1969. *Geology of a Portion of Western Marin County, California*. California Division of Mines and Geology Bulletin 202.

8. Hall, T. N., and David A. Hughes. 1980. Quaternary geology of the San Andreas Fault zone at Point Reyes National Seashore, Marin County, California. In *Studies of the San Andreas Fault Zone in Northern California*. California Division of Mines and Geology Special Report 140.

9. Hanna, G. D. 1951. Geology of the Farallon Islands. In *Geologic Guidebook of the San Francisco Bay Counties*. California Division of Mines Bulletin 154.

10. Hanna, G. D. 1951. Geology of the continental slope off central California. In *California Academy of Science, Proceedings*, 4th Series, 27 (9).

11. Kashiwagi, J. H. 1985. *Soil Survey of Marin County*. U. S. Department of Agriculture. Soil Conservation Service.

12. Kleist, J. R., ed. 1981. *The Franciscan Complex and the San Andreas Fault from the Golden Gate to Point Reyes, California*. The Pacific Section: American Association of Petroleum Geologists.

13. Page, B. 1966. Geology of the Coast Ranges of California. In *Geology of Northern California*, edited by E. H. Bailey. U.S. Geological Survey Bulletin 190.

14. Prescott, W. H., N. E. King, M. Lisowski, and J. C. Savage. 1985. *Deformation of the Pacific Plate near San Francisco, California*. U.S. Geological Survey, Menlo Park, Calif.

15. Quinn, A. 1981. *Broken Shore: The Marin Peninsula*. Salt Lake City: Peregrine Smith.

16. Rice, S. J. 1961. *Geologic Sketch of the Northern Coast Ranges*. California State Division of Mines, Mineral Information Service 14.

17. Ross, D. C. 1972. *Petrographic and Chemical Reconnaissance Study of Some Granitic and Gneissic Rocks Near the San Andreas Fault from Bodega Head to Cajon Pass, California*. U.S. Geological Survey. Professional Paper 698.

18. Spotts, J. H. 1962. *Zircon and Other Accessory Minerals, Coast Range Batholith, California*. Geological Society of America 73.

19. Taliaferro, N. L. 1951. Geology of the San Francisco Bay counties. In *Geologic Guidebook of the San Francisco Bay Counties*. California Division of Mines Bulletin 154.

20. Traganza, A. E., 1951. Old lime kilns near Olema. In *Geologic Guidebook of the San Francisco Bay Counties*. California Division of Mines Bulletin 154.

21. U.S. Geologic Survey. 1913. *Geologic Records Book #108*.

22. Weber, G. E. 1981. Physical environment. In *The Natural History of Año Nuevo*, edited by Le Boeuf and Kaza. Pacific Grove, Calif.: Boxwood Press.

Keith Hansen 1988

CHAPTER THREE

PLANT
COMMUNITIES
An Overlay of Influences

No poet has yet sung the full beauty of our poppy, no painter has successfully portrayed the satiny sheen of its lustrous petals, no scientist has satisfactorily diagnosed the vagaries of its variations and adaptability. In its abundance, this colorful plant should not be slighted: cherish it and ever be thankful that so rare a flower is common.

— Thomas Howell. *The Marin Flora.* 1970.

FROM THE FLOWER-STREWN HEADLANDS at Chimney Rock, through the swales, prairie, and scrub of the coastal plain, up the forested slopes of Inverness Ridge, and along the riparian corridor of Olema Valley, we pass through a mosaic of habitats, each grading into another, but each with a distinctive character and its own community of species. Few areas on the North American landmass host the variety of habitats found within the 100 square miles of the Point Reyes Peninsula. At 38° North Latitude, with a climate temperate enough to accommodate a wide range of physiological requirements, Point Reyes enjoys an overlap of floristic influences from north and south resulting in a patchwork of communities and a bountiful diversity of plants and animals.

The author of *Marin Flora*, Thomas Howell, lists 61 species of plants that are present on Point Reyes but absent from the rest of Marin County. In addition, he identifies 34 species that reach the southern limit of their distribution at Point Reyes and only 11 that reach their northernmost limit here. This three-fold predominance of northerly species results from the close affinity that the Point Reyes flora has with the North Coast Ranges, especially with the closed-cone pine and the Douglas fir forests.

In this chapter we venture first into the woodlands, then into more open country of the coastal strand, prairie, rangeland, scrub, and marshland, and, finally, into the marine algal community of the intertidal zone. For those species of plants whose common names are ambiguous or misleading, Latin names are given in parentheses following the common name.

BISHOP PINE FOREST

OVERHEAD, an osprey scribes concentric circles, repeating a piercing, liquid whistle. On a pale granite outcrop, silhouetted against the slate sky of summer, a bishop pine — trunk awry, limbs askew — stands sentry over the rolling grasslands that stretch toward the dunes of Great Beach and the swollen surf beyond. Hidden in the tufted clusters of long needles that splay from the ends of the smaller branches, a Steller's jay sounds a scolding "caw." Molded by the contrary forces of wind, substrate, and available moisture, these contorted conifers lend a twisted grace to the landscape and more than any other species, symbolize the unique and natural beauty that encompasses Point Reyes.

Although once widespread, **bishop pines** (*Pinus muricata*) now occur in relict stands, scattered along the humid coastal region of California from Humboldt to Santa Barbara counties, with isolated populations south to central Baja. Point Reyes hosts one of the most extensive and picturesque groves, and the variable growth patterns of the trees provide the local scenery with much of its distinctive character. In the summer fog, the silhouette of the forest is reminiscent of a romantic Japanese landscape.[34]

At Point Reyes the distribution of bishop pine is restricted to the north end of Inverness Ridge, almost entirely on soils of granitic origin. Derived from quartz diorite, this soil is a moderately deep, coarse, sandy loam with an effective rooting depth of 20 to 40 inches. Permeability is moderately rapid and water capacity is low. There is a similarity between the granitic rocks of Point Reyes and those of the Santa Lucia Range of Monterey and San Luis Obispo counties. Indeed, the bedrock of Point Reyes may have originated in the Santa Lucia Range from which it was rendered and pushed northward along the San Andreas Fault. Interestingly, it was in the Santa Lucia Range that the Irish botanist Thomas Coulter first discovered the bishop pine.[15, 19, 23]

> [This tree is] . . . unkempt and wild, as befits a tree breathed on eternally by the prevailing westerlies off the North Pacific. . . . But the true beauty of Bishop Pine is seen on the leeward side of Inverness Ridge, and at nearby Shell Beach, where the trees overhang Tomales Bay. Here, sheltered from the full force of the eternal winds . . . [the pines] form lovely groves, with picturesquely twisted stems, and flat-topped or dome-shaped crowns that interlock, tree with tree. So each tree takes protection from its brethren and all together they achieve an air of inviolable serenity and a sort of pagan sanctity.
> — Donald C. Peattie. *The Natural History of Western Trees.* 1953.

Influenced by soil, slope, and microclimate, bishop pines improvise shape and habit. If edaphic conditions permit, the trees grow lanky, straight, and tall, with few lateral branches, but inevitably are topped with a rounded tuft of foliage. At the forest's edge, individuals may grow apart from their neighbors and be free to branch broadly, twisting and bending under the constraints of wind and substrate. On barren granitic hogbacks of Inverness Ridge, where the soil is thin and nutrients are few, some trees become dwarfed, attaining only a few feet in height but developing cones and reaching full maturity. Such natural bonsai are found among other California conifers as well, most notably in the "pygmy forests" of coastal Mendocino County.

Other trees share the forest with the pines, but usually as secondary members of the community. These include bay laurel, madrone, California buckeye, California wax myrtle; and, to a lesser degree, coast live oak. The understory of the bishop pine forest

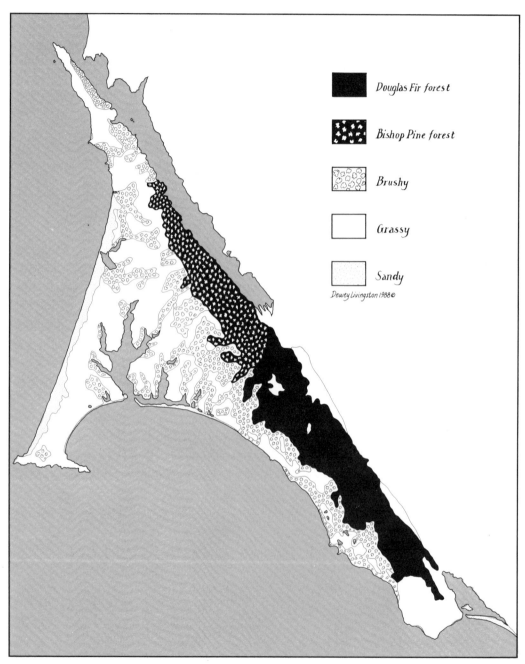

Map 5. Areal extent of the major plant communities at Point Reyes peninsula.

Deer Fern

Deer fern *(Blechnum spicant)*, a true fern that is rare locally, occurs in damp areas of the bishop pine forest, as in the vicinity of Ledum Swamp. It is unusual for a fern, because the male and female fronds are dissimilar, a condition known as sexual dimorphism. Pacific tree frogs — emerald green, black masked — take refuge within the damp recesses of the dense frond clusters. Winter wrens nest here too, climbing the stiff, ladder-like fronds, cocking their heads, and filling the forest with sweet notes.

varies with the growth pattern of the trees, which is a reflection of available moisture and soil. Beneath dense stands where the canopy is relatively closed and the substrate damp, the understory is usually crowded with California wax myrtle, coffeeberry, huckleberry, and salal. A good example of this closed canopy forest type is visible along Pierce Point Road or the Mount Vision Road. In drier forest with greater distance between trees and a more open canopy, many of the same substory plants dominate, but they tend to be less dense and there are more open grassy areas creating a park-like environment. In these drier forests, as on south-facing slopes, manzanita and ceonothus may be more prevalent than wax myrtle and salal. Along the forest edge, the bishop pine community mixes with coastal scrub, grassland, or Douglas fir forest.

Some of the most captivating growth patterns develop in areas where the trees of the forest are widely spaced and each individual has enough room to branch and twist freely. Several sites where the forest is particularly enchanted include: the windswept knob on the west side of the Pierce Point Road (seven tenths of a mile north of the intersection with Sir Francis Drake Boulevard); the Mount Vision Road; and the Bayview Trailhead off the Limantour Road.

Several rare or endangered species are associated with this habitat. **Bolinas manzanita** *(Arctostaphylos virgata)*, an early blooming shrub with hairy leaves and branchlets, is confined to rocky slopes at the forest's edge along Inverness Ridge. (This localized endemic also borders the redwood forest at Muir Woods and along Bolinas Ridge.) Another, species, the **Cushing manzanita**, is widespread, but a distinctive ecological form called **huckleberry manzanita** *(A. cushingia* f. *ripens)* grows only amidst the dwarfed bishop pines on granitic hogbacks on Inverness Ridge. This ecotype is small-leaved with a prostrate, matlike growth habit.[5,22]

Two varieties of *ceonothus*, a shrub commonly called "wild lilac" or "blue blossom," are listed as rare or endangered by the California Native Plant Society. **Mount Vision ceonothus** *(Ceonothus gloriosus* var. *porrectus)*, a low, spreading variety restricted to the bishop pine forest on the slopes of Mount Vision, Point Reyes Hill, Ledum Swamp, and near the summit of Point Reyes Road, is a candidate for endangered status. **Point Reyes Ceonothus** *(C. g. gloriosus)*, a prostrate coastal form, is found on exposed ridges on the edge of bishop pine forest along Pierce Point Road, as well as in the coastal strand and coastal shrub communities. John M. Bigelow, the botanist on the Pacific railway survey, first collected this species at "Punta de los Reyes" in 1845.[5, 21]

Bishop pines belong to an ecological category of conifers known as "closed-coned pines." All four species (bishop, Monterey, knobcone, and Santa Cruz Island pines) occur within the California floristic province. These species have an extensive fossil history which indicates that bishop pines were once widespread. The coastal species (bishop, Monterey, Santa Cruz Island) were derived from a common ancestor that was most common in the Pleistocene period (about one million years ago). The **Monterey pine**, the closest relative to the bishop, once occurred naturally in the Point Reyes vicinity, as indicated by fossils from Millerton Point on the east shore of Tomales Bay. The Monterey pine is desirable as an ornamental because it is faster growing and less temperamental than its native cousin (see page 50). Although the species are familiar, Monterey pines have three needles and bishops have only two (easily remembered because in each the number of needles is the same as the number of syllables in its name). Where the two species grow side by side, the fact that each has a different flowering time prevents rampant hybridization.[28, 29]

Closed-cone pines are adapted to periodic fires, which serve to open the cones, release seeds, and return nutrients to the soil. Such woodlands regenerate only after fires, which explains why groves are often made up of trees of uniform age. (Plants that regenerate through fire are known as "pyrophytes," and include most of the chaparral species as well as closed-cone pines and cypress.) Apparently, a fire-free period of 80 years or more might allow these relatively short-lived trees to die without reproducing.

The bishop's cones are arranged in tight whorls, their scales sealed closed with pitch. On a hot day in late summer or autumn, one can hear the cones crackle as the dried resins release the scales, freeing the seeds to fall or be eaten by finches and sparrows. Western gray squirrels also feast on the cones, but they will attempt to gnaw out the seeds before the scales have released their protective grip. Birds, rodents, and wind disperse the seeds. Undoubtedly, some seeds so dispersed find soil and moisture conditions suitable for propagation and growth; however, this method of regeneration does not compare to the abundance of saplings that sprout shortly following a forest fire that has cleared out the competing undergrowth and nutrified the soil. If fires are periodic, the kindling that litters the forest floor is sparse and the fires burn out quickly. Such conditions are ideal for the pines, because the fire is not so intense as to severely damage the larger trees. However, if fires are infrequent the litter will probably accumulate in such

The edge of the bishop pine forest, looking southwest from Pierce Point Road toward Mount Vision.

proportions that fire will burn long and hot, damaging the parent trees and destroying the vigor of the forest.[37]

As civilization has settled in fire-adapted habitats and periodic fires have been suppressed, changes have ensued. Although the bishop pine forest at Point Reyes appears healthy to the casual observer, systematic sampling is needed to determine if the forest is regenerating or approaching senescence. Current management practices include controlled burns as a regenerative tool for the health of the forest.

DOUGLAS FIR FOREST

A moonlight walk from Sky Camp along Meadow Trail down to Divide Meadow takes us through the heart of the Douglas fir forest. An onshore breeze cools the air and the trees whisper in conspiracy. Shadows dance in the duff on the path. Slightly unsettled, we stop to listen to the sounds behind the constant rushing of the limbs overhead. A repetitive whirring startles us — the warning patter of a woodrat's tail against the thimbleberry cane. Then a resonant, repetitive "hoo-hoo-hoo-hoo" — the mating call of a spotted owl — commands our attention, seeming to mute every other sound, even the wind. Silent minutes pass before we notice the trees again stirring their needles against the gusts high above. We have encountered the spirit of the old growth forest; somehow comforted, we continue on our midnight walk.

*   *   *

WHILE THE STRONGHOLD of the bishop pine is the north end of Inverness Ridge, **Douglas fir** *(Pseudotsuga menziesii)* in association with Monterey shale dominates the southern end of the ridge. Soils are of the Palomarin-Wittenberg complex — deep, well-drained soils derived from siliceous shale and sandstone on slopes that range from strongly sloping to very steep. Annual precipitation is higher than in the bishop pine forest, with 30 to 42 inches per year.

Like the bishop pine, the Point Reyes fir forest is a relict population whose distribution was more widespread and continuous in an earlier epoch. What remains is a southern outpost of an extensive northern forest that stretches nearly uninterrupted along the coast from Sonoma County north to British Columbia. The northern forest includes cedar, spruce, and hemlock — species that virtually disappear south of Mendocino and Sonoma counties. The drier forest at Point Reyes may be shared by the California bay, an occasional big leaf maple, and a varied substory of California coffeeberry, California hazel, red elderberry, ceonothus, poison oak, huckleberry, and thimbleberry. The understory species are similar to those of the bishop pine or the mixed evergreen forests that mingle with the Douglas fir.

Although these forests were heavily logged into the late 1950s, large virgin trees still stand, especially in the steeper, impenetrable canyons. Several areas logged over from 1958 to 1961 were reseeded with Monterey pine. One such plot, near Lake Ranch Gate on Inverness Ridge, was surveyed from 1972 to 1978 for changes in vegetation and bird-

Figure 5. Idealized cross-section of the Point Reyes peninsula from Inverness Park northwestward over Point Reyes Hill toward Abbott's Lagoon showing the distribution of the major plant communities.

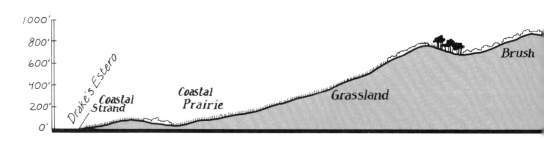

life. The plot was not clear-cut; several large trees were allowed to stand. Twenty years after the logging, the forest was dense with young Douglas fir and, characteristically, many of the shallow-rooted Monterey pine had blown over. It appears that the pine provided ample shade for the young fir and did not usurp the habitat, allowing the fir to reforest successfully.[13, 26]

The Douglas fir is a grand tree; some individuals within the Seashore rival redwoods in girth and height. Like bishop pine, Douglas fir forest thrives following fire. The seeds germinate readily, but only those seedlings survive that receive direct sunlight and whose roots come in contact with mineral soil. Therefore, before a new forest can become established, some event must clear the mother forest, provide a bed of mineral soil, and reduce competition from more shade-tolerant species. Fire is the only primeval event that provides these conditions.[37]

The deep forest is well represented along the Bear Valley Trail between Park Headquarters and Arch Rock. If you walk this trail in spring, Bear Valley Creek will be rushing loudly. Look for newts breeding in the still pools and back eddies, and listen to the cascading songs of the winter wrens that abound in the bracken fern along the damp slopes. As the spotted owl haunts the nocturnal forest, this tiny wren seems to fill the daylight with the sweetness of its endlessly varied lyric.

The Vedanta Trail, which parallels the Olema Creek, passes through a moist forest with a closed canopy. Here, search the damp forest floor for the dark, glossy green, heart-shaped leaves of **wild ginger** (*Asarum caudatum*). From March into July, if you lift a leaf you may find the flower – large but delicate, bell shaped with three elongated petals, a hidden treasure easily overlooked.

Drier Douglas fir forest is found along Inverness Ridge on the Bolema and Greenpicker trails; here the understory is brushier, with fewer ferns. In spring the lovely pink

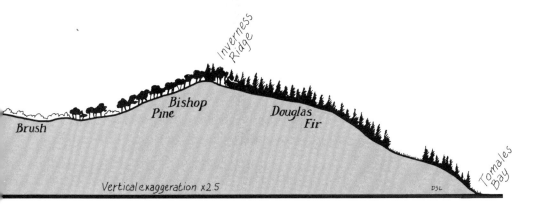

star flower *(Trientalis latifolia)* can be common. At Lake Ranch Gate, many of the dead "snags" are punctured with the large, oval excavations of the pileated woodpecker. Sometimes its maniacal voice *("kaka-kaka-kaka")* echoes through the old growth. Here, too, the riddled snags host a small colony of purple martins, a rare breeder on the coast. At Fir Top (elevation 1,325 feet), the fir opens into a grassy meadow with a view of Drake's Bay and, on a clear fall day, the Farallon Islands beyond. At this remote outpost, search the bare ground for tracks and scat of mountain lion, bobcat, badger, or gray fox. Here, too, western bluebirds raise their young, nesting in abandoned woodpecker holes and finding insects in the grassy opening. Audubon's warbler and hermit warbler, both rare breeders in Marin, sing atop the tallest ridgetop firs.

COASTAL STRAND

Perched atop a granite outcrop on the outer Point, scanning the horizon for flukes and spouts of gray whales, or huddled behind a dune at North Beach taking refuge from the wind, we are within the coastal strand. Desiccated by wind and salty spray, this habitat is sparsely vegetated, as the name implies. Proximity to the ocean moderates the temperature so that the growing season extends throughout the year, frost free. However, temperature may be the only moderate influence. The growth habit of the plants mirrors environmental stress. Most of the vegetation is low or prostrate owing to the consistent onshore winds. Many plants are succulent, an adaptation to drought. Fresh water is at a premium in the coastal strand due to the combined influences of low rainfall, rapid drainage in sandy or rocky substrate, and the dehydrating effects of the salty air.

The coastal strand at Point Reyes is similar to that of the north coast. From Point Reyes on northward, **beach grass** dominates the plant community. Perhaps the most familiar species is *Ammophila arenaria*, which lashes bare legs along the Limantour dunes. These grasses are not native to North America; they were first introduced to the Pacific coast of the United States from Australia (but originally from the Mediterranean) in 1896 to stabilize sand dunes in San Francisco on the site that eventually became Golden Gate Park. Beach grass serves to retard sand drift, forming foredunes parallel to the beach. **American dune grass** *(Elymus mollis)*, a native species, dominated the dunes prior to the introduction of the European beach grasses. Where *Elymus* is the dominant dune stabilizer, the dunes tend to form in lower ridges perpendicular to the beach. Dunes dominated by beach grasses generally support fewer plant species and fewer numbers of animals (burrowing arthropods) than do natural dunes. Mature stands of beach grass prevent recolonization by native plants and animals, and establish a rela-

Sand dunes, such as these coastal dunes at North Beach, support the plants of the coastal strand community. Large areas of these dune systems have been colonized by non-native vegetation over the last century. Ice plant (foreground, lower left) and beach grass (center left) dominate the habitat, stabilizing the dunes but relegating the native species to a secondary role.

tively permanent ecological presence. Another foreigner, equally detrimental to the native flora and fauna is **ice plant** *(Carpobratus edulis)*, introduced from Australia and now widely established from the coastal dunes and headlands to the median strip on Interstate Highway 5.[2,4,25,32,33]

Within the dunes are three subhabitats: foredune (nearest the shore), central dune, and hinddune. Few plants can survive the rigors of life in the foredune; indeed, the three common species are all introduced: two perennials, beach grass and ice plant; one annual, **sea rocket** *(Cakile maritima)*. Each of these hardy souls also survives in the central dune where some native species join the ranks: **beach morning glory**, the fragrant **ambrosia** (formerly franseria), and the succulent **sand-verbena**. The hinddune, with increased protection from the elements, hosts the greatest number of species, but even here diversity is low. In addition to the aforementioned plants, other members of the hinddune community include: **beach pea, bush lupine, dune lupine** (see below), **sand-verbena** (two species, one yellow, one pink), **salt bush, beach strawberry, Douglas bluegrass** (occurs only on the California coast from Mendocino to Monterey), **mock heather,** and **evening primrose.**

The most extensive dune system at Point Reyes borders Great Beach. In spring the central and hinddune blooms with some low-growing flowers, inconspicuous amidst the dominant yellow flowers of the bush lupine. **Curly-leaved monardella** *(Monardella undulata* var. *undulata)*, a rare annual in the mint family, blooms in May and June in barren sandy areas, often in association with **coast buckwheat** *(Eriogonum latifolium)* and **coast gilia** *(Gilia capitata)*. A lovely, small-leaved, low-growing coastal variety of **coyote bush** grows here too, hugging the contours of the dunes.

On "fresh dunes that have scarcely stopped moving" **dune lupine** *(Lupinus chamissonis)* is perhaps the most representative species of the coastal strand. Requiring a depth of clean sand for its roots, it is one of the first native species to colonize the dunes. It is a long-blooming shrub, its fragrant soft-blue flowers showiest in spring atop low-spreading limbs with silvery leaves.[30]

Above the dunes, on outcrops of pure granite or on the "Point Reyes Conglomerate" — a Paleocene mish-mash of chert, volcanic porphyrites, and granitic fragments in a bed of sandstone — is the headland strand. This community shares many of the environmental liabilities and several species with the dune strand. However, the flora of the headland strand is more diverse, incorporating some of the elements of coastal prairie or coastal scrub where the microclimate permits. **Lizard tail** *(Eriophyllum staechadifolium*

var. *artemisiaefolium)*, a small shrub "seemingly encrusted with the purest gold," is restricted entirely to these two strand communities. In June, the sandstone and shale cliff faces at Kehoe Beach host a resplendent bloom of lizard tail.

Several rarities are found along these precipitous headlands. The **coast rock cress** *(Arabis blepharophylla)* is one of the earliest blooming annuals. It magenta flowers brighten the shallow soils and rocky outcrops along the coastal headlands from the Lighthouse to Chimney Rock and at Tomales Point as early as February. Ice plant has colonized the hanging rock gardens of the headland strand, sharing the cliffs with the bushy **California phacelia** (meaning "clustered" in Latin) whose blue-violet blossoms open in February. Another less conspicuous phacelia, the delicate, violet-flowering annual **northcoast phacelia** *(Phacelia insularis continentis)*, finds its

Coastal cliff: lizard tail (Eriophyllum staechadifolium artemesiaefolium), live-forever (Dudleya farinosa).

southernmost station on the exposed Point Reyes headlands and around Abbott's Lagoon. A rare **rein-orchis** *(Habenaria elegans* var. *maritima)* with fragrant flowers occurs near McClure's Beach on dry bluffs.[5,6]

NORTHERN COASTAL PRAIRIE

*A*s early as mid-February, damp swales behind the coastal dunes brighten with the yellow blossoms of buttercups against deep green clumps of rushes. Yesterday a tropical storm raged, rain and wind unrelenting. Today the air is clean and clear, windless. From a low bush lupine a savannah sparrow cocks its head and sings a cricket-like buzz; it is answered by similar songs scattered evenly across the swale and up the grassy knoll. Spring starts early on the Point Reyes prairie.

*   *   *

THE NORTHERN COASTAL PRAIRIE is a narrow strip of habitat just inland from the coastal strand that occurs sporadically from San Francisco Bay north to the Oregon border. Coastal prairie has floristic affinities with the primeval valley grasslands of the Central Valley; however, the prairie has northern origins, while the interior grassland has more southern relationships. Each habitat has suffered a similar fate: conversion to agriculture. As early as 1793, when a Spanish lieutenant named De Goyoechea described the peninsula from atop Mount Vision as "very good pasture and springs in all parts, very appropriate for raising cattle of all kinds and very extensive," the fate of the pristine prairie was sealed.[27, 28, 36]

As a result of grazing pressure and intentional plowing, burning, and planting, most native perennial grasses were replaced by immigrants. The disappearance of antelope and elk soon followed.

> During the mission and rancho years . . . overgrazing, particularly in coastal areas, thinned the ranks of the bunchgrasses, enlarging the bare spaces . . . ready for the invasion into these areas were native annuals and aggressive newcomers.
> —Elna Bakker. *An Island Called California.* 1984.

Most of the original grasses of the coastal prairie were perennials. There are two kinds of perennial grasses: bunchgrasses and sod-forming grasses. To understand the changes that have affected this habitat since pre-European times, it is necessary to understand the ecological requirements of each type. Bunchgrasses are extremely long-lived and increase in size each year. An extensive root system penetrates deeply into the soil, provides water to the plant, holds the soil firmly in place, and reduces the erosional effects of wind, water, and grazing. The parent bunchgrasses produce an abundance of seeds, and these ultimately propagate the species. The sod-forming grasses spread vegetatively, that is, nonsexually by sprouting from root-like structures. **Saltgrass** (*Distichlis spicata),* of the upper salt marsh, is a well-known example. The seedlings of perennials fare poorly in competition with annual grasses, an important consideration in the decline of bunchgrasses from Point Reyes.

Coastal prairie survives at Point Reyes as a remnant of pre-European times. Over a century of grazing and use of the land for pasture has largely obscured this community of native grasses and forbs. There is some evidence that perennials return when grazing ceases, although coastal prairie may never regain pristine conditions because exotic species have taken such a firm hold (see "Coastal Rangeland" below for further discussion).[12, 36]

The coastal prairie at Point Reyes probably developed under light grazing pressure by elk and with frequent fires set by native peoples. The elk tended to roam seasonally from area to area, minimizing the intensity of their impact. There was probably a seasonal pattern to native burning practices as well. The shift from elk to cattle that accompanied European colonization changed the grazing pattern from seasonal to year-round, increasing the intensity of the grazing pressure and favoring a shift from prairie to rangeland.

Grazing pressure has been reduced since the establishment of Point Reyes National Seashore. In 1960 there were an estimated 10,500 head of cattle ranging on Point Reyes. By 1987 that number had been reduced to 5,100 head grazing on 20,659 acres of rangeland. Still, this density of one cow to every 4 acres is approximately twice the carrying capacity of one head to every 7 to 10 acres recommended by the Soil Conservation Ser-

Common grassland flowers: buttercup,
Douglas iris, California buttercup, pussy ears,
Ithuriel's spear, baby-blue-eyes, bi-colored lotus, blue-eyed grass, sun cups, checkerbloom.

vice. The current policy of the Park is aimed at further reducing grazing pressure in critical areas. [17, 39, 40]

A remnant plot of coastal grassland prairie, located on a windswept ridge shoulder along the Marshall Beach Trail on the bay side of Tomales Point, was studied in 1979. The plant community was composed of 75 percent native and 25 percent introduced species: 58 percent native perennials, 17 percent native annuals, 15 percent introduced annuals, and 10 percent introduced perennials. The most important species (42.6 percent relative dominance) was a native perennial bunchgrass, **Pacific hairgrass** *(Deschampsia holiciformis)*. Interestingly, the tufted hairgrasses are widely distributed and recover well from grazing pressure, which probably explains its continued presence at Point Reyes. [8, 36]

A comparative study of three grassland plots (heavily grazed, moderately grazed, ungrazed) near Point Reyes Beach North found that the removal of cattle caused a successional change in favor of native perennial grasses and a decrease in introduced annuals. The conclusion was that while climatic and soil conditions favor perennial plants, grazing pressure shifts the favor toward annual species. [12]

Some of the familiar plant species characteristic of coastal prairie include: hairgrass *(Deschampsia)*, oatgrass *(Danthonia)*, fescue, bracken fern, sedges, blue dicks, Douglas iris, blue-eyed grass, California buttercup, lupine, checkerbloom, gold fields, and footsteps-of-spring. [22, 27]

Two species of bentgrass are endemic to Point Reyes. **Awned bentgrass** *(Agrostis aristiglumis)* is found only at Point Reyes, on gravelly slopes near Home Ranch and near the Kehoe Beach trailhead; another, **Point Reyes bentgrass** *(A. clivola var. puntareyensis)*, discovered in 1967, survives only in crevices of sandstone or granitic outcrops along Pierce Point Road. [6, 7, 22]

COASTAL RANGELAND

By the 1800s dairy farms had been established in the Olema Valley, Point Reyes, Marshall, Tomales, and Chileno Valley areas . . . large numbers of hogs grazed and rooted the prairielands . . . the perennial grasses of the prairies on the Tomales Bay watershed received devastating blows during more than a century of heavy grazing by "hide" cattle, beef cattle, horses, dairy stock, hogs and sheep.

— Clarence Zumwaldt. Consideration of vegetation and soils on the Tomales Bay watershed. *Tomales Bay Environmental Study.* 1972.

THE TREELESS REACHES of rolling pasturelands that cover most of the western and northern sections of the Point are made up of a mosaic of habitats that differ subtly

Coastal rangeland looking southward from Mendoza Ranch toward Chimney Rock. Much of what is now coastal rangeland was northern coastal prairie prior to the introduction of European annual grasses and cattle.

from one another. Much of this grassland habitat is devoted to agriculture – the grazing of dairy and beef cattle. Interspersed with these ranchlands are "islands" of northern coastal prairie, seasonally wet swales, coastal strand, and coastal scrub. For our purposes, we will consider "coastal rangelands" as areas whose plant communities are determined by grazing pressure, areas dominated by non-native annual grasses.

Where grazing has ceased or not occurred, the combined influences of climate and soil type favor perennial plants. The summer fog plays an important role by extending the growing season, thereby giving perennials an advantage over annuals adapted to drier conditions (xerophytes). However, this natural advantage is overcome by domestic livestock. Intensive grazing causes a reduction in plant vigor and removes a critical amount of mulch, thereby tilting the balance in favor of exotic annual species. When cattle are removed the community tends to revert to native perennials, although it may never recover completely.[12]

Most of the grassland wildflowers are inconspicuous, masked by the rank growth of annual grasses. However, a winter or spring walk through the grassland offers an abundant native bloom. By late February, on damp slopes, **sun-cups** (*Oenothera ovata*) are easily found. Another early bloomer is the familiar **Douglas iris.** Like the sun-cups, the coastal iris' short stem helps to shelter it from the spring winds. In damp meadows and downs another member of the iris family, **blue-eyed grass** (*Sisyrinchium bellum*) sprouts leaves as winter ends, begins blooming in March, and attains its greatest splendor in early April. A close relative, **yellow-eyed grass** (*Sisyrinchium californicum*), is rarer and occurs in even damper situations; beginning in mid-March, look for it in the roadside swales that border the grassland along Sir Francis Drake Boulevard between Abandoned Ranch and North Beach. Farther south along the same road, also in a damp swale, a delicate yellow **meadow foam** (*Limnanthes douglasii* var. *sulphurea*) blooms from March to May. The most reliable spot to see this rare variety, classified as endangered by the Native Plant Society, is the sharp curve in Sir Francis Drake Boulevard, 0.4 miles south of Mendoza Ranch on the way to the Lighthouse. **California poppy** (*Eschscholzia californicus*), **buttercups** (*Ranunculus*), **checkerbloom** (*Sidalcea*), **owl's clover** (*Orthocarpus* species), and **baby-blue-eyes** (*Nemophila*) are other common members of the grassland's spring display.[5, 6]

Some of the rarities deserve our attention, for without it they could easily disappear, victims of uninformed land management practices. An example is a delicate little **swamp harebell** (*Campanula californica*) that occurs in coastal swales and shady canyons. Recently, keen observers discovered it in a wet drainage near Abbott's Lagoon. Because dairy cattle used the area freely, the Park Service fenced off the swale and re-routed the hiking trail to protect the population from inadvertant trampling by cattle or humans. Such stewardship ensures preservation of the diversity that enriches Point Reyes. Other rarities that occur in rangeland habitat and may be threatened by grazing include **Point Reyes blennosperma, Point Reyes horkelia, Point Reyes lupine, San Francisco owl's clover, Sonoma chorizanthe, Gairdiner's yampah,** and **northcoast phacelia.**[5, 6]

NORTHERN COASTAL SCRUB

TRAILS OF GRAY FOX and coastal mule deer weave through the coyote bush, boring openings through otherwise dense tangles of blackberry vine, poison oak, and sword fern. This is the coastal scrub, a "soft chaparral" where the songs of wrentits and white-crowned sparrows litter the hillside, scattered in abundance like the large, white

Table 1. Rare Plants of Point Reyes National Seashore.[6, 14]

P = Point Reyes National Seashore only; S = Southern limit; N = Northern limit; M = Marin only;
W = Widespread; E = Locally extinct.

Awned Bent Grass	*Argrostis aristiglumis*	P
Point Reyes Bent Grass	*Agrostis clivicola* var. *punta-reyesnesis*	S
Sonoma Alopecurus	*Alopecurus aequalis* var. *sonomensis*	S
Coast Rock Cress	*Arabis blepharophylla*	W
Mount Vision Manzanita	*Arctostaphylos uva-ursi* var. *marinensis*	M
Bolinas Manzanita	*Arctostaphylos virgata*	M
Point Reyes Blennosperma	*Blennosperma nanum* var. *robustum*	P
Thurber's Reed Grass	*Calamagrostis crassiglumis*	S
Swamp Harebell	*Campanula californica*	S
Point Reyes Paintbrush	*Castilleja leschkeana*	P,E
Mount Vision Ceonothus	*Ceonothus gloriosus* var. *porrectus*	P
Sonoma Chorizanthe	*Chorizanthe valida*	M
Franciscan Thistle	*Cirsium andrewsii*	W
North Coast Bird's-beak	*Cordylanthus maritimus* ssp. palustris	W
Yellow Larkspur	*Delphinium luteum*	S,E
California Bottlebrush Grass	*Elymus californica*	W
Supple Daisy	*Erigeron supplex*	S,E
Fragrant Fritillary	*Fritillaria liliaceae*	W
Point Reyes Horkelia	*Horkelia marinensis*	S
Beach Layia	*Layia carnosa*	W
Point Reyes Meadow Foam	*Limnanthes douglasii* var. *sulphurea*	N
Point Reyes Lupine	*Lupinus tidestromii* var. *layneae*	S
Curley-leaved Monardella	*Monardella undulata* var. *undulata*	N
San Francisco Owl's Clover	*Orthocarpus floribundus*	N
Gairdner's Yampah	*Perideridia gairdneri* ssp. *gairdneri*	W
North Coast Phacelia	*Phacelia insularis* var. *continentis*	S
Nodding's Semaphore Grass	*Pleuropogon refractus*	S
Marin Knotweed	*Polygonum marinense*	M
California Beaked-rush	*Rhynchospora californica*	S,E
Straggly Gooseberry	*Ribes divarticatum* var. *publiflorum*	W
Showy Indian Clover	*Trifolium amoenum*	N,E
Gray's Clover	*Trifolium grayi*	W

(Table 1 modified from Table 1 in Clark, R. A. and G. M. Fellers. 1986. *Rare Plants of Point Reyes National Seashore.* Technical Report No. 22. Cooperative National Park Studies Unit. University of California, Davis.)

flowers of cow parsnip.

This community extends in a discontinuous, narrow coastal strip from southern Oregon to Monterey County and is dominated by **coyote bush** *(Baccharis pilularis)* or **bush lupine** *(Lupinus arboreus)*. Coyote bush scrub communities are extensive on the westerly slopes of Inverness Ridge from the forest edge toward the coastal strand. Two assemblages of coyote bush community exist depending on the compass direction of the slope. On north-facing slopes the coyote bush provides a rather open canopy (about 26 percent cover) over an understory of sword fern (45 percent cover), with a mixture of salal, California hazel, western bracken fern, blackberry, and wild rye providing additional cover (27 percent). South-facing slopes are dominated equally by a shared canopy of coyote bush and coffeeberry with an understory of sticky monkeyflower, yerba buena, and western bracken fern. Other differences that result from moisture availability are canopy height, which on north-facing slopes averages about 5 feet while on south-facing slopes it averages about 3.3 feet; deciduous plant cover, which is less than 4 percent on north-facing slopes and more than 13 percent on south-facing slopes; and the fact that more species are found on north-facing slopes. Poison oak also enjoys the company of coyote bush, as the intrepid bushwacker will soon discover. On an "undisturbed, unburned" study plot on the coastal slope at Palomarin, poison oak was estimated as being 27 percent of the vegetative cover.[11, 16, 18, 27, 28]

On the drier slopes **California sagebrush** shares the coastal scrub community with coyote bush. The sagebrush, an aromatic shrub with finely feathered gray-green foliage, is a member of the southern coastal scrub community and extends northward only as far as Point Reyes, where the transition from southern to northern coastal scrub becomes complete. Moving north from about San Luis Obispo, drought-tolerant (xerophytic) species with southern affinities are replaced gradually by species that require more moisture (mesophytic).[2]

On the coastal slope, **pink flowering currant** *(Ribes sanguineum glutinosum)* blooms as early as February. This attractive shrub is uncommon but easily found amidst coyote bush on the shoulder of the road to Limantour Beach. This species tends to occur in moist environments, as on north-facing slopes; its presence along Limantour Road in south-facing coastal scrub may be explained by the increased runoff provided by the road surface as well as the persistent fog.

On the road to outer Point Reyes, between Pierce Point Road and Schooner Bay (the turnoff to Johnson's Oyster Company), the north-facing slopes are clothed with coastal scrub dominated by coyote bush. Beyond Schooner Bay the road passes agricultural pastures near the radio towers. Just beyond these facilities is a transition zone to coastal scrub dominated by bush lupine. The geology has changed; here is the Drake's Bay formation, the sedimentary siltstone interbedded with mudstone that reminded Sir

Francis Drake of the white cliffs of Dover. Soils are sandy and dune-like, formed by windblown deposits from nearby beaches. The coyote bush here (var. *pilularis*) is small leaved and low growing, hugging the ground in response to the onshore winds that besiege this flat plateau. The tallest shrubs are **coastal bush lupines** (*Lupinus arboreus*), whose yellow flowers emblazon the landscape by mid-May. The abundance, timing, and intensity of the bloom vary with winter rainfall, the wettest years producing the most spectacular displays. Although yellow is the most common color, various shades of violet to blue occur where this species hybridizes with **violet-flowered lupine** (*Lupinus propinquus*). The violet-flowered species is less common at Point Reyes, growing in more sheltered microclimates and heavier soils, as behind the dunes at Limantour Estero. Also at Limantour, and at the north end of Tomales Bay, hybrids occur with flowers of pure white. The ground cover beneath the bush lupine/coyote bush community is a sparse covering of grasses and forbs, depending on grazing pressure.

Both bush lupine and "prostrate" coyote bush invade grasslands when grazing stops. They also occur in the coastal strand and coastal prairie habitats.

One of the rarer California grasses, **California bottlebrush-grass** (*Hystrix californica*), a graceful, tall member of the barley tribe, grows amidst coastal scrub near the head of Drake's Estero. The habitat here is uncharacteristic for the species. Elsewhere within its range, from Sonoma to Santa Cruz, it is associated with coniferous forests. Perhaps the fog provides suitable moisture here.[8,22]

Since 1971, the Point Reyes Bird Observatory has been conducting research near Palomarin in three coastal scrub habitat types: disturbed, burned disturbed, and mature undisturbed. These studies are ongoing and provide information on the changing nature of the plant and animal associations within these three distinct types of coastal scrub. (Results are published in the journal *American Birds*, Vols. 25–39.)

Table 2. Extent of Habitats at Point Reyes Peninsula and Surrounding Wetlands.

Wetlands

Tomales Bay	9,290 acres (3,761 hectares)
Drakes Estero	2,070 acres (838 hectares)
Bolinas Lagoon	1,240 acres (502 hectares)
Abbott's Lagoon	1,724 acres (115 hectares)

Grassland, Prairie, and Scrub

Tomales Point	2,544 acres (1,030 hectares)
Pastoral Zone	21,135 acres (8,557 hectares)
Coast Prairie	6,610 acres (2,676 hectares)
Coast Scrub	8,536 acres (3,456 hectares)

Forest

Douglas Fir	12,395 acres (5,018 hectares)
Bishop Pine	7,700 acres (3,142 hectares)

Source: Lauer, D. T. 1972. Vegetation mapping at Point Reyes National Seashore. In *ERTS-1 Data as an Aid to Resource Management in Northern California*, edited by R. N. Colwell and G. Thorley. Berkeley: Center for Remote Sensing Research, University of California.

MARSHLANDS

T HE BOUNDARY BETWEEN salt, brackish, and freshwater marsh is not always distinct. Indeed, in pristine situations there tends to be a gradual transition, one plant community grading into the other as the influence of the ocean's salinity is diluted by freshwater runoff from the upland. At Point Reyes, before the influence of industrious American settlers altered the landscape, marshlands must have been more extensive than they are today. We can imagine the south end of Tomales Bay, unleveed, no tidegates or culverts, with a January flood tide extending its influence southward nearly to where Park Headquarters now stands. At Limantour, before man-made levees created the stock ponds at Muddy Hollow, Glenbrook, and Laguna Canyon, spring tidal surges must have extended up to where alder thickets now grow. Many of these transitional habitats have been sacrificed with the development of the peninsula for cattle ranching. By restricting tidal influence, man isolated fresh water from salt and created freshwater habitats — Muddy Hollow Pond, Drake's Beach Pond, and the upper ponds at Abbott's Lagoon — where brackish marsh must have existed before. Today, salt, brackish, and freshwater marshes tend to be separated by roads, levees, culverts, and fill. They are

Saltmarsh in July, Drake's Estero: sea lavender (Limonium californicum),
saltgrass (Distichlis spicata), quillwort (Isoetes nuttallii),
pickleweed (Salicornia californica), Jaumea carnosa.

often discrete from rather than integrated into surrounding wetlands.

Although marshes occupy less than 10 percent of the area of Point Reyes, they deserve our attention because they support some of the most diverse communities of flora and fauna and are subjected to the most extreme influences of nature and human activity.

Salt Marsh

Prior to the mid-1800s, tidal saltmarsh was more extensive than it is today. With the development of large-scale agriculture in the Point Reyes area, dikes and levees were built to restrict tidal flow and lowlands were filled to create pasture. The effects of leveeing are most apparent at the south end of Tomales Bay. When Easterners first settled the area, the unrestricted tide flowed south nearly to what is now Park Headquarters at Bear Valley. Then, with the construction of the Levee Road between Point Reyes Station and Inverness Park, what had once been brackish marshland became more of a freshwater marsh (now known as Olema Marsh or Bear Valley Marsh). Then, in the mid-1940s, levees were constructed in the Lagunitas Creek floodplain to create pasture and the salt marsh was further reduced in extent. In 1960 the levee system was extended, further reducing the influence of the tide. However, as these land use practices were removing salt marsh, other practices were inadvertently increasing its extent. The construction of a railroad along the east side of Tomales Bay in the 1870s isolated many small coves, causing them to fill with sediment and become vegetated with saltmarsh plants (especially pickleweed). Also, as the result of logging and increased grazing in the watershed, more sediment was carried into Tomales Bay, Bolinas Lagoon, and the coastside estuaries, raising the elevation of the deltas and permitting saltmarsh vegetation to grow over former mudflats. But overall there has been a significant loss of saltmarsh habitat and a reduction in size of the tidelands at Point Reyes since the mid-1800s.

Tidal salt marsh is restricted to the periphery of estuaries. There are approximately 1,000 acres of saltmarsh vegetation on the peninsula. They are distributed as follows: Bolinas Lagoon (240 acres); Limantour Estero (90 acres); Drake's Estero (160 acres); Tomales Bay (510 acres). The flora in these marshes is nearly identical to that in the San Francisco Bay marshes south of the San Rafael peninsula; however, two plants occur here that are absent from San Francisco Bay. The first, a small species of **gum plant** *(Grindelia stricta)*, finds its southernmost outpost in the Point Reyes marshes, and its yellow, sunflower-like blossoms lend a particular beauty to the upper edge of the marsh at the highest tide line from June into early fall. The other is an inconspicuous fescue-like grass *(Puccinelia grandis)* that mixes with the pickleweed/saltgrass community.[22]

The Point Reyes marshes differ in structure among themselves, depending on the amount of freshwater influence. The outer coast marshes in Limantour and Drake's

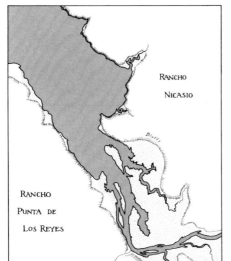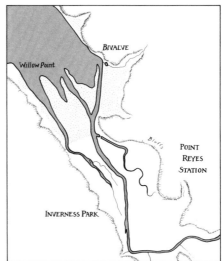

Map 6. The Southern Portion of Tomales Bay. The earliest hydrographic surveys, from 1860 to 1861, show deep water extending all the way up the Bay to Inverness and navigable channels to the towns of Point Reyes Station and Tomales. Even the smallest creeks entering the Bay show open water at their mouths, indicating that the tidal exchange exceeded the rate of sediment accumulation. In the ensuing century, disturbance of the watershed (logging, grazing, and leveeing of creeks for agricultural purposes) increased sedimentation rates, resulting in a reduction of the loss of Bay water volume, surface area, and tidal prism (the amount of water exchanged with each tide). (Source: A program for restoring the environment of Tomales Bay. State Coastal Conservancy. Tomales Bay Estuarine Enhancement Program, 1984.)

esteros, which receive less freshwater runoff, are quite saline and are covered mostly by low-growing pickleweed and saltgrass. The upper, less saline border, flooded only by the highest tides, is trimmed with two members of the thrift family: **sea pink** *(Armeria maritima)* and **sea lavender** *(Limonium californicum)*. The marsh at Limantour hosts the most fetching complement of thrifts. The soft pastel sea pinks bloom in late spring on long, delicate stems with strawflower-like bracts. By early summer the sea lavender (also called marsh rosemary) sends up its small blossoms, similar to the garden ornamental "statice." By fall, the large, rust-stained leaves of the rosemary combine with the complementary shading of the pink and lavender to lend the marsh a remarkable impressionistic beauty, recalling the muted shading of a canvas by Degas. **North coast bird's-beak** *(Cordylanthus maritimus palustris)* is a rare salt marsh plant which grows in association with sea lavender only in these protected outer coast marshes.

In the innermost reaches of Tomales Bay and Bolinas Lagoon, where perennial creeks feed the marshes with a steady flow of fresh water diluting the ocean's harsh salti-

Kehoe Marsh originates in damp swales near L Ranch and Kehoe Ranch (see Map 2) and follows the drainages westerly toward Kehoe Beach. One of the few freshwater marshes on the peninsula, its upper reaches support healthy populations of bog lupine and common yellowthroats. Unfortunately, cattle have trampled much of the marsh's lower reaches, eliminating these and several other marsh-dependent species.

ness, we find more luxuriant growth and the greatest variety of saltmarsh vegetation. These marshes, too, are dominated by a patchwork of pickleweed and saltgrass, with lavender and gum plant at the upper edges, but other species join the community. At the south end of Tomales Bay, where Lagunitas Creek drains a 223-square mile watershed, we find species rare or absent from the outer coast marshes: **alkali heath** *(Frankenia)*, **arrowgrass** *(Triglochin)*, and **jaumea**. At Bolinas Lagoon, where fresh water flows in through Pine Gulch Creek, there is a lush complement of brackish and even freshwater marsh plants grading into the salt marsh: sedges, rushes, cattails, alder, and willow.

Freshwater Marsh

Freshwater marsh is not extensive at Point Reyes, but what does exist hosts an impressive diversity of plant life. Olema Marsh, a large triangular wedge of alder-willow-cattail-tule marsh formed by the confluence of Olema, Bear Valley, and Lagunitas creeks is called "perhaps the best freshwater marsh in [Marin] County" by Thomas Howell.[22]

From the knoll at Kule Loklo we view Olema Marsh as a wide riparian jungle. Tall red alders are the dominant species, but yellow willow is abundant along the water course, and sedges line the outer edges of the willows. Amidst the sedges, we hear the sweet *"witchity-witchity-witchity"* song of a yellowthroat and finally we spot the lemon-breasted, black-masked warbler atop a deep purple spike of **bog lupine** (*Lupinus polyphyllus*). Walking north along the horse trail through the oak-bay woodlands, we cross several small streams that run down from the Douglas fir forest on Inverness Ridge to feed Olema Marsh. As we approach Bear Valley Road, the riparian corridor broadens; cattails mix with willows and hedge nettle and marsh monkeyflowers join the other wetland plants.

Ledum Swamp, at the junction of Sir Francis Drake Boulevard and Pierce Point Road, though smaller in extent than Olema Marsh, harbors a very diverse community of wetland plants. Other important areas that support freshwater plants include the borders of the upper ponds at Abbott's Lagoon, Kehoe Marsh, and the swales that feed it, Pine Gulch Creek on Bolinas Lagoon, and the upper reaches of Drake's and Limantour esteros. Of course, freshwater marsh habitat is not always separate and distinct from other habitats. Some marsh species occur in the wetter downs and swales of the grasslands. **Rushes** (*Juncus* species) and **marsh monkeyflower** (*Mimulus guttattus*) are the most conspicuous indicators of these wetland habitats. The **false lily-of-the-valley** (*Maianthemum dilatatum*) is a rare plant that occurs at Ledum Swamp, but also in moist ground around Abbott's Lagoon and in some swales on the outer Point; its distribution provides an example of the patchy distribution of freshwater marshlands on the peninsula.

INTERTIDAL PLANT COMMUNITIES

Marine Algae

THE SEAWEEDS of the intertidal and subtidal zones of the coast are often overlooked as plant communities. Yet, like the Douglas fir forest or the coastal prairie, they harbor a diverse array of organisms within the feathery forests of their blades and the tangled mazes of their "roots." There are myriad microscopic marine algae, but we will limit our coverage to the macroscopic species—the giant kelps and their kin that colonize the rocky shoreline and the still embayments where the substrate is stable enough for the young plants to take hold and grow to maturity.

Almost all of the marine plants are **algae,** plants without true flowers, leaves, or roots. Algae have blades (leaves), stipes (stalks), and holdfasts (roots). Rather than reproducing conspicuously like the brazen flowering plants, the algae are discrete, shedding microscopic spores into the sea. (The algae actually alternate generations, the asexual spore-producing generation giving rise to a sexual generation, the sexual generation giving rise to an asexual generation. For further discussion, see Dawson 1971).

There are three types of marine algae: green, brown, and red. Species of green algae are relatively few intertidally; **sea lettuce** *(Ulva)* is the most conspicuous since it occurs in shallow estuaries. The thin, lettuce-like sheets are a favorite food of coots on the tidal flats. The brown algae tend to be large and include the giant kelps, oar weeds, and sea palms. The cold waters of the California Current are particularly conducive to the growth of brown algae, and the kelp beds that stretch northward from Point Conception are some of the most extensive in the world. Most of the species of seaweed in the world belong to the red algae. Perhaps the most recognizable is the purplish *Porphyra* or **nori**, which is cultivated in the Orient and is now popular in the West as a food. Another familiar red algae is the large **"turkish towel" plant** *(Gigartina),* a flat, warty blade found commonly amidst the beach wrack.

The color used to classify each algal type is not necessarily recognizable to the human eye. Take, for example, the dayglow sheets of orange that emblazon the vertical cliff faces at Chimney Rock, the Headlands, and Tomales Bluff. We may suppose that these are lichens, but actually they are algae. Knowing this, we may suppose that they are red algae. Wrong. These are mats of a green algae, *Trentefolia aurea,* but the green

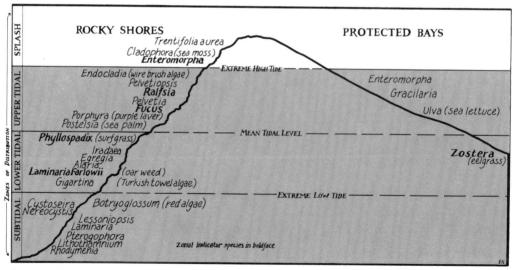

Figure 6. *Zonation (or vertical distribution) of intertidal plants along the coast at Point Reyes is determined largely by the amount of tidal exposure, wave action, and the ability of plants to compete with other species.*

chlorophyll is masked by a red pigment (haematochrome).

The only flowering plants that have adapted to coping with the rigors of marine life are **eelgrass** *(Zostera)* and **surfgrass** *(Phyllospadix)*. Both occur at Point Reyes; surfgrass is an important member of the rocky shore intertidal community and eelgrass supports its own fauna subtidally in protected bays. (See Chapter 4.)

The marine algae, like other intertidal organisms, are distributed vertically along the shoreline from the high splash zone to the lowest tideline. Beyond, in the areas never exposed to the drying air, is the subtidal. The major algae of each zone are listed in Figure 6 according to tidal exposure.

The major kelp beds are along the outer coast, where underwater shale or granite outcroppings are available for anchor and where powerful waves aerate the water. It is likely that these beds were more extensive prior to the 1800s, when sea otters still occupied the coast. With the extermination of the otters, the urchin population expanded, increasing the grazing pressure on young kelp. In other areas along the coast, offshore kelp forests have increased wherever sea otters have returned.[38]

Today, some of the most extensive kelp beds are at Sculptured Beach, near Coast Camp. Indeed, this wild cove has been selected as the best place to reintroduce sea otters to the Seashore. Ten to fifty yards offshore are luxuriant beds of **short kelp** *(Laminaria andersonii)* and **stalked kelp** *(Pterygophora californica)*. These two species also occur together nearshore below the Point Reyes Headlands and along the rocky coast from Kehoe Beach north to Tomales Bluff. (Stalked kelp is a favorite food of the red abalone.) Beyond, in deeper water, are patches of **bull kelp** *(Nereocystis luetkeana)* and **California kelp** *(Macrocystis integrifolia)*. The round flotation bulb of bull kelp, with blades and stipe attached, is often found shorecast on sandy beaches. California kelp also occurs at the confluence of Drake's and Limantour esteros, just inside the mouth, and along Drake's Beach.

In the areas least accessible to people, where the headlands and promontories jut into the most powerful surf, live the most remarkable of the local marine algae, the **sea palm** *(Postelsia palmaeformis)*. This brown algae is restricted to the cool waters of the North American Pacific, and grows only where the wave energy is the most intense. This annual plant begins growing in February and reaches its full stature of two to three feet by the summer solstice. The rhythm and drama of the rocky coast is well-embodied in the sea palm forest. With each breaking wave the rubbery stalks of the palms bend forward with the wave, then spring back upright with the outwash, always ready for the next breaker.

REFERENCES

1. Agee, J. 1973. *The Flora of Point Reyes.* National Park Service.

2. Bakker, E. 1984. *An Island Called California,* 2d ed. Berkeley: University of California Press.

3. Barbour, M. G., R. B. Craig, F. R. Drysdale, and M. T. Ghiselin. 1973. *Coastal Ecology: Bodega Head.* Berkeley: University of California Press.

4. Barbour, M. G., T. M. DeJong, and A. F. Johnson. 1976. Synecology of beach vegetation along the Pacific coast of the United States of America: a first approximation. *J. Biogeography* 3: 55–69.

5. California Native Plant Society. 1984. *The Inventory of Rare and Endangered Vascular Plants of California.* Special Publ. No. 1, 3d ed.

6. Clark, R. A., and G. M. Fellers. 1986. *Rare Plants at Point Reyes National Seashore.* Technical Report No. 22. University of California at Davis, Cooperative National Park Resources Studies Unit.

7. Crampton, B. 1967. New *Agrostis* from the California Coast. *Brittonia* 19: 174–177.

8. Crampton, B. 1974. *Grasses of California.* Berkeley: University of California Press.

9. Davidson, E. D., and M. C. Barbour. 1977. Germination, establishment, and demography of coastal bush lupine *(Lupinus arboreus)* at Bodega Head, California. *Ecology* 58: 592–600.

10. Dawson, E. Y. 1971. *Seashore Plants of Northern California.* California Natural History Guide 20. Berkeley: University of California Press.

11. DeSante, D., C. Isenhart, J. Tabbia. 1984. Winter bird population study: burned disturbed coastal scrub. *American Birds* 38: 55.

12. Elliott, H. W. III, and J. D. Wehausen. 1974. Vegetational succession on coastal rangeland of Point Reyes peninsula. *Madrono* 22 (5): 231–238.

13. Evens, J. 1978. Logged Douglas fir forest reseeded with Monterey pine. *American Birds* 32: 92.

14. Fellers, G. M., and V. Norris. 1990. A cooperative project at Point Reyes National Seashore. *Fremontia* 18 (4): 23–26.

15. Galloway, A. 1977. *Geology of the Point Reyes Peninsula, Marin County, California.* California Division of Mines and Geology Bulletin 202.

16. Grams, H. J., K. R. McPherson, V. V. King, S. A. MacLeod, and M. G. Barbour. 1977. Northern coastal scrub on Point Reyes peninsula, California. *Madrono* 24: 18–24.

17. Gogan, P. J. P. 1986. *Ecology of the Tule Elk Range, Point Reyes National Seashore.* Ph.D. dissertation. University of California, Berkeley.

18. Heady, H. F., T. C. Foin, M. M. Hektner, D. W. Taylor, M. G. Barbour, and W. J. Barry. 1977. Coastal prairie and northern coastal scrub. In *Terrestrial Vegetation of California,* edited by J. Major and M. G. Barbour. New York: Wiley Interscience.

19. Hill, M. 1984. *California Landscape: Origin and Evolution.* California Natural History Guide 48. Berkeley: University of California Press.

20. Houghton, M., V. Jensen, C. Thompson, T. Trapp. 1972. *Point Reyes National Seashore: A Study of Vegetation Distribution and Abundance.* Report to Drs. Harding and Foin, Environmental Studies 100. University of California at Davis.

21. Howell, J. T. 1952. California's bishop pines. *Pacific Discovery* 5 (1): 12–15.

22. Howell, J. T. 1970. *Marin Flora,* 2d ed. Berkeley: University of California Press.

23. Kashiwagi, J. H. 1985. *Soil Survey of Marin County, California.* Soil Conservation Service, U.S. Dept. of Agriculture.

24. Kuchler, A. W. 1977. *Natural Vegetation Map of California.* Dept. of Geography, University of Kansas.

25. Lamson-Scribner, F. 1898. Sand-binding grasses. U.S.D.A. *Yearbook* 1898: 405–420.

26. McDonald, K. 1972. Logged Douglas-fir reseeded with Monterey pine. *American Birds* 26: 983–984.

27. Munz, P. A. 1959. *A California Flora*. Berkeley: University of California Press.

28. Ornduff, R. 1974. *An Introduction to California Plant Life*. Berkeley: University of California Press.

29. Peattie, D. C. 1953. *A Natural History of Western Trees*. New York: Bonanza Books.

30. Roof, J. 1972. The big lupines of Point Reyes. *Four Seasons* 4 (2): 20–24.

31. Sawyer, J. O., D. A. Thornburgh, and J. R. Griffin. 1977. Mixed evergreen forest. In *Terrestrial Vegetation of California*, edited by J. Major and M. G. Barbour. New York: Wiley Interscience.

32. Shuford, W. D., and I. Timossi. 1985. *Marin County Plant Habitats*. Unpublished Ms.

33. Slobodchikoff, C. N., and J. T. Doyen. 1977. Effects of *Ammophila arenaria* on sand dune arthropod communities. *Ecology* 58: 1171–1175.

34. Stewart, R. 1972. *American Birds* 26: 981.

35. Vogl, R. J., W. P. Armstrong, K. L. White, K. L. Cole. 1977. The closed-cone pines and cypress. In *The Terrestrial Vegetation of California*, by J. Major and M. G. Barbour. New York: John Wiley & Sons.

36. Wagner, R. H. 1979. *A Northern Coastal Prairie Remnant on Point Reyes Peninsula, California*. National Park Service, Western Region.

37. Weaver, H. 1974. Effects of fire on temperate forests: western United States. In *Fire and Ecosystems*, edited by T. T. Kozlowski and C. E. Ahlgren. New York: Academic Press.

38. Wilson, S. 1984. California's surviving sea otters: still threatened. *Pacific Discovery* 37 (3): 16–20.

39. National Park Service. 1987. Personal communication.

40. Soil Conservation Service. 1987. Personal communication.

CHAPTER FOUR

FROM THE OCEAN'S EDGE TO THE SERPENT'S LAIR
Marine Invertebrates, Fishes, Amphibians, and Reptiles

Look deeply into the wind-furrows of the grass, into the leaf-stilled water of pools.
Think back through the silence, of the life that was and is not here now, of the strong
pastness of things — shadows of the end and of the beginning.

— John Haines. *Shadows.* 1982.

NOW WE MUST GET DOWN on our knees and peer under rocks, wade into the shallow
water with a fine-meshed net, roll up our sleeves and reach into the cool tide pools,
or peel bark off decaying branches — all in search of the "lower animals." In this chapter
we find the seldom seen creatures that inhabit the secluded reaches and crevices of the
peninsula — the shadow world where humans rarely venture.

From a human perspective, there is something otherworldly about most of the
animals discussed in this chapter, a strangeness that comes from their unfamiliarity. But
the strangeness of an anemone, a sturgeon, a salamander, or a snake stems, perhaps,

---

Water Temperature

Water temperature is of primary importance to the distribution of marine invertebrates. Along the California coast, the
major transition from cold to warmer
water occurs at Point Conception, nearly
300 miles south of Point Reyes. Point
Reyes is within the influence of the cold,
temperate waters of the California Current, with a relatively narrow range of
temperature. (See Chapter 2.) Point Reyes
is not at the southernmost or northernmost edge of distributional range for most
species, but closer toward the center.
Many of the species that occur here
extend southward to Southern California
or even Baja, and northward to British
Columbia or even the Gulf of Alaska.
However, there are exceptions.

The masking crab, *Loxorhynchus cris-
patus*, occurs from San Diego to Point

Reyes in the lowest intertidal zone, along
the rocky coast and in kelp beds. These
masters of disguise decorate their shells
with algae and animals — hydroids,
anemones, sponges — a concealment that
both protects them from predation and
allows them to approach their prey
undetected.

The small nudibranch, *Hallaxa chani*,
named after College of Marin marine
biologist Gordon L. Chan, was known
only from the tidepools in the high splash
zone at Duxbury Reef and Tomales Point
until 1981, when other populations were
discovered as far south as San Luis Obispo.
Still, Point Reyes is the northernmost
locale of this uncommon species.

from a memory — a dim thought that glows in our subconscious, our reptilian brain — a distant recognition of our mutual origins and an innate fear of our shared destiny.

We humans have learned to value some of these species: oysters, abalone, salmon, even frogs. They serve our purposes well. Others have commanded our attention: snakes, sharks, and even the microscopic *Gonyaulax,* the toxic microorganism that infests shellfish between May and October. But there are myriad others, about which even the most observant among us are only dimly aware.

Naturalists discover early that no organism is "insignificant," none is simple. The closer one looks, the more one sees. The smallest, most sessile limpet; the amorphous tunicate, difficult to identify as animal, vegetable, or mineral; the moss-like bryzoans that look more like algae than animals — each survives in a universe perfectly suited to its presence, and each goes about its business as earnestly as, and perhaps more efficiently than, the humans who pass by unnoticed.

Here we discuss some of those species that live out their lives beneath the water, beneath the forest's leaf litter, beneath the ground. This is a cursory review of the communities that surround us, but perhaps it will serve as a window into worlds seldom seen.

MARINE INVERTEBRATES

The peaceful pattern of Indian culture no doubt reflected their environment — a land of abundance. Food was no problem. The waters were full of fish and the sands were thick with clams to be dug at low tide.
— Harold Gilliam. *Island in Time.* 1973.

THE INTERTIDAL AND SUBTIDAL HABITAT that fringes Point Reyes is perhaps the least visited environment on the peninsula, but those few who venture below the tide line find a community populated by a richness and abundance of flora and fauna seldom found on dry ground. The intertidal zone, within the surge of two daily tides, is crowded with organisms with unfamiliar names — anemones, nudibranchs, chitons — creatures caught in the narrow world where land and sea overlap. The casual visitor into this diorama of unexpected beauty should pay heed to the sudden surges (sneaker waves) that have carried others off the reefs and rocks into the netherworld of the subtidal zone. The plants and animals that inhabit the intertidal zone on a daily basis have evolved mechanisms to withstand the force of pounding surf — byssal threads for mussels, holdfasts for sea palms; Top-Siders and Vibram soles do not function as well for humans. So, be forewarned! Choose your path into the intertidal carefully, certain that an escape route will still be available after the tide comes in. The lowest subtidal zones

Although the sandy beach often seems devoid of life, many organisms burrow under the surface to feed on detritus delivered with the wash of each wave.

are exposed on "minus" tides (less than 0.0 feet); remember that these lowest tides are accompanied by the highest tides. Visit the tidepools an hour before maximum ebb, and leave not more than one and one-half hours after low tide; give yourself plenty of time to get high and dry before the water rises.

*   *   *

It was one of the lowest tides of the year, mid-June, and we gathered on Agate Beach to follow the ebbing tide out across Duxbury Reef in search of nudibranchs — the multicolored "sea slugs" that, because of their delicate beauty, have been called "butterflies of the sea." Duxbury, the largest shale intertidal reef in North America, is renowned for its diversity of intertidal invertebrates, and more than 20 species of nudibranchs have been identified on a single visit. Although they occur in the higher tidal zones, as Ricketts says, "it is in the lower horizon that these brilliantly colored naked snails come into their own." So, this was our opportunity to delve into the seldom exposed depths in search of the elusive sea slugs.

With babies on our backs, and Light's Manual *in our day packs, we wandered slowly out along slick rock that was wrapped in a shimmering cloak of marine algae —* Porphyra, Egregia, Laminaria, Iridea *— subtle shades of purples, greens, blues, and browns iridescent in* *the summer light. In the upper zones, the animals are familiar: mussels, turban snails, acorn barnacles, hermit crabs. Farther out we raked our fingers through surfgrass in a still pool and someone yelled "Rostanga!," excited to find the first species of nudibranch of the day. More raking reveals more; the pool is rich with* Rostanga. *These tiny, bright scarlet, shell-less snails forage on red siliceous sponges that they find by scent.*

With each few steps we are lured farther and farther out into the intertidal zone, discovering more species of nudibranchs in the clear tidepools — Dialula, Anisodoris, Triopha, Hermissenda *— losing track of everything other than the strange and beautiful creature treasures hidden in the pristine pools. We are now a quarter of a mile out on the reef, in the low intertidal zone, refuge of red abalone, sea cucumbers, and graceful plumed hydroids. One of us looks up and is suddenly alarmed by the tide. In our preoccupation we had failed to notice the incoming water; we are stranded on an island of the reef, now surrounded by water, several hundred yards offshore. Slightly panicked, we begin wading toward shore, children and gear held above our heads. Fortunately, the water is only waist deep and we arrive ashore safe, if shaken.*

*   *   *

The preceeding story illustrates the need to exercise caution while exploring the seductive coast of Point Reyes. Always consult a tide book and plan your escape route before wandering along the rocky shore. Also consider taking along the valuable pocket guide to the common species, Joel Hedgepeth's *Seashore Life.* For those interested in delving deeper into the lives and times of animals and plants of the intertidal and subtidal regions of Point Reyes, several excellent references are available. *Light's Manual of Intertidal Invertebrates of the Central California Coast* is the bible, and *Between Pacific Tides*, by Ed Ricketts and Jack Calvin, is the "book of common prayer" for the intrepid marine naturalist. For the home library, *Intertidal Invertebrates of California* by Robert Morris, Donald Abbott and Eugene Haderlie is an excellent reference.

Distribution of marine invertebrates is regulated to a large degree by the temperature of the water. Along the California Coast, the major change from cool to warm temperatures occurs to the south, at Point Conception. Therefore, Point Reyes, with a relatively narrow range of temperature throughout the year (see Chapter 1), shares the same species with much of the coastline from about Point Conception north to about British Columbia, the cold, temperate waters under the influence of the California Current. The relative coldness and consistency of the ocean temperature in this region account for the high diversity of species found here. While water temperature is important to distribution over a broad geographical range, distribution from the high tide line (upper zone) to the subtidal (lower) zone is determined by exposure to the drying effects of immersion in the upper zone and by competition in the lower zones.

The intertidal habitats at Point Reyes can be divided into three major types: (1) sandy beach, (2) rocky shoreline, and (3) protected bay or estuary. Each type supports its own organisms; the following text summarizes the major species found in each habitat. Each habitat may also be subdivided into "zones," areas with their own complements of plants and animals based on the extent of tidal exposure. Each zone has its characteristic species. The vertical zonation of species is well illustrated by the distribution of crabs; the highest zone is inhabited by the little striped shore crab (*Pachygrapsus*), the middle zone by the purple shore crab (*Hemigrapsus*), and the lowest zone by the large rock crab (*Cancer*). A succinct discussion of zonation, one of the guiding subjects of intertidal biology, is available in *Between Pacific Tides* or *Seashore Life*.[12, 13]

Sandy Beach

The outer coast of Point Reyes is graced with long, sweeping beaches. More than 20 miles of undeveloped sandy beach qualifies this as the most extensive of the shoreline habitat types on the peninsula. Point Reyes Beach, facing west-northwest into the prevailing weather, parallels the riptide breakers for 11 miles — one of the most beautiful expanses of unspoiled shoreline in North America. Limantour and Drake's beaches are more protected, facing southwest onto the calmer waters of Drake's Bay; together they form an eight-mile semicircle that extends from Sculptured Beach nearly to the Fish Docks. The smaller Wildcat Beach (approximately two and one-half miles) and Kelham Beach (about one mile) are backed by steep coastal cliffs and offer little or no refuge on the highest flood tides. Protected pocket beaches are scattered along the shore of Tomales Bay; many of those on the west shore are accessible to the public. Each of these locations, because of their sandy granite substrate, shares many of the same inhabitants.

On the upper beach, beneath the shorecast wrack, we find "beach hoppers," small **amphipods** that scavenge decaying seaweed and plant detritus. Although less than one-half inch in length, by using its abdomen as a catapult and flipping its body one and one-half times through the air, it can leap nearly three feet! These animals burrow in the sand, and different species occur in fine-grained rather than in coarse-grained beaches. Although amphipods are one of the most common animals in the intertidal zone, the beach hopper of the upper tidal zone is the only one commonly encountered by the casual observer.[17]

Another abundant resident of the sandy beach is the **sand crab** (also called mole crab), which lives in the wet sand at the surf's edge. These creatures are very mobile, able to move quickly in any direction either by burrowing, swimming, or crawling. This mobility is an adaptation to the shifting sands and to the crab's feeding strategy, that is to bury its body in the area of the beach washed in waves with only the eyes projecting above the surface, watching the ocean. As the wave breaks and then begins to recede, the mole crab unfurls feathery feeding antennae with which it strains minute organisms

"By-the-Wind Sailors"

In the spring, with onshore winds accompanying the northward shift of the Pacific High, the tide line along the Point Reyes beaches may be strewn with a strange debris. When dried by the wind and sun, this refuse looks like crumpled pieces of cellophane, transparent, each piece an inch or two long. Some years they are abundant, some years sparse. On close inspection, a certain symmetry is noticeable — an oval, flat, ridged plate with a half oval attached at right angles along the main axis. It seems like some human-made object. But these are animals — hydroids named "by-the-wind sailors" (*Velella velella*) — which have adapted to a pelagic life, drifting far offshore. When alive, *Velella* is royal blue with an erect sail (the half oval) and short jellyfish-like tentacles below, but on the beach the soft tissue soon shrivels and the color fades.

The famous teleologist Al Molina has proposed an interesting hypothesis concerning *Velella* as a weather forecaster. Years of *Velella* abundance portend a dry winter the following year, years of *Velella*

Velella velella

scarcity portend a wet winter ahead. Twenty or so years of observation indicate that *Velella* occurrence is about as accurate at forecasting weather as any other method available.

from the flowing water. The crab then recoils its antennae, eats the contents, and awaits the next wave. Mole crabs can be very abundant in the wettest sand, packed nearly "shoulder to shoulder." They have to be abundant to survive, for this is the primary food of many of the shorebirds we see chasing the waves up and down the gently sloping beaches. Sanderlings and willets are the most common predators on the outer beach, but plovers and whimbrels also eat mole crabs.[5]

Ricketts and Calvin note that the female mole crab is larger than the male and that the population as a whole migrates "up and down the beach with the tide, staying more or less in the zone of breaking waves." Because of the size difference, males tend to occur higher on the beach than females. However, the species is hermaphroditic; an individual is a male in the early stages of life, then becomes a female with age! (This condition, called "protandrous hermaphroditism," is not unique to mole crabs; some oysters and fishes also change sex as they mature.) The cast shell (carapace) — light orange, egg-shaped, tailless, and not more than two inches long — is a common sight along the tideline, amidst shorecast wrack on which the beach hoppers feast.

Another closely related species, the **spiny mole crab**, occurs below the low tide line and reaches its northernmost distribution at Drake's Beach. This is a rather rare scavenger that does not migrate up and down the beach like its common cousin. Indeed, the spiny mole crab, nearly twice the size of the sand crab, depends on dead sand crabs as its primary food source!

Although the sandy beach supports the lowest diversity of intertidal invertebrates of any of the three habitat types, there are animals hidden underfoot for the curious naturalist. **Red bloodworms** burrow in the damp sand at the mid-tide line where they survive by eating sand. Apparently these small worms digest nutrients off the surface of the sand grain as it passes through their bodies. Studies at Drake's Beach found dense colonies of bloodworms (about 100 worms per square inch) and reported that it was the only location in Marin County where they occurred. Bloodworms are preyed upon by shorebirds and possibly by a segmented worm (*Nephtys*).[4, 17]

Other species to look for along sandy beaches are Pacific razor clams, purple olive snails, bay mussels, sand dollars, shore crabs, and periwinkles.

Rocky Shoreline

Although more restricted in extent than the sandy beach, the rocky shoreline supports one of the most diverse communities of animals on the peninsula. Duxbury Reef, Double Point, Sculptured Beach, Point Resistance are formed of shale. The Point Reyes Headlands, Bird Rock, and Tomales Point are granitic promontories. The Headlands,

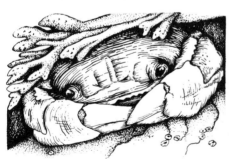

Lined shore crab

approximately three and one-half miles of rocky coast from Chimney Rock to the Lighthouse, encompass the most important rocky shoreline habitats on the peninsula. Although pocketed with small beaches, it is essentially an uninterrupted stretch of rocky coast, which has been designated as a protected area because of its importance to invertebrates, marine mammals, and seabirds. People are not allowed here because of the potential for disturbing wildlife and because of the treacherous surf. However, access is allowed at Chimney Rock, the easternmost point of the Headlands. Even here, the tide can be fatal, so along with your field guides and lunch, carry precaution.

Because so few humans visit this outer headland rocky shore, **abalones** are fairly common. There are eight species of abalone in California, but four are in warmer water south of Point Conception; only one, the red abalone, is common at Point Reyes. Black abalone occurs rarely here intertidally, and pinto and flat abalones are deepwater species. Central California is the area of maximum abundance for the red abalone, and the subtidal area off Tomales Point may have the densest population within the range. It is the largest of the abalone species and the one taken by humans as a food item. This slow-growing animal averages a growth rate of about one-half inch per year with the rate slowing with age. Adults of legal size (six and one-half inches) may be well over ten years old. Red abalone are found mostly under low intertidal rocks where they may cluster together. The shells found on the cove beaches adjacent to the rocky shore are often pocked with small holes caused by the workings of a yellow boring sponge.

Like abalone, the **owl limpet,** named for the owl-shaped pattern on the underside of the shell, is a marine shell that has suffered severe predation by hungry humans. These largest of the limpets occur in the mid-intertidal zone of heavy surf. Because they are large and tasty, they are favored by humans now as in the past; the shells are quite common in kitchen middens of the coastal Indians. As a result of this continuing pressure, owl limpets now occur only on the least accessible portions of the outer coast.

Another species to look for at Chimney Rock, rare at more heavily visited sites, is a large, beautifully shaded **seastar** (starfish) variously known as the 20-rayed star, the many-rayed star, or the sunstar. These occur in the lower intertidal region where there is luxuriant growth of seaweed. Perhaps because they have so many arms (up to 24), sunstars are the fastest and most active of the several species of seastars. They prey primarily on sea urchins, which they envelop and digest, leaving only empty shells (tests) behind. Three other seastars also occur on the rocky shore: the little six-rayed star, the purple or ochre starfish, and the batstar. The little six-rayed stars, perhaps the most common, tend to occur in groups and eat small snails, barnacles, and limpets. The purple starfish, rather large and having the familiar "starfish" shape, is able to insert its stomach into the shell of a clam or mussel and digest the contents. The batstar (or the sea bat) is easily recognized by its short, webbed rays and its bright orange or red color (although some individuals can be white, greenish, brown, or even blotched). Because of their bright color, batstars are easily found in the low intertidal zone, especially on rock surfaces with an abundant growth of surfgrass protected from the continual pounding of the surf.

The big **gumboot chiton** frequents large pools protected from the surf. Chitons are vegetarian grazers, subtidal sheep. The odd body looks like an oblong scrap of leather, a misshapen football, but inside are a row of eight plates shaped like butterflies. Because the chitons cannot grip the rocks as tightly as an abalone or seastar, the bodies are often washed up on the beach during storms. The presence of these chiton plates in Indian middens suggests to some that the gumboots were taken as food. Although possible, it seems more likely that the plates may have served as tools or ornaments. Chitons are extremely tough and unpalatable; indeed, even otters do not eat them.

Other common animals at rocky shore sites include aggregating anemone, giant green anemone, hermit crab, porcelain crab, shore crab, black turban snail, brown turban snail, rock whelk, red sea urchin, purple sea urchin, acorn barnacle, goose barnacle, white-cap limpet, California mussel, and various species of nudibranchs.

Bays, Estuaries, and Lagoons

Estuaries — wetlands where freshwater runoff mixes with ocean water — encompass approximately 18.3 square miles of Point Reyes, about 16 percent of the total area of the peninsula. Sizes of these habitats are as follows: Tomales Bay, 6,780 acres; Drake's Estero, 2,380 acres; Bolinas Lagoon, 1,450 acres; Limantour Estero, 818 acres; and Abbott's Lagoon, 282 acres. Ecologists might argue that some of these sites (especially Tomales Bay) are actually marine bays, but for the purposes of this chapter, we will call them estuaries.

Salt marshes, like the one at Limantour pictured above, are some of the most productive habitats on earth. They harbor myriad invertebrates in the substrate, and waterbirds roost and forage on the emergent vegetation when the tide has covered the adjacent mudflats.

Abbott's Lagoon, which is rarely influenced by tides, is really a 200-acre brackish lagoon connected by a spillway to two freshwater ponds (about 80 acres in extent). Little research has been done on the invertebrate fauna at Abbott's, but we might expect it to host some of the same species of clams, snails, and burrowing worms common in other protected bays and estuaries. The large concentrations of shorebirds that forage along the water's edge, especially in fall, indicate that a large invertebrate population is present. The most common fish in the lagoon is the **threespine stickleback**, an anadromous species in a family of mostly freshwater, but salt-tolerant, fishes.

The other sites, under the influence of daily tidal influence, fit well into the estuarine category and each site supports many of the same organisms. These estuarine animals must be able to withstand the physiological stress caused by daily and seasonal changes in the water's salinity. In general, marine organisms are better adapted to dealing with reduced salinities than are freshwater organisms to surviving increased salinity. Therefore, within the Point Reyes wetland system, where the ocean's influence is strong and the freshwater runoff is minimal, marine organisms predominate.

Within each estuary, many animals and plants are distributed according to the nature of the substrate, the influence of freshwater inflow, the volume of tidal flow, and temperature. The habitat preferences of the more common clams illustrate distribution determined by the character of the substrate: the **Washington clam**, or butter clam, occurs in coarse sand or coarse mud; the **white sand clam** occurs in medium- to fine-grained sand or sandy mud; the **gaper**, or horseneck clam, occurs in finer mud. Each of these species occurs at each estuary, but abundance varies depending on the availability of suitable habitat.

The importance of the texture of the substrate has to do with the burrowing and feeding strategies of each species. Perhaps this is best illustrated by the **ghost shrimp,** a close relative of the mole crab of the outer beach discussed previously. Two species of ghost shrimp are rather common in these estuaries, though because of their burrowing habit they are rarely seen. Indeed, each lives its entire life in its burrow and tunnel system and will die shortly if removed. Both feed by pumping water into their burrows and sifting detritus and plankton from the current. Their presence is betrayed by low cones on tidal flats, similar to small anthills, which surround the opening to their burrows. The **pink ghost shrimp** occurs in sandy areas, usually close to shore, and is quite common at Bolinas Lagoon and Tomales Bay. The **blue ghost shrimp** occurs in the lower tidal zone in muddier substrate and is rather common at Drake's Estero. The burrow system of each species is a kind of invertebrate apartment house, hosting a variety of smaller animals that freeload off the ghost shrimp's largess. Ecologists refer to animals that exploit the host's hospitality without damage or benefit to the host as *commensals*. Some of the common commensals found in ghost shrimp burrows include **pea crabs,**

scale worms, a **red copepod** (a small crustacean), several small clams, and a **goby fish**. Ghost shrimps are a favorite bait for fishermen, who extract them from their burrows with "slurp" guns, pipes that are used to suck up the sand or mud and the ghost shrimp with it. This common practice has undoubtedly had a deleterious effect on the shrimp population, especially along the east shore of Bolinas Lagoon and near the mouth of Tomales Bay where the pressure on pink ghost shrimp is intense. The long-billed curlew, a large shorebird with a foot-long curved bill, is especially well adapted at finding and eating ghost shrimp. From July through March, curlews patrol the tidal flats of Bolinas Lagoon, probing the burrows.

The most abundant species in estuaries may also be the most seldom seen. Beneath the mudflats at Drake's Estero are vast nations of **phoronid worms** (also known as green-plumed worms), named for their tentacles, feathery tufts that are unfurled from the buried tube into shallow water and serve for feeding and respiration. The vast colonies of plumed worms that carpet the mudflats of Drake's Estero and Tomales Bay are unique *in the world.* Outside of central California these are rather rare animals.[4]

Also beneath the surface are the several clams mentioned previously and the huge geoduck, the largest and deepest burrowing of the local species. **Geoducks** (pronounced "gooey-duck," perhaps from a Chinook word for "deep digger") burrow to a depth of four feet in fine-grained mud and extend their long siphon to the surface. This siphon, which resembles a baby elephant trunk, is so long that it cannot be retracted into the shell. Apparently the end of the siphon is sometimes nipped off by skates or rays. Healthy geoduck beds are located near shore in Drake's Estero; however, Gordon Chan, marine biologist at College of Marin, has expressed concern that these colonies represent "a remnant of a vanishing species in California."[4]

No discussion of bay and estuary habitats would be complete without mentioning the giant **moon snail**. Moon snails are most often seen on the sandy tidal flats of the protected inner estuaries. Although less common than many of the species mentioned above, they are more obvious and familiar to the casual observer; empty shells are rather common on the Limantour flats. The nearly circular shell grows to four or more inches in diameter, and when fully extended the foot is three or four times larger than the shell. These slow-moving animals are predators on clams, especially sand clams, and even cannibalize one another. Gulls often try to prey on these hardy beasts, carrying the snail, retracted in its shell, high into the air and dropping it on the sand in a vain attempt to break the heavy shell.

Occasionally, egg cases of the moon snail are found on the exposed tidal flats. The eggs are shed in a continuous gelatinous sheet that becomes entirely encrusted in sand grains and forms a delicate, beautifully fluted circular collar. The uninitiated who finds this oddly symmetrical casting may well be mystified by its origins.

Oysters

The species of oyster native to California, *Ostrea lurida,* also known as the Olympia, was once widely distributed in shallow bays and estuaries and was an important food to native Californians. Today, it is the least important of the three species harvested for human consumption. The Eastern oyster and the Japanese oyster are favored species in the industry. The advantages of Japanese and Eastern oysters over the native species are size and growth rate. Though delicious, the native oyster is small, taking several years to grow to two inches; the exotic species grow twice the size in as many years.

Ostrea lurida

Eastern oysters were first planted in Tomales Bay in 1875 for the purpose of supplying the San Francisco market. The industry operated in fits and starts for about 50 years. By the late 1930s the oyster-growing industry in San Francisco Bay was abandoned due to pollution, and the demand for oysters from Tomales Bay increased. Japanese oysters were introduced to California when they were planted in Tomales Bay in 1928. By the late 1930s commercial production of Japanese oysters was well established there. In 1932

small numbers were planted in Drake's Estero. These experimental plantings were so successful that the effort was enlarged and continues today. Oysters were raised in Bolinas Lagoon from the mid-1950s to the mid-1960s; the area was used for seed beds and the oysters were then transplanted to Drake's Estero. Although Eastern oysters are still cultivated locally, the Japanese variety has proved hardier and now dominates the market.

During the 1980s there was a resurgence of the aquaculture industry in Tomales Bay. Several small oyster companies were established and they succeeded in growing several new varieties of oysters commercially – a small Japanese oyster called the Kumomoto and another Eastern species, *Ostrea virginica.*

Both Japanese and Eastern oysters require warm water temperatures to spawn, temperatures rarely available in the cool California current. As a result, local growers import spats (young oysters) each year, plant them in spring, and grow them for two or three years before harvesting.

The introduction of an exotic species into any community can have unforeseen results. The oysters introduced to these waters have brought with them parasites and "hitchhikers." Some of these have become naturalized, establishing their own independent populations. Newcomers to Tomales Bay (and perhaps Drake's Estero) include the predatory "oyster drills"; a dog whelk; a parasitic copepod (which lives in the digestive tract of mussels and has decimated the mussel industry of France); a horse mussel; a horn snail; and the Japanese littleneck clam.

Eelgrass Beds

> This flowering plant is important as food, whether eaten directly . . . or as a source of detritus when it decays. It also influences the community structure because the rhizomes [roots with buds] help stabilize the mud and because both rhizomes and leaves provide refuge for animals.
>
> — Michael Barbour et al. *Coastal Ecology.* 1973.

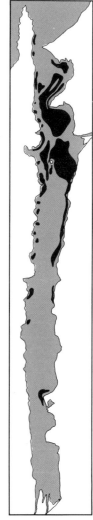

A fourth habitat, the eelgrass beds, deserves special attention because of the unique community of animals it supports, and because of its abundance, especially in Tomales Bay and near the center of Drake's Estero. **Eelgrass** is really a subtidal plant; it grows in dense meadows in quiet waters. Unlike most "seaweeds," which are really marine algae, eelgrass is a true flowering plant, one of the few species (along with surfgrass) that has adapted to life in the ocean. It provides a substrate for various invertebrates, a nursery for fishes (see "Pacific Herring," below), and foraging habitat for birds. (See Chapter 5.)

The blades of the grass support abundant growths of **coralline algae**, large **diatoms** ("shelled protozoans" — Foraminifera), and **bryzoans** (colonial "moss animals"), each of which provides a broad base for the estuarine food pyramid. These in turn are grazed by tiny snails, skeleton shrimp ("the praying mantises of the sea"), and others. Hydroids attach themselves to the blades and are fed on by small sea slugs (nudibranchs), which seem particularly abundant here. Two species that have been found commonly in the eelgrass beds at Limantour but are rare elsewhere at Point Reyes are the large *Melibe* and *Triopha*. A close relative of the nudibranchs, sea hares (opisthobranchs) tend to be common here, especially *Phyllaplysia*, which lives almost exclusively on eelgrass and whose color, green with longitudinal black stripes, perfectly mimics the blade, rendering the animal nearly invisible. Even more common than *Phyllaplysia* is *Haminoea*, which deposits its bright yellow stringy egg masses amidst the blades of grass. Another opisthobranch, the brown sea hare, is much larger than *Phyllaplysia* or *Haminoea*, and rather than crawling along the blade, gracefully swims through the forest, grazing on the grass.

Map 7. Distribution of eelgrass beds in Tomales Bay. Eelgrass beds appear black. (Adapted from Spratt 1981.)

One of the strangest looking fishes in the nearshore and estuarine waters, the **bay pipefish**, frequents the eelgrass beds of Tomales Bay. These fish look like sea horses that have been straightened out and elongated; indeed, they are closely related to the more tropical sea horses. The narrow body shape and deep green color of the pipefish allow it to resemble the blades of eelgrass and must serve as camouflage. The similar **snubnosed pipefish** ranges from central Mexico northward only as far as Tomales Bay; it is browner and smaller than the bay pipefish.

FISHES

WINTER BRINGS THREE SEASONAL EVENTS that infuse the Point Reyes area with a combination of anticipation, excitement, and hope: the first rains and the salmon run that accompanies them, gray whale migration, and the herring run. Of these, the last goes unnoticed by some, but to many it is the highlight of winter.

San Francisco and Tomales bays have supported healthy commercial fisheries since at least the mid-1800s, although the first catch records go back only to 1872. The richness of these cold waters is attested to by the large number of fishing ports established in the Point Reyes vicinity, especially in the shelter of Tomales Bay: Dillon Beach, Hamlet, Nick's Cove, Blake's Landing, Blue Baie Tavern, Marshall, Marconi, Millerton, Bivalve, Point Reyes Station, Inverness, Drake's Bay, Bolinas Bay. Through the years, herring has been the leading species of the Tomales Bay fishery, but other species landed include salmon, crab, sole, shark, and ling cod, with lesser numbers of surf perch and smelt. Oysters are grown commercially from planted spats. Formerly there were Chinese shrimp camps on Tomales Bay, but they were abandoned before 1897.[21]

The overall effect of the commercial fishery on these populations is nearly impossible to assess. Furthermore, the long-term effects of changing water temperatures may mask the short-term effects of fishery depletion. There have been extended warm-water periods in the mid-1800s, 1926, 1957–59, 1972–73, 1983, and 1989–90, with intermittent cool-water periods. Certainly the fish populations that are sensitive to water temperature altered their distributions and abundances in response to these environmental changes. Regardless of the cause, we know from the accounts of early naturalists that fish were much more abundant than they are today.

> The Californians [1841–1842] . . . eat no fish because they have no boats to catch them, but when a westerly gale has driven millions of sardines on the strand, they do not take the trouble of cooking what Dame Nature has poured into their laps.
> —G. Gaylord Simpson. *Narrative.* . . . 1930.

Sardines

The sardine fishery was one of the largest resource industries in California from 1920 into the 1940s. The fishery peaked in 1936 when up to a million tons were harvested; in subsequent years the catch began to fluctuate. Finally, the bottom dropped out when the sardine population crashed about 1945. Few sardines were left north of Point Conception by the early 1950s; the population had contracted its range southward. The decline may have been attributable to overfishing, changing ocean temperatures, or, most likely, a combination of influences.

The Pacific sardine and the northern anchovy are "ecological equivalents" with similar life histories and distributions. However, the mature sardine is nearly twice the size of the mature northern anchovy, and most of the sardines that occurred off central California were large adults.

Because larger predators are more efficient at exploiting the larger sardines, the decline of the sardine in the Gulf of the Farallones was accompanied by a decline in the largest cormorant (double-crested), the largest alcid (tufted puffin), and the largest sea lion (northern sea lion), each of which preyed on sardines. Although anchovies had always been present in the waters of the California Current, as sardines disappeared in the late 1940s and early 1950s, northern anchovies increased in abundance, in effect filling a vacant niche. The increase in the anchovy population may help explain the concurrent increase in animals that eat anchovies—northern fur seal, rhinoceros auklet— but does not account directly for the increase in the elephant seal or California sea lion!

ANADROMOUS FISHES

A NADROMY (from the Greek: *"ana"* = up + *"dromo"* = running) is migration from the ocean to brackish or fresh water for the purpose of breeding. At Point Reyes, few freshwater drainages are suitable for anadromous fishes. The mouths of some meet the sea with a precipitous drop, impassable to a migrant fish. Others have been dammed to create stock ponds for cattle. The flows of others have been altered by culverts, tide gates, or levees, thereby increasing siltation and destroying habitat. Despite these obstacles, salmon, trout, sturgeon, and herring are still found, though in increasingly reduced numbers, within the Point Reyes watershed. Fortunately, the Park Service and other regulatory agencies are committed to watershed restoration. If sound management practices and the tenacity of the species prevail, we may see the revival of the depleted populations within the century.

Herring

Pacific herring, an ocean fish closely related to the sardine, groups into large schools in the early winter and migrates inshore to deposit its eggs (spawn) in coastal bays and estuaries. The eggs are attached to subtidal vegetation, especially the abundant eelgrass which accounts for 75 percent of the vegetation in Tomales Bay. The herring do not enter the bay en masse, but in several pulses that can occur from December through March. The causes for the timing of these pulses are not well known; however, most spawning occurs when the highest daily tides are at night. The nocturnal nature of these spawning runs may help avoid predation, which can be severe; estimates suggest that predation by birds may deplete 90 percent of the eggs.[24]

Historically, Tomales Bay was one of the major spawning grounds of herring in California, in some years providing up to 75 percent of the total harvest. From the 1930s until 1973, herring landings in Tomales Bay varied from 200 up to 1500 tons per season. Up to that time the market was small, the price was low, and the fishing effort was small. In the early 1970s the Russians stopped providing the Japanese with herring roe and the local fishery grew to accommodate the new market. One of the lowest catches (110 tons in 1983–84) corresponded to El Niño warm water. It took a few years for the population to recover, but by 1986–87 the local fleet netted 867 tons, their best season since the roe fishery began. In subsequent years, however, the take diminished precipitously. The 1988–89 catch of 40 tons was the lowest on record. Since 1989 the fishery has all but disappeared. The decline is probably related to several interactive factors, including warmer ocean waters, damming of creeks, a decrease in fresh water inflow, overharvesting, and a population shift to San Francisco Bay.[19]

Silver ("Coho") Salmon

There was a time, when herds of tule elk were stalked by grizzlies and Miwok people gathered abalone at Palomarin, when the silver salmon run must have been bountiful. In the fall, as the sun shone at an oblique angle and the expectation of the rainy season approached, the people gathered to celebrate and encourage the coming of the salmon. By the winter solstice, as the rivers were swelling, Olema Creek, Pine Gulch, and Lagunitas creeks must have teemed with the swirls and shimmering sides of salmon, swimming upstream to spawn and die. In years when the salmon were abundant great feasts were held.

Silver salmon

After settlement of West Marin and the vicinity by Europeans, Tomales Bay supported a large silver salmon fishery. Salmon are now rare here, the result of overfishing, siltation, and the damming of rivers. Overfishing of adult salmon probably had less impact than siltation of the stream beds. With increased human use of the watershed – logging, intensive grazing, damming – the gravel beds have been covered with silt, limiting the availability of spawning habitat and reducing the numbers of aquatic insects available to the fry. Much habitat has also been lost due to dams and reservoirs on Lagunitas Creek.

The life history of silver salmon is more regimented than that of the steelhead; silvers are less flexible, less able to adapt to changes in the environment. The first year is spent in the freshwater creek of their birth where they live a solitary existence, defending territories in back eddies and shallow rills from others of their kind. Mortality can be high, especially in dry years. At the end of the first year, in April or May, most "finger-lings," now about three inches long, gather in small schools and migrate downstream to the Pacific where they spend the next two years. The change from a fresh to a saline environment requires physiological adjustments, a process known as "smolting," during which the fish undergoes biochemical changes that enable it to survive in salt water. Once they are in the ocean, they remain in schools in nearshore waters and grow quickly on a diet of invertebrates and small schooling fish, such as herring.

Schools join schools, and soon the congregation is journeying around the Pacific, through uncharted waters. Many fall prey to seals, sharks, and fishermen. Then, after two years abroad, at the onset of the winter storms, the salmon begin to gather outside the mouths of the creeks of their birth. (Some males mature and return after one year.) If rainfall is sufficient, the surviving salmon, ripened and gravid, enter the watershed of their birth to lay or fertilize eggs in a series of gravel or sandy nests (redds). The female will select a redd site away from the most turbulent water, but where the current is strong enough to supply sufficient oxygen for the eggs. After the female deposits a few hundred eggs in her chosen redd, the male immediately follows and fertilizes them with his "milt"; the female then covers the eggs with gravel and repeats her movements. This will be the last effort of their lives.[7,14]

Steelhead Rainbow Trout

Of the vertebrates, the trouts are among the most variable of all . . . of the trouts the Steelhead is one of the most variable.
—L. Shapovalov and A. C. Taft. *Life Histories.* 1954.

Silver salmon and steelhead are very similar in appearance but very different bio-logically. Unlike silver salmon, which exist within a relatively narrow range of param-eters, steelhead are flexible. Silver salmon will not spawn unless they enter the ocean first, and they die after spawning once. Steelhead are able to remain in the stream, mature, and spawn without entering the ocean, and are capable of spawning more than once. The spawning season of the steelhead is much longer than that of the silver. Steel-head run in fall and spring where conditions permit, but Point Reyes hosts a fall run population. Steelhead will run toward the ocean at various ages and may spend a varying amount of time there. It would seem that the flexibility of steelhead would serve the species well in its struggle to survive the obstacles placed in its way by humans.[22]

There are also many similarities in life history between steelhead and silver salmon. Both migrate upstream on rising and falling water levels, but cease movement during peak flow. In both species, the onset of upstream migration seems to be triggered by an increase in stream flow, but does not always coincide with the first heavy runoff. Perhaps they must wait until the stream reaches a critical volume of flow, or until the water clears. Both species migrate during daylight hours. Females of both species select the redd site, but steelhead select smaller gravel than silvers. Steelhead tend to select a site at the upstream head of a riffle, at the foot of a still pool.[7,22]

Steelhead are not taken commercially, though sports fishermen take large numbers.

AMPHIBIANS

Salamanders

THE SIX SPECIES OF SALAMANDERS that occur at Point Reyes can be divided into two ecological groups: those that breed in water (Pacific giant salamander, California newt, rough-skinned newt), and the so-called woodland salamanders which breed on land (*Ensatina*, California slender salamander, and arboreal salamander).

With the first winter rains the aquatic newts migrate from their subterranean haunts and the inner depths of rotten logs to still-standing ponds or slow-flowing streams to find a mate and complete ancestral obligations. As salamanders go, newts are conspicuous. Both species might be seen during the wetter months, especially as they migrate from their solitary hideouts to communal breeding waters where they lay their eggs. Because of this overland movement, these are the most commonly encountered species on the peninsula; whether they are actually the most abundant is not known. Two other species, the **Ensatina** and the **California slender salamander**, rarely wander out in the open, but remain in or under wet and decaying logs where they lay their eggs.

*   *   *

In the last days of February, after a dry winter, we wandered into the damp lowland forest near Lake Ranch. By this late date the rains should have soaked well into the ground, but this season the skies had been reticent, promising storms with angry morning clouds that degenerated into gray mists, then sunshine. We had come to see if the drought had visible effects on the innermost forest. We stood on the end of a fir log that was colonized by polypody ferns and extended out into a shallow pond of muddy water. Overhead, we heard a flock of chickadees and kinglets in the highest branches, the occasional high-pitched notes of a brown creeper, and the ventriloquial creaks of a tree frog. Another sound whispered through our ears, a soft sloshing at our feet. Down we looked and found a knot of orange and brown flesh, about the size of an apple, spinning slowly just beneath the surface of the muddy little pond — newts entwined. We had stumbled upon an amphibian orgy.

Upon closer inspection we noticed that the male, using all four legs, held his mate beneath his body. Other newts approached from the depths of the clouded water, attempting to join the pair. The mating male, his cloacal orifice swollen to an almost grotesque size, seemed larger than the intruders; perhaps they were females? The scene became slapstick as the interlopers tried to attach to the mating pair; they grabbed with their forelegs, but kept slipping off and spinning the couple in place. (Although the male newt becomes smooth-skinned during the mating season, the palms of his hands become rough, developing "nuptial pads," presumably to aid in holding on to his slippery mate.) For a brief time four newts were embraced in a tumbling ball of salamander sexuality. Finally, the mating male mustered the strength to squirm out of the tangle and swim to the bottom with a few strokes of his broad tail. The knot unraveled and the others followed the male to the murky depths. Having been transfixed on the activities of this foursome, we raised our heads and looked about the pond. Soon we noticed other soft swirls breaking the water's surface: at least a dozen other knots of newts were entangled in the same ritual.

People are intruders into such gatherings and we watched in silent awe. Such communions — rutting of deer, denning of lions, nesting of birds — are common in nature but seldom observed by humans. For us, this congregation of solitary beings to perpetuate their own in a small forest pond in the middle of the Point Reyes peninsula was a gift from the wilderness — a gift of participation in the timeless process of renewal, an image of the perfection of uncontaminated nature. Such phenomena are regenerative to the human soul, and therein lies the mystery of nature and the value of wilderness to humanity's urbanized spirit.

*   *   *

The newt knots that we discovered happened to be composed of **rough-skinned newts,** one of the most water-loving of the North American species and one of the most common at Point Reyes. Rough-skins are very similar in appearance to the closely related **California newt,** which also occurs on the peninsula. Although the skin of each species is covered with small wart-like bumps, when the male arrives in his wet wedding place his skin loses its roughness, becoming smooth, while his tail broadens, enabling him to scull through his aquatic breeding habitat. The two species are distinguished from one another by the color of their lower eyelids: dark brown in the rough-skinned, orange in the California. At Point Reyes, rough-skinned newts are quite common on the coastal slope, in the humid fog belt; Californias seem to be less common and occur in drier areas.

Another species, the **Pacific giant salamander,** is also rarely seen, but when found it never fails to thrill the observer. There is something otherworldly about salamanders in general, about Pacific giants in particular. Perhaps it is their relative rarity or their large size; perhaps their broad head and large eyes suggest some vaguely human characteristics. Whatever the origin of their mystery, it prevails.

We tend to associate Pacific giants with the dampest redwood forests and the

Pacific giant salamander

wettest canyons, but at Point Reyes they also occur in the drier bishop pine forest and even in the coastside drainages, as at Laguna Ranch and in the coastal scrub near the old RCA Station. In spring the larvae can be found in the colder streams of these drainages. These most primitive of the amphibians display the remarkable tendency toward "neoteny," the ability to remain in a larval condition and even to breed in that form. The environmental conditions that inhibit transformation into the adult form are not well known.

The **slender salamander** is a dark, small, skinny species with tiny legs; on first glance one may mistake it for an earthworm or a little snake. These are the most easily found of the woodland species: nearly every log in the damp broadleaf forest harbors one or two underneath, though they are easily overlooked. Ensatinas and **arboreal salamanders** are seldom seen and they are likely rather rare here. Ensatinas may be more common than the few sightings indicate, but arboreals are probably restricted to the few live oaks that border the eastern flank of the peninsula.

Frogs

Through the evenings of the first drenching rains of November, the swales, ponds, and marshes resonate with the choruses of **Pacific treefrogs.** As the song of the swainson's thrush and the osprey's whistle herald the birth of spring at Point Reyes, the frog symphony announces that winter is well underway. At Olema Marsh, or Kehoe Marsh, or Muddy Hollow Pond, we hear a myriad of voices repeating their creaking sounds together, seeming to encourage one another toward crescendo, then suddenly stopping, simultaneously. How does the population preform in such unison? What cue prompts the sudden silence? It reminds us of the seemingly telepathic ability of shorebird flocks to wheel through the air in synchrony.

Although treefrogs occur in several color forms, and individuals may change color quickly, many local treefrogs are a beautiful bright green with a striking black mask.

Red-legged frogs are most easily found in the winter or spring, in ponds and, especially, in slow-moving coastal streams. They are not as vocal as treefrogs and their croaks are low-pitched and gutteral. It is likely that they were more common before bullfrogs were introduced into California as a food item early in this century. **Bullfrogs**, larger than red-leggeds, are rapacious and consume both tadpoles and adults of other species. We do not know when bullfrogs first became established at Point Reyes, probably in the 1930s or later. They are now abundant in freshwater ponds. At Five Brooks, for example, one may see hundreds of bullfrog heads emerging from the water's surface in spring; conversely, red-legged frogs are rare or absent there. One can only wonder if red-leggeds can sustain their numbers with the continued depredations by their larger cousins from east of the Rocky Mountains.

The more terrestrial **western toad** is rarely encountered on the peninsula, perhaps because of its nocturnal habits in this portion of its wide range. The additional habit of burying itself in loose soil, leaf litter, and even woodrat lodges makes it even harder to find.

REPTILES

Turtles

THE ONLY "LAND TURTLE" at Point Reyes is the **western pond turtle.** We call it a land turtle to distinguish it from the sea turtles, but in fact this species is entirely aquatic, occurring in nearly all freshwater ponds, streams, and even drainage ditches that have sufficient aquatic vegetation. Some individuals, usually fertile females, migrate overland. Western pond turtles are most often seen on warm days as they emerge from the water and bask on logs or the muddy shores of marshes and stock ponds. Five Brooks and Muddy Hollow ponds are the best places to find pond turtles.[25]

The sea turtles, as a group, occur mostly in the warm waters of the tropics and subtropics: rarely do they wander into the relatively cool waters of the Gulf of the Farallones. Based on sightings and strandings along the Pacific coast from Monterey Bay north, the green turtle and the leatherback are the species most likely to occur. The few records of sea turtles at Point Reyes are of beach-stranded individuals, dead or dying. In 1989 and 1990 summer water temperatures were warmer than usual in the Gulf of the Farallones and leatherbacks were sighted frequently from June to November by fishermen and naturalists. A rare Pacific Ridley turtle was found stranded on McClure's Beach in January 1987. The specimen is now at California Academy of Sciences.

Lizards

Four species of lizard are found at Point Reyes, but only one, the **western fence lizard**, is abundant. These "blue-bellies" belong to a family known as the "spiny lizards," named for the sharp, overlapping scales that give them a rough, textured look. Fence lizards are ubiquitous here, occurring in nearly every habitat except the dampest innermost forest and the tidal salt marsh. They are usually seen basking in sunshine on bark, fences, or the unpainted wood siding of buildings. The males have a deep blue throat that they show-off while they do push-ups in place, a mating posture that may also function as a threat display. Often we find a fence lizard with a stubby tail. As in other lizards, the tail is weakly attached to the spine and easily broken off when grabbed by a potential predator, perhaps a kestrel, a shrike, or even another fence lizard (they are known for cannibalism).

Alligator lizards, with their small rectangular scales, have smoother skins than fence lizards and their body shape, with long thin torso and relatively small limbs, gives them a more snake-like appearance. They are also less commonly encountered at Point Reyes, where two of California's three species occur. One, the more common **northern alligator lizard**, lays eggs. The northern is slightly smaller, less bulky, and has a shorter tail than the **southern alligator lizard**. The northern is also darker, usually with a coppery brown ground color; the southern is lighter with a brassy yellow ground color. The condition of having two similar species co-exist in the same geographic region is known as "sympatry." That these two alligator lizards are sympatric here suggests that they occupy separate ecological niches within the environment. They may have separate breeding seasons, utilize different food sources, and occur in different habitats. We know little about their natural history, except that northerns are more common and are probably more tolerant of colder and more humid microclimates.

Snakes

Most snakes, like most lizards, are creatures of warm and dry environments; therefore, the humid environment at Point Reyes limits the population sizes of several species. Of the ten species that occur here, only four are fairly common; the others are uncommon to extremely rare. (All ten are listed in the species list in the Appendix.)

Western rattlesnakes have been found on the peninsula, but they are extremely rare and the few individuals discovered were in villages around human habitations; it is possible that they arrived here in firewood or other deliveries that were brought in from drier inland areas. Rattlesnakes do occur with regularity in chaparral and rocky areas on Mount Tamalpais and Bolinas Ridge, just east of the San Andreas Fault. Hikers, campers, and picnickers within the Seashore need not be overly concerned about rattle-snakes; there is only one documented case of a person being bitten at Point Reyes. No other poisonous reptiles are found here.

Gopher snakes resemble rattlesnakes, and may even mimic the rattling sound that serves as a warning, but gopher snakes do not have rattles at the end of their tails. Although they will threaten humans, especially on warm days, they are harmless and should be allowed to continue on their way, unharmed. Gopher snakes are rather common at Point Reyes and are an important predator of rodents and birds.

The most commonly encountered snakes are the small and graceful garter snakes, diurnal species that tend to be found near fresh or brackish wetlands. Three distinctly marked species may be found at Point Reyes, another example of sympatry. Of the three, the **western terrestrial garter snake** (also called the "coast garter snake") is the most commonly seen, especially in lowland swales, in damp fields near streamside thickets, or even out in coastal salt marsh. Although this species varies in color and pattern throughout its range, at Point Reyes it has an olive or tan head and a distinct dull yellow stripe down its back.

The **California red-sided garter snake** (also called the "common garter snake") is seen less frequently, although it can be quite common around Limantour and Abbott's Lagoon, and is the most striking of the three species. Indeed, this is one of the most beautiful snakes in North America. It has a brilliant red head, red- and black-checkered flanks, and a pastel bluish belly.

The third and least common species is the **western aquatic garter snake.** It is plain-looking compared with the other two species, lacking the elaborate patterning on the flanks, which are drab olive in color. The stripe down the back is a brighter yellow than in the western terrestrial, and the bright yellow throat is unique to this species. Although the other species will also enter water, this is the most aquatic of the three. It feeds on tadpoles, frogs, small fish, and probably aquatic invertebrates.

REFERENCES

1. Ainley, D. A., and T. J. Lewis. 1974. The history of Farallon Island marine bird populations, 1854–1972. *Condor* 76: 432–436.

2. Barbour, M. G., R. B. Craig, F. R. Drysdale, M. T. Ghiselin. 1973. *Coastal Ecology: Bodega Head.* Berkeley: University of California Press.

3. Barrett, E. M. 1963. *The California Oyster Industry.* California Department of Fish and Game, Fish Bulletin 123.

4. Chan, G. L. 1971. *A Report on the Survey of Major Marine Organisms at Point Reyes National Seashore Park.* College of Marin, Sea Grant Project GH-48.

5. Cubit, J. 1969. Behavior and physical factors causing migration and aggregation of the sand crab *Emerita analoga* (Stimpson). *Ecology* 50: 118–123.

6. Fitch, J. E., and R. J. Lavenberg. 1975. *Tidepool and Nearshore Fishes of California*. California Natural History Guide 38. Berkeley: University of California Press.

7. Fry, D. H. 1973. *Anadromous Fishes of California*. Department of Fish and Game.

8. Goddard, J. H. R. 1981. Range extension and notes on the food, morphology and color pattern of the dorid nudibranch *Hallaxa chani*. *Veliger* 24: 155–158.

9. Goslinger, T. M., and G. C. Williams. 1970. The opisthobranch mollusks of Marin County, California. *Veliger* 13: 175–180.

10. Goslinger, T. M., and G. C. Williams. 1973. Additions to the opisthobranch mollusk fauna of Marin County, California, with notes on their natural history. *Veliger* 15: 252–253.

11. Hardwick, J. E. 1973. Biomass estimates of spawning herring, *Culpea harengus pallasii*, herring eggs, and associated vegetation in Tomales Bay. *California Fish and Game* 59: 36–61.

12. Hedgepeth, J. 1968. Beyond the tides: the uncertain sea. In *Between Pacific Tides*, 4th ed., edited by E. Ricketts and J. Calvin. Stanford, Calif.: Stanford University Press.

13. Hedgepeth, J. 1971. *Introduction to Seashore Life of the San Francisco Bay Region and the Coast of Northern California*. Berkeley: University of California Press.

14. Hershey, M. C. 1973. *The Silver Salmon of Muir Woods*. Muir Woods-Point Reyes Natural History Association.

15. Light, S. F. 1975. *Light's Manual: Intertidal Invertebrates of the Central California Coast*, 3rd ed. Berkeley: University of California Press.

16. Miller, D. J., and R. N. Lea. 1972. *Guide to the Coastal Marine Fishes of California*. Department of Fish and Game, Fish Bulletin 157.

17. Morris, R. H., D. P. Abbott, and E. C. Haderlie. 1980. *Intertidal Invertebrates of California*. Stanford, Calif.: Stanford University Press.

18. Peabody, F. E., and J. M. Savage. 1958. Evolution of the coast range corridor in California and its effect on the origin and dispersal of living amphibians and reptiles. In *Zoogeography*, edited by C. L. Hubbs. American Association for the Advancement of Science, Publication No. 51.

19. Ricketts, E. F., and J. Calvin. 1968. *Between Pacific Tides*, 4th ed. Stanford, Calif.: Stanford University Press.

20. Scofield, W. L. 1952. The Tomales Bay herring fishery. *California Fish and Game* 38: 499–504.

21. Scofield, W. L. 1954. *California Fishing Ports*. California Department of Fish and Game, Fish Bulletin 96.

22. Shapovalov, L., and A. C. Taft. 1954. *The Life Histories of the Steelhead Rainbow Trout* (Salmo gairdneri gairdneri) *and Silver Salmon* (Oncorhynchus kisutch) *with Special Reference to Waddell Creek, California, and Recommendations Regarding their Management*. California Department of Fish and Game, Fish Bulletin 98.

23. Simpson, G. 1930. *Narrative of a Voyage to California Ports in 1841–1842*. San Francisco: The Private Press of T. C. Russell.

24. Spratt, J. D. 1981. *Status of the Pacific Herring*, Culpea harengus pallasii, *Resource in California 1972 to 1980*. California Department of Fish and Game, Fish Bulletin 171.

25. Stebbins, R. C. 1966. *A Field Guide to Western Reptiles and Amphibians*. Peterson Field Guide Series. New York: Houghton Mifflin Co.

26. Stebbins, R. C. 1972. *Amphibians and Reptiles of California*. California Natural History Guides 31. Berkeley: University of California Press.

CHAPTER FIVE

BIRDS
The Sky People

Keith Hansen 1988

> The eagle ranges far and wide over the land, farther than any other creature, and all
> things there are related simply having existence in the perfect vision of this bird.
>> — N. Scott Momaday. *House Made of Dawn.* 1966.

THE "FIELD CHECKLIST OF THE BIRDS OF MARIN COUNTY" refers to the area as a "hot-bed" of birdlife. It is. About 425 species have been recorded at Point Reyes and adjacent waters and new rarities are discovered each year. Indeed, Point Reyes supports as great a variety of bird species as any other area of equivalent size in North America (a distinction shared by coastal areas of Florida, Texas, and Southern California). Several factors contribute to this diversity of birds that have been recorded at Point Reyes: a temperate climate, a mosaic of habitats, varied topography, and the peninsula's coastal position at the western edge of the continent.

At latitude 38°N, the peninsula lies near the northern extent of influence of the Pacific High, a stable mass of cool air that presses down on the ocean about 1,000 miles offshore. (See Chapter 1.) The Pacific High protects the peninsula from polar or tropical storm fronts as effectively as a mountain range. Even as nearby as Mendocino County, the moderating winter influence of the Pacific High decreases: fresh water freezes, fewer plants bloom, sap runs more slowly, rainfall increases. Here at Point Reyes, however, the climate is milder, more hospitable, survivable. The constancy of the climate cooperates with the availability of a variety of habitats to ensure that large numbers of birds find Point Reyes suitable as a productive breeding ground, a dependable refueling station during migration, and a hospitable wintering ground.

Each species found at Point Reyes occurs elsewhere, but here we have an unusual variety of rarities, that is, species one would not expect to occur here. Often it seems that the peninsula is a refuge for the lost birds of the continent. Indeed, fully one-half of the species are rare or extremely rare (Species list 4: pg 205). There are few other places where a brown shrike (from Eurasia) and a scissor-tailed flycatcher (common in the southwestern United States) may be seen on the same morning, where an American golden plover and a Pacific golden plover may be seen in the same flock, or where there is a possibility of finding *nine* species of owls in one day. However, it is not only rarity that distinguishes Point Reyes, it is also abundance, and each season has its complement of plenty: songbirds in spring, fledglings in summer, migrants in fall, waterbirds in winter.

*   *   *

In Bolinas, early September 1975, our wedding celebration was interrupted when the hori-
zon darkened with a flock of shearwaters that stretched along the shore as far as we could see in

either direction. The excited crowd, many naturalists among them, found three different species amidst a million sooty shearwaters.

*   *   *

Following a particularly intense Pacific storm in November 1976, we stood on the shore of Tomales Bay, scanning the water's surface, which was littered with flittering red phalaropes, tiny shorebirds usually seen only far offshore. Attempting to count the inestimable numbers, we came up with a lame census of 10,000; there were probably twice that many.

*   *   *

It was one of those typical spring days, March 31, 1980, clear sky, the wind out of the northwest, relentless. We stood on a promontory at Bull Point and aimed our telescopes to Drake's Estero, taking a census of black brant for the Department of Fish and Game. The small geese seemed restless. Squadrons flew from one arm of the estero to another; other groups reached underwater with necks outstretched, grazing eelgrass from submerged pastures. The flock, 4,000 strong, must have taken refuge here to refuel as it struggled against the headwinds northward in migration from Baja to Alaska. Whatever the reason, the estero provided nourishment and refuge for the hungry congregation.

*   *   *

In this chapter we consider types of birds (the avifauna) in the region seasonally, for it is in the seasonally changing assemblages of species that the peninsula hosts a unique community of birds.

WINTER RESIDENTS

*A*T ABBOTT'S LAGOON, *a treeless plain, the only vegetation is verbena, nearly succulent, scattered in sparse clumps in the damp sand. We stand on the flat shore, watching a large flock of small shorebirds, several thousand dunlin, wheel over the tidal flat in an aerial display of remarkable synchrony, all turning in unison, flashing silver-gray then immaculate white in the bright November sun. As the dunlin pass over water, a raft of sea ducks, surf scoters, struggle to get off the surface with wild wings. We hear the whistle of a million flight feathers. Then another in the duck family, the wigeon, jump off the water, hundreds rising quickly from the surface, in orderly chaos. Scanning the sky we see the provocateur — a peregrine falcon, broad-chested, sickle-winged, strafes the water scattering the multitude. Soon, almost suddenly, the hurried flight, the feathered confusion, the noise (save the soft whistles of a few nervous wigeon) stop. The flocks alight again on water and shore. The birds resume their feeding, apparently un-*

*Gulls and shorebirds may be found on the outer beaches during any season,
but they reach peak numbers during the winter months.*

*concerned with the large falcon, now roosted on a fence post, a still shorebird grasped in his talons.
As the peregrine bows to begin his meal, the fading light of the orange winter sun touches the
gray Pacific.*

Shorebirds

Winter is the season of greatest abundance. From October through March, the
tidal flats and sandy beaches bustle with the activity of myriad shorebirds. Many of the
most common species — black-bellied plover, dunlin, sanderling, least and western sandpiper — breed on the Canadian and Alaskan tundra. Others — long-billed curlew, willet,
marbled godwit — breed in grasslands of the American prairie. A few — killdeer, snowy
plover, black oystercatcher — nest within the Seashore. In winter, shorebird flocks
gather here because of the abundance of food (invertebrates, mostly) available in the
estuaries. Tomales Bay, Limantour and Drake's esteros, and Bolinas and Abbott's
lagoons comprise about 18 square miles of estuarine habitat. This abundance of wetlands, complemented by about 25 miles of sandy beach and rocky shoreline, provides
wading birds with a network of choice wintering habitats. Birds move between estuaries
daily. When the mudflats in Schooner Bay are flooded at high tide, flocks of small
shorebirds will fly to forage or roost at Abbott's Lagoon, where the shore is unaffected
by the tide. (For this reason, it is best to look for birds at Abbott's Lagoon at high tide.)
Egrets are often seen flying along the beach at Limantour, presumably commuting

between Bolinas Lagoon and Drake's Estero as food availability or foraging conditions change. Some species, most notably black-bellied plovers, gather in agricultural pastures to feed when the preferred tidal flats are flooded.

Seabirds

On open water, in the swelling ocean and at the mouths of bays and estuaries, loons, ducks and cormorants gather and disperse with the movement of fishes. Mid-winter, scaup and scoter, perhaps cued by the ever-vigilant gulls, stream into Tomales Bay to feast on the herring spawn. (Researchers estimate that gulls, diving ducks, and fish consume 56 to 99 percent of herring spawn.) At the height of the spawn, the numbers of birds present on the bay waters can be impressive. Surf scoter and greater scaup are most abundant, each numbering in the tens of thousands. In former days, many thousand **black brant** wintered on Tomales Bay and Drake's Estero. From 1931 to 1932 the Point Reyes population averaged 8,000 brant. Since the mid-1950s the winter population has decreased, never exceeding 450, although hundreds still pause during spring migration. In the mid-1960s the entire population shifted its wintering grounds from the Pacific states to the Gulf of California. The shift may be attributable to depletion of the eelgrass beds (a primary food source), a change in feeding habits, human disturbance, or some combination of the three. Whatever the cause of the decline, the bays are less vital in the absence of this magnificent "sea goose."[7, 25, 28]

Leeward of Point Reyes, in the calm waters of Drake's Bay, thousands of scoters and grebes gather in loose rafts protected from the surge and swell of the misnamed Pacific. The careful observer will soon discover that the species in the flock can be grouped into assemblages of three: surf, white-winged, and black scoters; western, Clark's, and horned grebes; common, red-throated, and Pacific loons. From the low promontories near Chimney Rock or Drake's Beach one can look down on the still waters and watch western grebes dive and propel themselves through the water like feathered torpedos.

Raptors

The greatest numbers of birds of prey (raptors) visit Point Reyes in winter as well. Red-tailed hawks and American kestrels, the two most common species, breed here in spring and summer, but the numbers increase in fall when birds from the north and the interior arrive to spend the winter. The size of the winter raptor population varies greatly from year to year, depending on continental weather patterns or the local abundance of prey. When there is a mild fall and winter in the Pacific Northwest or the Great Basin, many raptors may not move this far south, but remain on more northerly wintering grounds. In other years, a local abundance of prey might attract large numbers of raptors to Point Reyes.

The most dramatic recent examples of years of raptor abundance were the winters of 1979-80 and 1980-81, when there was a "population explosion" of small rodents, mostly meadow voles. Red-tailed hawks, primarily rodent eaters, were particularly common; in October and November 1979 about 70 red-tails were estimated hunting the open agricultural fields of the outer Point. Other rodent eaters also arrived to feast on the multitude of mice, including unprecedented numbers of black-shouldered kites, ferruginous hawks, northern harriers, barn owls, short-eared owls, and long-eared owls. Several of these species congregate in impressive concentrations when food is abundant. During November 1979 the dense stand of Monterey pines along the Estero Trail hosted 35 long-eared owls and 20 barn owls. At Muddy Hollow, 14 long-eared owls roosted in an alder grove and up to 30 short-eared owls clustered together in the Limantour dunes. That same fall, 25 black-shouldered kites hovered over the Olema Creek floodplain. How those birds discover a localized population of mice and communicate that information to one another remains a mystery. The following anecdote describes such an occurrence at Point Reyes.[31, 57]

*   *   *

We trudged toward the end of Limantour Spit, out where the stabilized dune that forms the sandy finger loses its continuity and begins to break into hummocks of sand vegetated only with beachgrass and lupine. Driftwood and wrack deposited by the highest winter tides form a ring around the base of each hill. After walking through two miles of wet sand in rubber boots against a damp January wind, counting shorebird flocks that seem to flush each time we've estimated half their number, we are ready to climb the dune and take a sandwich break. The beachgrass, waist-high and densely clumped, stings our thighs as we highstep up the slope. Suddenly we are startled by a large, tawny-colored bird that flushes just a few feet away. We hadn't noticed it roosted behind the dense clumps of vegetation. Silently it climbs into the air on broad, outsized wings that seem to pump its body up and down. "Short-eared owl!" We rarely see them anymore, especially on the coast. The bird circles back and flies close, as if to inspect us with his fierce, yellow eyes. Then from beneath his flight path others spring into the air, to our amazement. Soon twenty-eight birds are circling the dune, flushed from their temporary day roost by a couple of windblown naturalists.

We begin searching the sandy roost area for owl pellets, the regurgitated remains of undigestible prey items. Soon we've found several, each a small, oblong package of hair and tiny bones. We pull the pellets apart and find perfect little rodent skulls, still intact. The pattern of the teeth, especially the molars, forms an unmistakable "W," and identifies the prey as Microtus, the meadow vole.

Landbirds

In many respects coastal central California is, for landbirds, a more favorable area for wintering than for breeding.

— Dave DeSante. *The Avifauna of the South Farallon Islands, California.* 1980.

In late September and October, landbirds flock to Point Reyes. Many are north coast or montane breeders, absent from the peninsula in summer, who migrate southward or coastward to find winter refuge in this relatively temperate climate. By mid-October, such species as ruby-crowned kinglet, varied thrush, fox sparrow, and golden-crowned sparrow have returned to the peninsula's forests and brushlands, often in large numbers.

Some species breed here and remain through the winter, but their numbers are augmented by individuals who only winter here. For example, white-crowned sparrows are a common breeder on the coastal slope at Point Reyes, but in late September birds from the north coast, Puget Sound, and even Alaska swell the ranks of the resident population. Other local breeders whose populations increase in fall with the arrival of winterers include winter wren, American robin, brown creeper, golden-crowned kinglet, yellow-rumped warbler, rufous-sided towhee, savannah sparrow, and song sparrow. Another pattern of occurrence involves species like the hermit thrush, which breeds here then leaves to winter elsewhere, only to be replaced by another wintering population of hermit thrushes from breeding grounds to the north. Some species, like the band-tailed pigeon and the mourning dove, may breed here in summer, then leave to be replaced by individuals from other populations. Of the winter arrivals, several are particularly attracted to the abundance of berries found here in the winter months. Toyon (Christmas berry) trees, laden with bright clusters of red berries in December and January, attract robins and hermit thrushes especially. Flocks of band-tailed pigeons haunt canyon bottoms and moist hillsides feasting on madrone berries and acorns.

Other wintering species are "irruptives," coming to Point Reyes sporadically, present some years, absent others. Most notable are red crossbill, evening grosbeak, and red-breasted nuthatch. Most years crossbills are rare at Point Reyes, but occasionally the Douglas fir trees on Inverness Ridge will produce an abundant crop of cones and seeds, the favored food of crossbills. Such a year was 1984 when the old firs drooped under the weight of their cones; by mid-October, flocks of over 100 crossbills were common near the summit of the Limantour Road. Throughout winter, the species was common wherever there were conifers within the Park. How strange that by mid-March the forest was suddenly void of crossbills; their familiar *"kip-kip"* flight call, heard all winter, was missing. The nomads had disappeared, gone to some other mountainside where some other forest would provide a copious supply of seed and nourishment.

A PLURALITY OF PELICANS

USE OF THE TERM "WINTERER" to describe the seasonal status of a species can be misleading. Perhaps "nonbreeder" would be more appropriate for some species. For example, brown pelicans have a common association with Point Reyes; their processions sail effortlessly within inches of the surf along Limantour Beach. Brown pelicans spend the nonbreeding season at Point Reyes – they "winter" here. However, they are present at Point Reyes from May or June through December, arriving here from Baja California or the Channel Islands where they begin breeding in mid-winter. The brown pelican responds to the changing productivity of fish populations and its arrival in these waters varies with the seasonal warming of ocean temperatures and the success or failure of the breeding colony in the Gulf of California.

> Pelicans seem always to know exactly where they
> are going.
>   –John Steinbeck. *Log of the Sea of Cortez.* 1971

Brown pelican

Luckily for those who spend time here, Point Reyes is one of the places pelicans go. Indeed, here is one of the few places in North America where two species coexist; such is the bounty of Point Reyes. The **California brown pelican**, strictly marine in distribution, breeds on offshore islands of Southern California south into the Sea of Cortez and Mexico. The **American white pelican** also breeds on islands, but on landlocked lakes of the North American West: the Great Salt Lake, Pyramid Lake, Klamath Lake, to name a familiar few. Both species arrive here from their nesting grounds to spend the nonbreeding season roosting on remote beaches and feeding in the fish-full waters.

A Very Strange Bird is the Pelican . . .

At first glance, the two species are similar. Each has the characteristic pelican shape, comical to human eyes: stout body atop short legs with huge webbed feet, long neck, and broad, rounded head with small eyes, an absurdly large bill underhung by a distensible "gular pouch," which according to the familiar rhyme can ". . . hold more food than its belly can." Although these birds may seem awkward on land, few sights are as captivating as an effortless flight of pelicans on the wing.

The careful observer will first distinguish species by aeronautical style. Brown pelicans tend to fly single file low over the breakers, nearly skimming the water with the tips of their deeply cambered wings. Occasionally they will dip into the wave's trough, or flap to gain altitude then dive vertically into the water. White pelicans tend to soar higher in single file or in classic V formations, wheeling in great circles with wings held horizontally flat.

White pelicans do not tuck their wings and dive vertically the way browns do. While the brown pelicans are busy diving headlong into nearshore waters, groups of white pelicans will gather on the surface of a shallow estuary or bay and flail about with wings loosely held akimbo as they "herd" fish into a concentrated school; then each bird will begin madly dunking its big bill in the water, gathering as many fish as it can.

The two species are superficially similar in appearance. The adult brown pelican has a white head (sometimes with a yellowish wash), which might cause some confusion to the uninitiated observer. Few people ever get close enough to see the pale yellow iris, scarlet eyelids, and cobalt blue bare facial skin that signal a bird is old enough to breed. The body of the brown pelican is a dark gray-brown and the wings do not show the black wingtips contrasting with white plumage that is characteristic of the white pelican at any age. Brown pelicans take at least four years to mature into full adult plumage; first-year birds are entirely brown, while second- and third-year birds gradually acquire adult plumage characteristics.

Except for black wingtips, the plumage of the white pelican is entirely white. Breeding birds have light blue eyes and also scarlet eyelids; the bare facial area is yellowish orange. During the breeding season, both sexes develop yellow plumes on the back of the head and a peculiar two-inch "horn" that grows atop the bill; this horn (fibrous plate) is shed after the eggs are laid; its function is unknown. The white pelican, with a wingspan of eight to nine-and-a-half feet, is about 20 percent larger than the brown pelican.

From late spring through early fall, brown pelicans can be seen in any saltwater habitat around Point Reyes. Traditional roost sites include Tomales Bay, Bolinas Lagoon, Limantour Spit, and offshore rocks in the vicinity of the Lighthouse, Tomales Point, and along the Coast Trail. Traveling flocks can be seen at most leeward beaches; Limantour Beach seems to be a favored foraging area.

At Point Reyes, brown pelicans arrive earlier and occur in greater numbers than whites. In early May, the first brown pelicans arrive along the outer coast with numbers increasing gradually through summer to peak in August. Biologists at Point Reyes Bird Observatory have counted as many as 2,500 at Bolinas Lagoon, although the usual population is only several hundred birds. Occasionally larger numbers will concentrate in response to an unusual abundance of prey items. In 1984, as a result of the anamalous warm-water temperatures associated with the El Niño phenomenon, there was a remarkable concentration of anchovies in nearshore waters offStinson Beach and Bolinas. Observers reported flocks upwards of 7,500 brown pelicans amidst the hordes of gulls and terns that had arrived to exploit the bounty of fish. The timing of peak numbers corresponds to the warming trend of the Pacific. As waters begin to cool in November, numbers of brown pelicans decline. By Christmas only a few stragglers remain.

Historically, white pelicans begin arriving in August, with numbers reaching a peak in October, then declining through January. Since the late 1980s some white pelicans have been staying through summer. Whites are less common than browns at Point Reyes, with high counts of 200 to 350 birds. Year after year large flocks roost at traditional locations, which include the mouth of Drake's Estero, the mouth of Tomales Bay, and Bird Rock near Tomales Point. The birds choose these sites for their proximity to fishing grounds and isolation from disturbance. It is advisable for human and canine Park visitors to afford these wild beings plenty of elbow room.

Threatened Populations

The populations of both species have histories of decline. Brown pelican populations experience wide annual variation in reproductive success, depending on oceanographic conditions and availability of food. Their large size, low reproductive rate, and their position at the top of the food chain make them vulnerable to environmental variability. From the 1950s through the early 1970s, this natural vulnerability was exacerbated by environmental pollutants (primarily DDT and related chlorinated hydrocarbons), which further reduced reproductive potential and caused the California population to decrease by an estimated 90 percent over a 20-year period. As a result of the banning of DDT and the classification of the brown pelican as an endangered species, their numbers have increased substantially. Indeed, the population seems so healthy that the U.S. Fish and Wildlife Service has removed it from endangered status.

Although not classified as endangered, the American white pelican has also suffered a substantial decline. Many lakes where the species formerly bred have been drained for agricultural purposes or dried up because of drought. Also, lethal doses of pollutants continue to be found in California birds, particularly the insecticides eldrin and DDE, a metabolic by-product of DDT. The sources of these contaminants are as yet unknown, but their effects on the pelicans are disastrous.

SPRING AND FALL: Migrants Visit the Peninsula

P EOPLE TEND TO THINK OF BIRD MIGRATION as a concentrated event, an intense passage in a short time. But at Point Reyes the spring and fall seasons are protracted, extending into summer and winter and obscuring the seasonal boundaries. Bird migration, too, obscures seasonal boundaries. Indeed, at nearly any month of the year migration is apparent if one knows where to look under what conditions.

A month-by-month review of major migratory events of the year illustrates that migration is a year-round phenomenon at Point Reyes. Even in mid-winter, migration is evident. On New Year's Day, Pacific loons may be seen streaming southward — low over the water, single file, necks outstretched — offshore from the headlands.

Tree and barn swallows

During February or even late January, Allen's hummingbirds — resplendently iridescent — return from Mexico, visiting feeders and eucalyptus flowers. By March, black brant migration is on, as is most evident from the beach at Limantour, since many fly into Drake's Estero to feed. Large flocks of these small geese can be seen from shore flying into the northwesterly winds characteristic of the season. Flocks of swallows, first seen in February and March, gather above freshwater ponds and rivers. Late March and April host the return of landbird migrants from the tropics — western flycatcher, warbling vireo, Wilson's warbler, black-headed grosbeak — and the departure of most of the shorebirds that have wintered on the estuaries. By May, pelicans begin to return from southern breeding islands, surf-sailing nearshore, banking and diving beyond the breakers. Caspian terns, some probably from recently established nesting colonies in San Francisco Bay, fly along the beaches or roost on the tidal flats. By late June to early July, migrant shorebirds are returning to the estuaries, back from a brief Arctic breeding season. Heerman's gulls (the small, dark gulls with a blood-red beak that play Pancho Sanza to the brown pelican's Don Quixote) are now migrating northward along the beaches. But autumn is the true migratory season. The first pulses in August escalate into a frenzy of nervous excitement by September when shearwaters bound for Australian breeding grounds mingle with western gulls from the Farallones and common loons from the Arctic. The movement of most species is sustained well into October, then dwindles through November. The first winter storms force goldfinches and bluebirds to flee the immediate coast, but push the flocks of loons and waterbirds southward along these shores.

The notoriety of Point Reyes as a birdwatcher's paradise derives primarily from its being one of the most reliable places on the west coast to find unusual species. Most of these "vagrants" are migrants who have wandered away from the main migratory paths of their species. However, several of the most common vagrants – American redstart, blackpoll, Tennessee and palm warblers – can be found as far north and west as Alberta, British Columbia, or Alaska and, although most of these populations migrate east of the Rocky Mountains, a small percentage move down the west coast to include Point Reyes in their regular route. Many species qualify as true vagrants; birds that breed only east of the Continental Divide (prothonotary, prairie, and hooded warblers) occur at Point Reyes only occasionally.

The question presents itself: Why does this remarkable phenomenon occur? What is it about Point Reyes that concentrates such a variety of migrants? There is no single answer, and researchers continue to seek explanations. The geographical position of the peninsula on the coast, jutting westward into the Pacific, must be a major factor. But other land masses share this peculiarity – Año Nuevo, Cape Mendocino, Point Arena – without concentrating such a diversity of migrants. Other factors must be at play as well. To identify those factors, we must look to the birds themselves. Most of the vagrants that occur here are nocturnal migrants. They also tend to arrive on nights when a high overcast obscures the stars. The Point Reyes Lighthouse casts its bright beacon seaward for many miles on such nights, and the glow reflects on the underside of the cloud cover. We can imagine the vast "catchment basin" created by the Lighthouse as it beckons mis-oriented warblers, vireos, orioles, and sparrows from hundreds of square miles of ocean and shoreline. But the Lighthouse is not the only factor that attracts the migrants. Once they arrive, these migrants find protective cover and sustenance in the islands of cypress and lupine that are scattered across the outer point.

Most landbird vagrants occur at Point Reyes in the fall, most are nine-primaried (warblers, vireos, sparrows), and most (about 95 percent) are immature birds, aloft on their first migration. Each of these phenomena has an explanation. The predominance of young birds is expected. Since most migratory species hatch more than two chicks each year, there are simply more young birds around in the fall. Also, although a species' migratory route may be hundreds of miles wide, the juveniles of most species tend to cut the widest migratory swath, therefore hitting the coast during migration, a phenomenon known as the "coastal effect."[45]

The explanation of the fact that most are "nine-primaried" is more complex, but of major importance. The nine-primaried (meaning each wing has nine, rather than more, flight feathers or "primaries") species, especially the wood warblers, are prone to wandering beyond the range of the species' usual distribution. Why? The nine-primaried species are relatively "new" – recently evolved – and therefore genetically variable, with

During spring and fall, migrants flock through the woodlands and streamside thickets at Point Reyes. The riparian vegetation that borders Lagunitas Creek (pictured here just south of Point Reyes Station) is one of the best habitats to find migrant landbirds as they stop to forage and refuel en route from their breeding to their wintering grounds.

more potential for genetic "mistakes" to occur.

It is likely that several different factors cause vagrancy in migratory birds; however, so little is known about how birds migrate correctly that it proves difficult to explain how they make errors. Dave DeSante, landbird biologist at the Point Reyes Bird Observatory, has suggested that vagrancy arises from two possible mechanisms: disorientation or misorientation. Disorientation (the inability of an individual to follow any consistent orientation) might arise from a failure to inherit or to learn a consistent compass direction. Disoriented birds would be expected to fly in random directions or to drift downwind. Misorientation (the inability of an oriented bird to follow the correct direction) is more complex; the bird's movement is not random but is consistently wrong. The bird may have inherited or learned the wrong compass direction and, as a result, is consistently offcourse. DeSante detects a pattern to this misorientation, what he calls "mirror-image orientation," in which the bird tends to orient along the mirror-image of the correct direction for the species. For example, most of the blackpoll warblers leaving the Yukon in fall head southeast, toward their wintering grounds in Venezuela. A misoriented vagrant heads southwest, following a mirror image (relative to a north-south axis) of its species' normal route, toward the California coast.[17, 18]

While mirror-image orientation seems to be a plausible explanation for vagrancy and perhaps accounts for many of the regular vagrants that occur here (American redstart, blackpoll warbler, Tennessee warbler, palm warbler), it seems likely that disorientation is also a factor in the arrival of some of the lost birds that wind up at the Point Reyes Lighthouse.

So, aloft on its first migratory flight, misoriented on a star pattern genetically misinherited, a prairie warbler encounters an extensive cloud cover that obscures its reference point, perhaps Sagittarius, the brightest cluster in the southwest sky of the Milky Way. Now, not only misoriented, but disoriented as well, it flies toward the brightest light it can see – emanating from the Point Reyes Lighthouse. It circles the headlands, chipping repeatedly, hoping to hear a response from one of its kind. From the cypress trees nearby it hears a few *"chinks"* and *"wheets,"* not other prairie warblers but at least a redstart and a hermit thrush, other birds equally dependent on the safety of cover. The warbler, now tired from its hapless flight, nearly 50 miles in the last several hours, descends to the relative security of the cypress. Here, in the morning, it will find sustenance and safety for a few days before returning aloft – urged on by a change in the barometric pressure, the direction of the wind, and an undeniable zeitgeist – to resume its quixotic journey.

Although the vagrants receive a great deal of attention at Point Reyes, the vast majority of the migrant landbirds (about 85 percent at the Farallon Islands and presumably a higher percentage at Point Reyes) breed or winter along the coast of central California. These common migrants tend to arrive in massive "waves," large-scale movements that result from the combined effects of changing weather patterns: low-pressure systems preceding storm fronts, electromagnetic disturbances, and changing wind directions. Despite their magnitude, they may go unnoticed by the uninitiated. These waves are most noticeable in areas where there are islands of vegetation surrounded by expanses of open land, as on outer Point Reyes, where the only available cover is a cypress grove or a few small willow patches. In the forests of Inverness Ridge or along the riparian corridor of the Olema Valley, the migrant flocks disperse through the foliage and may escape our notice.[18]

Still, knowing where and when to look, it is possible to witness migration in the forest as well. The season of greatest movement is autumn, between mid-August and mid-October, peaking from late August through September. Areas where fresh water is available to the birds, as indicated by riparian vegetation (mostly willows and alders), are the best places to check during these months. Although migrant flocks may occur in any tree or bush, the most reliable birding spots in the Point Reyes area are Pine Gulch Creek at Bolinas Lagoon, Five Brooks Pond, along Bear Valley Creek from Park Headquarters to White House Pool (known as Olema Marsh), the watercourses at Laguna Ranch and Muddy Hollow canyons, the riparian strip from Ledum Swamp to the

Estero Trail turnoff on Sir Francis Drake Boulevard, and the willow patches between Upper Pierce Point Ranch and McClure's Beach.

The first arrivals, in late July or early August, are species that winter far to the south, in Central America. These flocks may be composed of a single species – violet-green swallows, pine siskins, Western tanagers – but more often include a colorful mix of transient warblers (black-throated gray, Townsend's, orange-crowned, yellow, and Wilson's) and warbling vireos joined by some resident species such as chickadees or bushtits. Later, in early October, the species that winter at more northerly latitudes – red-breasted nuthatch, ruby-crowned kinglet, varied thrush, hermit thrush, yellow-rumped warbler, fox sparrow – arrive. Some will stay the winter, others will continue onward, presumably south along the coast.

The spring migration of landbirds tends to be concentrated inland from Point Reyes, especially amidst the moist oak canyons of the inner coast range where transients can depend on the cyclical emergence of insects. Live oaks are sparsely distributed here at Point Reyes, but those few areas where they do occur are the most likely places to encounter mixed flocks of spring migrants. The flocks seem to avoid the outer coast where they would have to contend with the prevailing longshore winds. One particularly productive spot is the knoll above the Earthquake Trail at Bear Valley. Here, the oaks meet the bay forest and grade into the riparian vegetation along Bear Valley Creek. The overlap of habitats proves attractive to migrants in late April and May, and it is one of the few spots on the peninsula where birds characteristic of the oak woodlands – Nuttall's woodpecker, plain titmouse, lazuli bunting, and sometimes house wren – occur with any regularity.[23]

SUMMER: The Breeding Season

FOR MOST SPECIES THE BREEDING SEASON is synonymous with the longest days of the year when availability of food is at a peak – sunlight to leaf to caterpillar to beak. Yet many other species, especially the year-round residents, breed earlier, each attuned to the season of greatest resource abundance. Anna's hummingbird is one of the earliest breeders. Soon after the winter solstice, on bright days in late December, the males begin their dazzling aerial display – arching over a scarlet, flowering twinberry. By January, western gulls have already started to visit their nesting sites atop Chimney Rock, each pair ensuring its claim to the best real estate.

About 130 species of birds breed on the peninsula. Most species nest in the same habitats at about the same time year after year. Every May at Chimney Rock or Arch Rock, one can find pelagic cormorants balanced on the precipitous coastal cliffs, pigeon guillemots in a natural crevice, or black oystercatchers on the ledge of a sea stack near shore. In the wetlands, marsh wrens and yellowthroats commence singing every March. From riverine thickets, Wilson's warblers and song sparrows fledge young each spring. In the grove of Douglas firs near Bear Valley, acorn woodpeckers, tree swallows, and a pair of red-shouldered hawks carry on their annual breeding rituals, each propagating their species. Such is the cyclical rite of nature.

There are a few species, however, whose breeding status here is sporadic. The local nesting in 1979 of two species of owls — long-eared owl and short-eared owl — was most likely the result of the abundance of rodents in that year. At Palomarin, rufous-crowned sparrows nest erratically, often with several years lapsing between each effort. Red-breasted sapsuckers attempted to nest along Bear Valley Creek in 1980, only to have their nest raided and the nestlings killed by acorn woodpeckers. Tricolored blackbirds, a species that is nomadic by nature, nested around the pond at Drake's Beach in 1980, an event that has not been repeated since.[31, 49]

Vagrants, too, have nested on rare occasions. These species are far from their normal breeding ranges, and the fact that *two* birds of the opposite sex managed to find one another, find appropriate nesting habitat, and attempt to nest is a reflection of the peninsula's amazing suitability as bird habitat. Northern parula, a colorful warbler that occurs east of the Rocky Mountains, nested near Five Brooks Pond in 1977, and in 1984 successfully hatched young in an alder grove near Inverness Park, while an equally rare American redstart sang from the same grove. Cassin's kingbird nested near Palomarin in 1972, far from its normal haunts in the dry interior foothills of Southern California. An indigo bunting sang from the top of a bay tree near Kule Loklo every spring beginning in 1976; finally in 1983 he settled for a closely related lazuli bunting and the pair produced a hybrid brood.[10, 56]

The saw whet owl, though seldom seen at Point Reyes, is a fairly common breeder in the coniferous forests of Inverness Ridge and can occasionally be found in riparian thickets and woodland edges. A monotonous, repetitive whistle echoing through the forest on a moonless night most likely belongs to this tiny gnome-like owl.

Point Reyes is at the edge of the range of several other species and each may breed regularly or occasionally, but in very small numbers. Those that probably breed regularly in small numbers include ashy storm-petrel (10 to 12 pairs at Bird Rock in 1972); American bittern (Abbott's Lagoon and Glenbrook ponds); wood duck (Olema Valley); tufted puffin, rhinoceros auklet, and rock wren (Point Reyes Headlands); pygmy owl, Vaux swift, pileated woodpecker, and purple martin (Inverness Ridge); hermit warbler (the tops of the tallest firs). Those that may breed only on occasion, when environmental factors are favorable, include blue-winged teal, poorwill, dipper, house wren, blue-gray gnatcatcher, black-chinned sparrow, and red crossbill.[1, 42, 48]

But let us focus on two breeding species that have fluctuated dramatically at Point Reyes: common murre and osprey. The history of each illustrates the effects — sometimes positive, sometimes negative, usually inadvertent — that the activities of humankind can impose on the environment. Common murres have probably been here since before humans, while ospreys are apparently new arrivals; the fate of each is an unfinished chapter.

Common Murre

Below the Lighthouse, at Bird Rock, or on the sea stacks off Point Resistance gather penguin-like hordes of sooty, black-and-white diving birds, described by someone as "footballs with wings" — common murres. Prehistorically, hundreds of thousands of these deep-diving fish eaters must have occupied the nutrient-rich waters of the Gulf of the Farallones. However, beginning with the arrival of New England sealers in the early nineteenth century, there followed a series of human disturbances that would drastically reduce the multitudes. The natural history of the common murre intertwines with that of San Francisco, the Farallones, and Point Reyes — past and present.

To understand the impact of civilization on the murre population it is necessary to understand something of the bird's biology. Murres are marine birds; most of their life is spent on the ocean surface or diving in search of small schooling fishes — rockfish, anchovy, smelt. They resort to land only to breed, and even then choose sites at the water's edge, inaccessible to predators — sea cliffs, ledges, islands, and sea stacks. The common murre is a colonial species; on breeding sites thousands of birds may be packed shoulder to shoulder, each with a single egg resting between its large webbed feet. The egg is extremely large and pear shaped, an adaptive advantage on narrow ledges without a supporting nest, since its shape causes the egg to roll around its pointed end rather than off the edge of the cliff. After hatching, the precocious chicks stay beneath the parent for about three weeks, then, half-grown and as yet unable to fly, the chicks tumble off the cliffs into the ocean, where, accompanied by a parent, they learn to dive and forage. Often these young murres will drift shoreward. In August we see them along the beaches, usually accompanied by a much larger parent.

The nesting colonies are susceptible to human disturbance, inadvertent or intentional. When a human approaches a colony, all the birds may flush, leaving the eggs or chicks vulnerable. Gulls, waiting around the periphery of the colony for just such an opportunity, descend and devour whatever protein happens to be unprotected. An estimated 400,000 murres bred at the Farallones when the first sealers, Bostonians on the vessel *O'Cain*, arrived in February 1807. It is likely that human disturbance continued regularly from then through 1968 when the population had dwindled to about 6,000 birds and the islands became a National Wildlife Refuge.

Not all disturbance was unintentional. In 1854, commercial egg companies began collecting eggs to sell in the San Francisco markets. Over the ensuing 25 years, 12 million eggs were taken. Eventually, the establishment of poultry farms in Petaluma provided cheaper eggs, and the egg companies folded in 1880. However, the Lighthouse keepers and their families continued collecting eggs until at least 1905; by 1910 only about 20,000 murres remained. By now San Francisco had grown into a thriving port. Ships passing the Farallones routinely flushed their bilges before entering the Golden Gate; the subsequent oil slicks must have killed many birds. During the 1930s, only a few thousand murres survived. These low numbers, maintained by the continuing disturbances of human visitors and domestic animals, persisted through the 1960s.[2, 11]

Threats to the murres continued: unusually warm ocean temperatures in 1957–58; paralytic shellfish poisoning in 1967–1968; a large oil spill in 1971; eggshell thinning due to DDT contamination throughout the 1950s and 1960s. Each event was detrimental to the population. In 1969, with the population down to about 6,000, the U.S. Fish and Wildlife Service designated the islands as a National Wildlife Refuge, protecting the breeding grounds from further disturbance. Despite some oil spills and the as yet undetermined effects of leaking canisters of nuclear waste in the nearby ocean waters, the response to protection was dramatic. The colony increased at a rate of about 15 percent per year to 88,000 individuals by 1982! By then the population, vigorous and healthy, had increased also at Point Reyes and other appropriate sites along the central coast.[9]

The future looked rosy for murres. Then several catastrophic events coincided, conspiring to devastate, and perhaps ultimately threaten, the population. In the early 1980s, gill-net fishing practices increased pressure on the population. Because of their deep-diving habits, murres were extremely prone to becoming entangled and drowning in gill nets. Each year, as the fishery increased in size with an influx of netters from Southeast Asia, more murres drowned. At the same time, in 1982–83, the warm waters of the El Niño phenomenon undermined the productivity of the Gulf of the Farallones, resulting in little available food. The murres laid few eggs and fledged fewer chicks.[11, 29] In a newsletter article a Farallones biologist summarized the problem: "While El Niño was causing nearly total reproductive failure, gill netting was exacting a much higher toll. The California Department of Fish and Game estimated that between

Large flocks of murres gather on the rocks and sea stacks along Point Reyes's shoreline. Some favored roost sites include Stormy Stack, Point Resistance, and the rocks below the Lighthouse.

The common murre, about the size of a football with wings, reminds many people of a penguin. Penguins evolved in the southern hemisphere, however, and alcids, the family to which murres belong, evolved in the northern hemisphere. As deep-water divers that eat fish and shrimp-like organisms, both types of birds have evolved similar body types and life histories to fulfill similar ecological roles.

25,000 and 30,000 murres were killed in the gill net fishery in the Gulf of the Farallones in 1983."[11]

Then, in the fall of 1984, there was another oil spill and dead murres washed up on the beaches from Monterey to Point Reyes. Had the population not had the decade of relative freedom from 1969 to 1979 to rebound, it is likely it would not have survived this deadly triangle of catastrophes from 1982 through 1984. As of 1987, both the central California colonies and those at Point Reyes continue to decline. At Stormy Stack, off

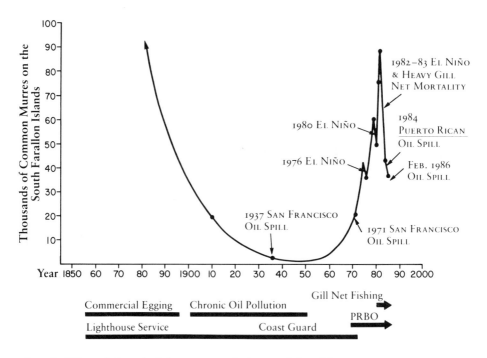

Figure 7.   This graph shows the decline, recovery and subsequent decline of the common murre in the Gulf of the Farallones. The causes for the various influences on the local murre population are labeled in the figure and discussed at length in the text. (From Carter and Ainley 1987.)

Double Point, a colony of 12,500 murres has lost nearly 80 percent of its numbers since 1986; just north, near Miller's Point, another colony has declined by 60 percent.[12]

The primary cause of the current disappearance is halibut gill netting. (Research in Northern California, where gill netting is not a factor, has shown that those murre populations have recovered from the reproductive failures that followed the El Niño year.) The primary victim is the common murre, although cormorants, grebes, shearwaters, seals, sea lions, and porpoises are also dying. In an attempt to reduce mortality of these "non target" species, legislation has been passed that prohibits gill nets from Point Reyes north, from inside 40 fathoms south of Point Reyes, and within 3 miles of the Farallon Islands.[29]

Osprey

The nest, as wide as a man's outstretched arms, sits atop a bishop pine on Inverness Ridge, positioned with a view of Tomales Bay, Drake's Estero, and the Pacific — an eyrie fit for an eagle. But this is the domain of an osprey, the eagle's regal cousin. It is May, and the two chicks — heads white, eyes fiercely orange — are whistling hoarsely toward the empty sky, hungry for some fish. Finally, an adult sails over the ridge on cambered wings. It is the female of the nesting pair, with a large fish still struggling in her talons. She alights on the nest's rim, embeds her beak in the flounder's flank, and presents the nestlings with their second meal of the morning.

Osprey

By mid-summer, the young from this nest, and from the half-dozen other nests scattered along the east slope of Inverness Ridge, will soar above the canyons and waters of Point Reyes, piercing the sky with their clear whistles and breaking the bay's surface with their foraging dives. Today, so graceful and visible a raptor is quickly noticed and admired by even the most casual observer; yet this "fish hawk" has not always been held in such esteem.

Early in this century, William Dawson, the author of *The Birds of California*, describes the osprey in his inimitable prose:

> Whether or not fish is proper brain food depends more upon the brain than it does upon the fish. An exclusive diet of fish has not made the fish hawks either brainy or valiant. We need not be troubled on the latter score, though, for in a family [birds of prey] where prowess and tyranny are almost synonymous, it is a comfort to find birds who mind their own business and exhibit a proper humility.

Although osprey are now fairly common, there is scant evidence available on their nesting status at Point Reyes prior to the 1970s. This dearth of information probably reflects an absence of birds. One 1933 text, *Birds of Marin County*, lists osprey as "very rare"; another, from 1944, makes no mention of breeding records for Marin.[28, 52]

During the first half of the twentieth century (and probably earlier) osprey suffered declines throughout its range due to persecution by man and environmental poisoning. In the early 1960s, researchers noticed the decline of a breeding colony of osprey along the Connecticut River and implicated agricultural pesticides as the cause. This important study inspired subsequent studies of other raptor species (bald eagles, kestrels, Cooper's hawks, and peregrines in the United States, white-tailed eagles and sparrow-hawks in Europe) and identified the organo-chlorine family of pesticides (especially DDT) as the primary culprit in reducing breeding success. The various data showed that bird and fish-eating predators were most susceptible to the deleterious effects of pesticide contamination; reproductive success decreased primarily due to egg-shell thinning. Among birds of prey, those which displayed the most severe egg-shell thinning included peregrine falcon, sparrowhawk, and osprey. Ospreys then, as obligate fish-eaters, had the dubious distinction of becoming an ideal environmental indicator species.[38]

After 1972, when DDT was banned, ospreys began to show signs of increasing in areas where their numbers had previously declined. During the 1960s and 1970s another phenomenon was boosting the osprey population, especially in the western states. With agricultural and urban development in the arid West came an increasing need for the impoundment of water. The construction of dams and reservoirs provided habitat that ospreys proved capable of colonizing. Which brings us to Point Reyes . . .[30, 38, 54]

The Local Population

On the north slope of Mount Tamalpais, the construction of Peters Dam in 1954 flooded the narrow canyons of Lagunitas and Big Carson creeks, creating a large reservoir (Kent Lake) where redwoods and silver salmon used to reign. An extensive fire in 1945 had severely pruned, or even killed, many of the redwoods and the bases of many others were drowned with the rising level of the reservoir. As a result, there are numerous "snags" that the osprey have appropriated as nesting sites. The availability of nesting sites is not the only quality that makes Kent Lake so attractive to osprey. In the absence of public roads, the area is relatively remote and free of human disturbance. The water is clear and well stocked with fish, providing a ready food source, particularly for recently fledged individuals, and it is relatively close to the outer coast at Bolinas Lagoon (four and a half miles away) and Tomales Bay (nine miles away), well within the foraging flight of an osprey.

Ospreys probably colonized Kent Lake in the late 1960s (first known nest in 1967); by 1980, there were 11 active nests, and by 1990 there were 32 active nests. We do not know when osprey began to nest on Inverness Ridge, but there has been a marked increase since the late 1970s. By 1990, 15 active sites were located on Inverness Ridge. It seems likely that as the Kent Lake population increased, it "spilled over" to Tomales Bay, and that the two populations are related.

This history of the osprey illustrates the fragility and resilience of one species, as well as the accommodations that are made when humans manipulate the environment. In this case, redwoods and salmon were sacrificed for water and, inadvertently, ospreys benefited. We can no longer dismiss the "fish hawk" with William Dawson's glib judgment of it as neither "brainy or valiant," for subtler qualities are at play here. Today, when we see an osprey circling over Mount Vision we realize that its gyre encompasses our

The osprey, Pandion haliaetus, *a large bird of prey often mistaken for an eagle, is a common sight along the Point Reyes shoreline, especially at Bolinas Lagoon and Tomales Bay.*

shared history and our shared destiny. Two decades ago low reproductive success in ospreys alerted us to the otherwise invisible threats of organo-chlorine contamination. In the decades to come, a decline in the local osprey population could flag the destructive effects of acid rain or some other as yet unidentified environmental threat. For now, we watch the birds with an appreciative eye, knowing that their presence here is as transitory as ours.

Thus far, we have discussed two large, conspicuous species, osprey and common murre, whose natural histories are closely interwoven with our own. A third, Nuttall's white-crowned sparrow, is small and inconspicuous; few people notice these sparrows, yet their sweet songs are as much a part of the coastal environment as the wind and the fog, and they provide us with a particularly interesting representative of summer breeders on the peninsula.

White-crowned Sparrow

The white-crowned sparrow occurs commonly as a breeder on the coastal slope, amidst the coyote bush and the morning fog. In fact, the breeding distribution of this species is restricted to the fog belt. The clear song is often heard at Abbott's Lagoon, Limantour, or Palomarin, but is largely absent from the spring symphony on the east slope of Inverness Ridge, where the coastal fog seldom creeps. The race that breeds at Point Reyes is known as "Nuttall's" white-crowned, after an eighteenth-century naturalist. The Point Reyes population is "sedentary," residing the year around on the coastal slope, never wandering beyond the fog's influence. This sedentary habit has caused the population to differentiate into smaller subpopulations (demes), each somewhat isolated from its neighbor. As a result, the songs of Point Reyes' white-crowns have dialects, and these variations have been studied in detail.

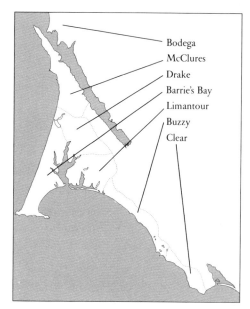

Bodega
McClures
Drake
Barrie's Bay
Limantour
Buzzy
Clear

Map 8. The geographic distribution of dialect populations of white-crowned sparrows on the Point Reyes peninsula. The dashed lines on the map outline the geographic distribution of the subpopulations of Nuttall's white-crowned sparrows, each of which has a distinct song type, or "dialect." See text for further discussion. (Source: Tomback et al. 1983)

In thorough studies of the Point Reyes population, researchers recognized six distinct dialects on the peninsula. (See Map 8.) Each dialect population adjoins its neighbor, but the transitions between song types are abrupt and there is no mixing of dialect. (Interestingly, in the urban population in San Francisco, dialects do mix.) The birds apparently differentiate between dialects when they hear a neighbor's song. For example, males at Palomarin ("clear dialect") tend to respond in song more to tapes of adjacent dialects than to their own dialects, whereas males from the Limantour group respond more to tape playbacks of their own dialect than to playbacks of the most distant (non-neighboring) dialect. The biological significance of these observations is still being debated, but there are several possible explanations of how these distinct dialect populations are maintained: (1) Young birds are imprinted with the songs of their parents and tend to stay within their natal area, rather than wander across dialect boundaries. (2) Females select males who sing their dialect over a neighboring male. (3) Males act more

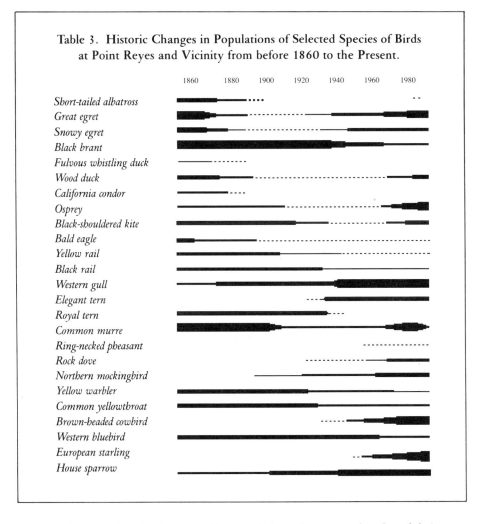

Table 3. Historic Changes in Populations of Selected Species of Birds at Point Reyes and Vicinity from before 1860 to the Present.

aggressively toward males from neighboring dialects than toward males of their own dialect, thereby discouraging outsiders from crossing dialect boundaries.[7,55]

HISTORIC CHANGES

Today Point Reyes hosts a diversity of bird life nearly unparalleled in North America. Yet if we look at the historical evidence, several species occurred here in earlier days and have become extinct or decreased in numbers under the influence of in-habiting peoples.

The Coast Miwok used feathers of spiritually powerful species (hawks and eagles) for ceremonial purposes, and those of brightly colored species (red-winged blackbird epaulets, red-shafted flicker quills, and acorn woodpecker scalps) for ornament. Brown pelican skins were fastened with abalone buttons and fashioned into dance capes. There is no evidence that the native peoples exterminated any of these species. However, bones from Ohlone middens (refuse heaps) indicate that there was a flightless scoter-like duck that occurred along the California coast between 3,500 and 5,000 years ago that was probably harvested to extinction by the aboriginal peoples.[36]

Several species that occurred at Point Reyes into the nineteenth century have since disappeared, not because of any local change in the environment but because of widespread human influences that have caused these species to decrease throughout their ranges. Perhaps the California Condor is the most poignant example.

The **California condor** once ranged along the California coast north to the Oregon border, but has not been reported from Marin County for over a century. Today, with the species extinct in the wild, we can only imagine a mixed flock of condors and vultures feeding on the remains of a whale carcass freshly flensed (stripped of blubber and skin) on the beach of the Bolinas whaling station. With the depletion of the whale populations along the coast (and fewer dead whales awash on the beaches), and the disappearance of herds of elk and (possibly) antelope, the California condor, like the grizzly bear, was deprived of its primary food source. Additionally, the changes that accompanied the shift from Spanish ranching to American farming—such as the use of carcasses laced with poison to control predators—must have had a negative impact. The last sighting from this area was of a lone condor circling Mt. Tamalpais in the mid-1950s; that bird must have seen Point Reyes from its widening gyre and may have noticed that the skies were empty of its kin. The likelihood of a California condor ever again soaring over this peninsula, or any other wild landscape, daily becomes more remote, soon approaching the vanishing point.[28, 52]

Seabirds

Just as the shore whaling stations must have first attracted condors, other birds must have been lured ashore toward the easy feast. One 1871 text mentions three species—Pacific fulmar, short-tailed albatross, giant petrel—foraging on floating whale blubber in Monterey Bay, which could have easily applied to Point Reyes. The reference to giant petrel, also known as Antarctic giant-petrel or "gong," is enigmatic. The only evidence that these large Southern Hemisphere breeders ever occurred on the coast of California is hearsay from early accounts. Perhaps these accounts were referring to the short-tailed albatross. The northern fulmar still visits the Gulf of the Farallones in the winter and is occasionally seen picking at the carcass of a beached gray whale. The short-tailed albatross was a common sight off the coast of California in the nineteenth century; it undoubtedly visited these shores in fall and winter as it wandered the eastern North

Pacific. In the early twentieth century, millions were slaughtered for their feathers on their nesting grounds on islands off Japan; by the 1940s the species was considered extinct. In 1954 a small population (10 pair) was discovered on Torishima Island and, under zealous protection, it has been growing slowly since. Still, with a total population of about 200 individuals, it is one of the world's most endangered birds. In the fall of 1985, a single short-tailed albatross was spotted by Inverness naturalist Rich Stallcup as it soared on seven-foot wings over the upwelling swells of the Cordell Banks, due west of Point Reyes. The possibility of such encounters increasing in the future provides an encouraging counterpoint to the predictable fate of the California condor.

The historic impacts of human activity on common murres have been recounted above. The numbers of other species of seabirds have fluctuated up and down, often as the result of humans exploiting the prey base and thereby changing the abundance or distribution of the predator. The decline of the California sardine population and the subsequent explosion of the anchovy population in central California, for example, has affected the populations of several species of marine birds and mammals.

As the sardine fishery peaked in the early 1940s, the stock began to decline drastically and the population retreated southward (south of Point Conception). The decline was probably the result of overfishing, the retreat probably the result of an extended period of cold water temperatures. The northern anchovy, a close relative of the sardine and, though smaller, its "ecological equivalent," soon filled the vacancy left by the sardine and increased in number. As might be expected, sardine eaters — **double-crested cormorants** and **tufted puffins** — decreased in number. Puffins disappeared entirely from Point Reyes; however, there is some indication that a few pair are again breeding in the cliffs near the Lighthouse. Anchovy eaters, like **rhinoceros auklet**, began to increase. After being absent for about a century, in the early 1970s "rhinos" began recolonizing the Farallon Islands and visiting the Point Reyes headlands.[2]

Today, **harlequin duck**, one of North America's most beautiful species, is a rare winter visitor to Tomales Bay and the turbulent waters along rocky shorelines. Yet one researcher states that "Tomales Point has the most regular population" in central California. In 1918 "hundreds" were reported in fall and in 1944 "flocks" were noted in early winter on Tomales Bay. There is even a summer record of "flocks at Point Reyes" in June 1880. In the 1950s, a flock of seven harlequins off Tomales Point was collected by a museum ornithologist "for science." With the exception of such senseless slaughter, the cause for decline here is not clear. Harlequins formerly bred along mountain streams in the Sierra Nevada, but there have been few records for the last 30 years. This decrease in the California breeding population is the likely cause of the decrease at Point Reyes.[13, 27, 28, 32, 33]

One of the most familiar species to Park visitors is the "sea gull." Actually, fifteen species of gulls have been recorded at Point Reyes and nine of those occur regularly. The most abundant, and the only one that breeds on these shores, is the large, dark-backed **western gull**. Gulls, and particularly western gulls, have increased dramatically in this area with the urbanization of the Bay Area and the increase in landfills and refuse dumps, which these scavangers visit daily. It is possible that a bird breeding on the sea stack at Chimney Rock might commute to the Berkeley dump and back in a given day. The impact of increased gull populations on other nesting species, especially those marine birds susceptible to predation by gulls, is inestimable.

Another species that has increased because of human manipulation of the environment is the **Caspian tern**. These, the largest of the tern species, have increased as a nesting species in San Francisco Bay since the early twentieth century when the south bay was leveed to create salt evaporation ponds, an increase that continued at least until about 1980. Point Reyes is within the 35-mile foraging range of the San Francisco Bay colonies, and the Caspians we see on the tidal flats of the peninsula's estuaries from March through October are likely from those colonies. (It should be noted that, although Caspian terns have increased in San Francisco Bay, there has been a concurrent decrease of most inland colonies due to drainage and filling of wetlands.)[25]

Marsh Birds

Several species of birds are intimately associated with wetlands, particularly birds in the rail family. The few marshes and swales of Point Reyes have been dramatically altered to accommodate the ranching industry, thereby affecting marsh birds. The most extensive change has been caused by the leveeing and filling of the south end of Tomales Bay. Photographs from the early 1900s show tidal marshes extending southward to Lagunitas and Olema creeks. Now, much of what was formerly marsh has been converted to agricultural pasture. (See Map 6, page 65.) As a result, habitat for rail has been greatly reduced. Also, cattle graze up to the edge of the marsh, destroying the transitional vegetation between marsh and upland. On extreme high tides, the rails are forced out of the protective cover of the marsh vegetation and, with no upland cover available, are exposed to predation by egrets, herons, and hawks. **Black rails** still occur in the tidal marshes of southern Tomales Bay, but in recent years they have disappeared from smaller marshes within the Seashore. At Kehoe Marsh, black rails used to be found annually, but cattle have been allowed to roam freely, trampling the vegetation and fouling the water; black rails have not been found there since 1978. At Olema Marsh, the cause of disappearance is different. The floods of January 1982 caused tremendous deposition of sediment in the marsh, altering the substrate and, apparently, excluding black rails, which have not been detected since the fall of 1981. We can only hope that each marsh will be restored to health, and black rails, classified as "threatened" by the

Table 4. Seasonal Use Patterns of Point Reyes Wetlands by Estuarine Birds*

BREEDING

Breed Regularly

Pied-billed Grebe
Great Blue Heron
Great Egret
Mallard
Cinnamon Teal
American Coot
Snowy Plover
Killdeer

Breed Irregularly

Gadwall
Ruddy Duck

**Nonbreeding
Oversummering Individuals**

Common Loon
Double-crested Cormorant
Snowy Egret
Black-crowned Night Heron
Brant
Greater Scaup
Lesser Scaup
Surf Scoter
White-winged Scoter
Red-breasted Merganser
Black-bellied Plover
Willet
Whimbrel
Long-billed Curlew
Marbled Godwit
Bonaparte's Gull
Ring-billed Gull
California Gull
Western Gull
Caspian Tern

MIGRANT

**Primarily Spring and
Fall Migrants**

Cinnamon Teal
Whimbrel
Short-billed Dowitcher
Red-necked Phalarope
Red Phalarope
Bonaparte's Gull
Caspian Tern

**Winter Populations
with Spring and Fall
Migratory Peaks**

Common Loon
Surf Scoter
White-winged Scoter
Red-breasted Merganser
Semipalmated Plover
Black Turnstone
Western Sandpiper
Forster's Tern
Sanderling

**Winter Population with
Spring Migratory Peak**

Brant

WINTER

**Winter Populations with
Fall Migratory Peak**

Western Grebe
Double-crested Cormorant
Mallard
Killdeer
Willet
Least Sandpiper
Dunlin
Ring-billed Gull
Mew Gull
California Gull
Western Gull

**Winter Populations with
No Migratory Peak**

Pied-billed Grebe
Horned Grebe
Eared Grebe
American White Pelican
Brown Pelican
Snowy Egret
Black-crowned Night Heron
Green-winged Teal
Northern Pintail
Northern Shoveler
Gadwall
American Wigeon
Canvasback
Greater Scaup
Lesser Scaup
Common Goldeneye
Bufflehead
Ruddy Duck
American Coot
Black-bellied Plover
Snowy Plover
American Avocet
Long-billed Curlew
Marbled Godwit
Long-billed Dowitcher
Common Snipe
Herring Gull
Glaucous-winged Gull
Heermann's Gull
Elegant Tern

*Rare species are excluded from this summary.

(Source: G. Page. 1984. "Waterbirds in Winter." Point Reyes Bird Observatory Newsletter 65.)

Great egrets on the shore of Bolinas Lagoon.

California Department of Fish and Game, will recolonize.[24,57]

The **yellow rail** is a species that formerly bred in freshwater marshes of interior California and migrated to the coast to winter in salt marshes. Although the species has always been considered rare in California, it apparently used to occur with some regularity in the marshlands of Tomales Bay, and six specimens were collected in November-December during the years 1898–1905. The 1982 *Field Checklist of the Birds of Marin County* listed yellow rail as "extirpated." Although there have been two sightings on Tomales Bay in recent years, it is unlikely that yellow rails will visit Point Reyes with regularity in the near future. The breeding marshes, particularly those east of the Sierra, have largely dried up or been overgrazed by ranching interests. This pressure, coupled with a decrease in the available wintering habitat, condemns the species to a bleak future.[28,48]

What is now known as "Olema Marsh," the extensive alder-willow thicket that stretches from near Park Headquarters north to "White House Pool," is one of the most diverse habitats for breeding, wintering, and migrating birds in the Point Reyes area. Breeding bird censuses have recorded over 40 breeding species, and winter population studies have tallied over 80 species within this small area. Before the establishment of the Seashore, the Bear Valley Country Club managed the wetland ("swamp") for the benefit of nesting waterfowl. From at least 1900 until about 1920 the willows were burned annually to open up the habitat. This probably decreased the suitability of the habitat to migrant landbirds, but controlled the cattails and left more open water for nesting ducks.[5]

From the accounts of naturalists in the early 1900s we know that the "marshes near Olema" formerly supported American bittern, black-crowned night heron, Virginia rail, "white-tailed" kite (now called black-shouldered kite), "red-bellied" hawk, tule wren, green heron – all wetland species that still occur here, though several rarely. Other marsh habitat has been created within Point Reyes during the last 50 or so years, especially around the borders of stock ponds where wetland vegetation – cattails, sedges, rushes – has established itself. These habitats now support marshland species – bitterns, Virginia rails, coots, marsh wrens, yellowthroats – in places where they were formerly absent. Most of these ponds are on the southwest drainages of Point Reyes Hill and Mount Vision: Devil's Canyon, Laguna Ranch, Muddy Hollow, Glenbrook, Home Ranch, and the unnamed drainages feeding Limantour and Drake's esteros. These ponds provide open freshwater habitat for waterfowl that now occur commonly but apparently were uncommon or did not occur in the early 1900s: gadwall, cinnamon teal, northern shoveler, ring-necked duck, and, though rarely, hooded merganser.[52]

Bats of the
Point Reyes Peninsula

Big-eared bats

Of the 40 species of bats in North America, 24 occur in California. Of these 24 species, nearly one-third are listed as "Species of Special Concern" by the California Department of Fish and Game. They are of special concern because their populations are declining throughout the state, primarily due to habitat loss resulting from human disturbance.

The 12 species of bats that occur at Point Reyes are listed in the mammals list in the appendix (Species List 5). Five of these are breeders; the rest are transients. Perhaps the most common transient is the hoary bat. In the spring and fall large numbers of hoary bats migrate through Point Reyes. By day they rest in trees or – where trees are not available, as on the Farallon Islands or along the immediate coast – cling to cliff faces.

Of the breeding species, the Yuma myotis is the most common, with roosts of several hundreds gathering in the rafters of barns and abandoned buildings. The Red Barn at Park headquarters hosts an impressive roost, where pregnant females congregate to bear their young. (In many species the pregnant females gather together to give birth; the males roost at the periphery of the cluster or elsewhere.) Two other species also roost amidst the Yuma myotis, the fringed myotis and the Mexi-

can free-tailed bat. A fourth species, the pallid bat, tends to segregate into single-species roosts and is found fairly commonly in old buildings at Point Reyes. Their existence is often revealed by the presence of Jerusalem cricket legs, their favored food item, littering the floor beneath the roost.

Most interesting was the recent discovery of a roost of Townsend's big-eared bats in an abandoned building at Point Reyes. This roost of approximately 150 animals is the largest known colony on the Pacific coast. Elsewhere the species has undergone dramatic population decline due to habitat loss and other human disturbance, but at Point Reyes the colony seems to be maintaining its historic population level.

Big-eared bats have very specific habitat requirements. Their roosts must be rather large chambers with an opening large enough for the animals to enter and exit in flight. The western subspecies (*townsendi*) tends to use abandoned mine shafts or buildings. However, even slight human disturbance may cause the colony to abandon the roost. Many of the mine shafts along coastal California are closed at the entrance and many of the abandoned barns and outbuildings are razed for development purposes, thereby eliminating potential roost sites for big-eared bats.

Unlike many bats, big-eareds are non-migratory; indeed, they rarely range more than about five miles from their roosts. This sedentary habit has made them more vulnerable to habitat loss than migratory species that are able to pioneer new habitats. The establishment of the Point Reyes National Seashore, with its policy of allowing historic landmarks, old barns, and mines to continue to exist, has preserved the local population of big-eared bats.

Although the local bat populations seem to be relatively stable, there is a widespread decline throughout the New World. As insect eaters, bats are particularly prone to the detrimental effects of agricultural pesticides, but habitat loss and disturbance of maternity roosts and hibernating sites have also contributed to this decline. Conservation of habitat and diminishing use of long-lived pesticides will be necessary to ensure that these important animals survive and thrive. In the long run, hosts of bats filling the twilight skies will be far more effective at checking populations of insects than the indiscriminate broadcasting of pesticides that has characterized modern agricultural practices and plagued our planet.

Landbirds

There have been changes in landbird population as well. The most dramatic changes must have resulted from the conversion of the flat and rolling coastal terraces from perennial grasslands and coastal scrub to agricultural pasture dominated by annual grasses. Species that have increased as the outer peninsula has become pasture may include red-winged, Brewer's, and tricolored blackbirds, European starling and house sparrow—each of which is now common in winter. **European starlings** were introduced to North America from Europe shortly before the turn of the century. Starlings were first recorded in California in 1942 and at Point Reyes by 1949; the California population began exploding in the early 1960s, increasing 1,600 percent over the next decade. Today it is a common breeder at Point Reyes, where it competes with other cavity nesting species (e.g., western blackbird) for nest sites. **Brown-headed cowbirds** have increased phenomenally throughout California since European settlement and now gather in sizable flocks around the cattle ranches on the outer Point in the fall. **Savannah sparrows** are perhaps the most abundant breeders in agricultural fields today, but they probably bred in coastal prairie as well. Several shorebirds—killdeer, black-bellied and lesser golden plovers—visit plowed and short-grass fields in fall and winter; whether they also visited the coastal prairie prior to its conversion to pasture is moot. The northern coastal prairie at Point Reyes, now just a remnant habitat, probably supported larger breeding populations of horned lark, savannah sparrow, and grasshopper sparrow than occur here now.[16, 26, 28, 50]

If pasture replaced coastal scrub there must have been a decrease in the populations of the most common scrub-breeding species. Bird population studies of an undisturbed plot of coastal scrub, which have been conducted annually since 1971 at Palomarin, inside the southern boundary of the Seashore, found the following species as the most common coastal scrub breeders: wrentit, white-crowned sparrow, rufous-sided towhee, song sparrow, and Bewick's wren. Interestingly, each of these species is a year-round resident. (A sixth, Allen's hummingbird, is migratory, but returns in late January or early February to begin breeding in winter, like its neighbors.) As grazing pressure decreases on the outer Point, and coastal scrub recolonizes pastureland, we might expect an increase in those species.[20]

Suppression of wildfire has affected most of the habitats within the Seashore. Population studies of bird communities within "disturbed" (burned) bishop pine forest and unburned bishop pine forests in Tomales Bay State Park were conducted for five years from 1972 to 1978. The results of those censuses illustrate predictable differences between burned and unburned forest. After fire, the understory growth is vigorous, creating habitat for several species not found in the undisturbed "climax" community. The disturbed forest supported higher densities of undergrowth nesters like Bewick's wren, Swainson's thrush, wrentit, Wilson's warbler, and rufous-sided towhee. Perhaps most significantly, the disturbed forest, with a dense understory of salal and huckleberry, held high numbers of **Allen's hummingbird** (up to 55 per 100 acres of habitat); hummingbirds were absent from the climax forest. Although each plot had similar numbers of breeding species, the burned plot supported much higher densities of territorial males. In the pristine environment, wildfires probably occurred rarely but regularly, therefore creating a cycle of destruction and renewal of undergrowth; bird populations must have fluctuated accordingly.[53]

Sections of the Douglas fir forest on Inverness Ridge were logged as recently as 1961. Subsequently, breeding bird censuses of logged and unlogged (virgin) stands revealed differences in the avian communities that closely paralleled those found in the bishop pine habitat. Like the disturbed bishop pine forest, the logged Douglas fir had a dense understory (especially of huckleberry) and, predictably supported greater densities of species that nest in that habitat, especially California quail, Swainson's thrush, Bewick's wren, wrentit, and rufous-sided towhee. Allen's hummingbird was the most common species in the logged-over area; it was absent from the mature forest. In the mature forest, western flycatcher, Wilson's warbler, and pine siskin were more common; and brown creeper and golden-crowned kinglet were present in the mature forest, absent from the logged area.[3, 21]

In other regions of California, the introduction of exotic vegetation, especially ornamental shrubs and trees, has increased the number and variety of birds. Because the native vegetation is relatively intact at Point Reyes, this effect is less apparent than at many other coastal locations. There are several examples, however, of species that are able to exist here now, though they were formerly absent. The **northern mockingbird**, originally restricted to the dry habitats in Southern California, has expanded its range northward with European settlement. Over the past 20 years it has become an increasingly familiar sight around the highly cultivated gardens in Inverness and Point Reyes Station, especially near orchards.[6,43]

Eucalyptus trees, introduced from Australia, seem to have attracted orioles to Point Reyes. The large grove around Park Headquarters hosts a small population of northern orioles from March to July. Some species of eucalyptus flower in mid-winter; the sap is a favored food of hummingbirds, warblers, and orioles. It seems likely that the eucalyptus has encouraged an increase in numbers of overwintering birds and extended the seasonal occurrence of several nectar-eating species. In the third or fourth week of January, flowering eucalyptus is the most likely place to encounter the first Allen's hummingbirds of the year, returning from their wintering grounds in Central America.

Cedar waxwings have probably always visited Point Reyes, but the establishment of cotoneaster (a native of China) and other berry-producing ornamentals has probably increased their presence. Buildings, especially abandoned barns, have increased nesting habitat for barn and cliff swallows, and for barn owls. Black phoebes have probably benefited from road construction; every culvert in the area seems to host a phoebe nest.

REFERENCES

1. Ainley, D. G. 1972. A Marin County, California, breeding site for ashy petrels. *California Birds* 3: 71.

2. Ainley, D. G., and T. J. Lewis. 1974. The history of Farallon Island marine bird populations, 1854–1972. *Condor* 76: 432–446

3. Akers, E. 1975. Breeding bird census: mature Douglas fir forest. *American Birds* 29: 1128.

4. Ames, P. L. and G. S. Mersereau. 1964. Some factors in the decline of the osprey in Connecticut. *Auk* 81: 173–185.

5. Arndt, Lefty. 1984. Personal communication.

6. Arnold, J. R. 1980. Distribution of the mockingbird in California. *Western Birds* 11: 97-102.

7. Baker, M. C., D. B. Thompson, G. Sherman, and M. A. Cunningham. 1981. The role of male vs. male interactions in maintaining population dialect structure. *Behavior, Ecology, Sociobiology* 8: 65–69.

8. Bellrose, F. C. 1976. *Ducks, Geese, and Swans of North America.* Harrisburg, Pa.: Stackpole Books.

9. Boekelheide, B. 1984. Farallon Islands common murres. *Point Reyes Bird Observatory Newsletter* 64.

10. Campbell, K. F., and R. LeValley. 1984. The nesting season: Middle Pacific Coast Region. *American Birds* 38: 1056–1060.

11. Carter, H. R. 1986. Rise and fall of the Farallon common murre. *Point Reyes Bird Observatory Newsletter* 72.

12. Carter, H. R., and D. G. Ainley. 1987. Disappearing murres. *Point Reyes Bird Observatory Newsletter* 75.

13. Cogswell, H. L. 1977. *Water Birds of California*. California Natural History Guides 40. Berkeley: University of California Press.

14. Cooper, J. G. 1871. Monterey in the dry season. *American Naturalist* 4: 756-758.

15. Dawson, W. L. 1923. *The Birds of California*, Vol. 4. San Diego, Los Angeles, San Francisco: South Moulton Company.

16. DeHaven, R. W. Winter population trends of the starling in California. *American Birds* 27: 836-838.

17. DeSante, D. F. 1983a. Vagrants: when orientation or navigation goes wrong. *Point Reyes Bird Observatory Newsletter* 61.

18. DeSante, D. F. 1983b. Annual variability in the abundance of migrant landbirds on Southeast Farallon Island, California. *Auk* 100: 826-852.

19. DeSante, D. F. and D. G. Ainley. 1980. The avifauna of the South Farallon Islands, California. *Studies in Avian Biology* No. 4.

20. DeSante, D. F., D. Fortna, G. Geupel, D. Seimens, and P. Super. 1984. Coastal scrub breeding bird census. *American Birds* 38: 129.

21. Evens, J. 1975. Breeding bird census: logged Douglas fir reseeded with Monterey Pine. *American Birds* 29: 1127-1128.

22. Evens, J. 1986. *Reproductive Success of Osprey at Kent Lake, California, 1986*. Report to Marin Municipal Water District. 10 Dec. 1986.

23. Evens, J., and R. LeValley. 1981. The spring migration: Middle Pacific Coast Region. *American Birds* 35: 857-862.

24. Evens, J., and G. Page. 1986. Predation on black rails during high tides in salt marshes. *Condor* 88: 107-109.

25. Gill, R. E. and L. R. Mewaldt. 1983. Pacific coast Caspian terns: dynamics of an expanding population. *Auk* 100: 369-381.

26. Gordon, B. L. 1974. *Monterey Bay Area: Natural History and Cultural Imprints*. Pacific Grove: Boxwood Press.

27. Grinnell, J., and M. W. Wythe. 1927. Directory to the bird life of the San Francisco Bay region. *Pacific Coast Avifauna* 18.

28. Grinnell, J., and A. H. Miller. 1944. The distribution of the birds of California. *Pacific Coast Avifauna* 27.

29. Heneman, B. 1987. Gill nets: the search for solutions. *Point Reyes Bird Observatory Newsletter* 75.

30. Henny, C. J. 1983. Distribution and abundance of nesting ospreys in the United States. In *Biology and Management of Bald Eagles and Ospreys*, edited by D. M. Bird. Quebec: Harpell Press.

31. Laymon, S. A., and D. W. Shuford. 1980. Middle Pacific Coast Region. *American Birds* 34: 195-199.

32. Mailliard, J. 1904. A few records supplementary to Grinnell's check-list of California birds. *Condor* 6: 14-16.

33. McCaskie. G., P. DeBenedictis, R. Erickson, J. Morlan. 1979. *Birds of Northern California*. Berkeley: Golden Gate Audubon Society.

34. Moffitt, J., and C. Cottam. 1941. *Eelgrass Depletion on the Pacific Coast and its Effect upon Black Brant*. U.S. Fish and Wildlife Service Wildlife Leaflet 204.

35. Moffitt, J. 1943. Twelfth annual black brant census in California. *California Fish and Game* 29: 19-28.

36. Morejohn, G. V. 1976. Evidence for the survival to recent times of the extinct flightless duck, *Chendytes lawi* Miller. *Smithsonian Contributions to Paleobiology* 27.

37. Newton, I. 1979. *Population Ecology of Raptors*. Vermillion, S.D.: Buteo Books.

38. Nowak, J. H., and G. Monson. 1965. Black brant summering at Salton Sea. *Condor* 67: 357.

39. Page, G. 1984. Waterbirds in winter: patterns of use in coastal embayments. *Point Reyes Bird Observatory Newsletter* 65.

40. Page, G., B. Fearis, and R. M. Jurek. 1972. Age and sex composition of western sandpipers on Bolinas Lagoon. *California Birds* 3: 79-86.

41. Page, G., L. E. Stenzel, and C. M. Wolfe. 1979. Aspects of the occurrence of shorebirds on a central California estuary. In *Shorebirds in Marine Environments*, edited by F. Pitelka. Studies in Avian Biology 2.

42. Page, G., W. D. Shuford, J. Evens, and L. Stenzel. 1983. *The Distribution and Abundance of Aquatic Birds in Wetlands of the Point Reyes to Bodega Area*. Point Reyes Bird Observatory: Report to Point Reyes-Farallones Marine Sanctuary.

43. Pitelka, F. A. 1942. High population of breeding birds within an artificial habitat. *Condor* 44: 172-174.

44. Point Reyes Bird Observatory. 1983. Avian migration. *Newsletter* 61.

45. Ralph, C. J. 1971. An age differential of migrants in coastal California. *Condor* 73: 243-246.

46. Rice, D. W. 1984. Albatrosses. In *Seabirds of Eastern North Pacific and Arctic Waters*, edited by D. Haley. Seattle: Pacific Search.

47. Shallenberger, R. J. 1984. Fulmars, shearwaters, and gadfly petrels. In *Seabirds of Eastern North Pacific and Arctic Waters*, edited by D. Haley. Seattle: Pacific Search Press.

48. Shuford, W. D. 1982. *Field Checklist of the Birds of Marin County, Alta California*. Bolinas, Calif.: Point Reyes Bird Observatory.

49. Shuford, W. D. 1985. Acorn woodpecker mutilates nestling red-breasted sapsuckers. *Wilson Bulletin* 97: 234-236.

50. Sibley, C. G. 1952. *The Birds of the South San Francisco Bay Region*. San Jose State College. Mimeo.

51. Sorrie, B. 1978. Disturbed bishop pine forest breeding bird census. *American Birds* 32: 90.

52. Stephens, L. A., and C. C. Pringle. 1933. *Birds of Marin County*. San Francisco: Audubon Association of the Pacific.

53. Stewart, R. 1978. Bishop pine forest breeding bird census. *American Birds* 32: 90.

54. Swenson, J. E. 1981. Status of the osprey in southeastern Montana before and after the construction of reservoirs. *Western Birds* 12: 47-51.

55. Tombark, D. F., D. B. Thompson, and M. C. Baker. 1983. Dialect discrimination by white-crowned sparrows: reactions to near and distant dialects. *Auk* 100: 452-460.

56. Winter, J., and J. Morlan. 1977. The nesting season: Middle Pacific Coast Region. *American Birds* 31: 1183-1188.

57. Winter, J., and S. A. Laymon. 1979. Middle Pacific Coast Region. *American Birds* 33: 310.

CHAPTER SIX

LAND MAMMALS
Opossums to Pronghorns

Keith Hansen 1988

In a few minutes we thought bedlam broke loose: bears, deer, wildcat and coyotes darted out in all directions [Indian hunters with dogs were beating the brush]. . . . Mr. Richardson and I singled out a big brown grizzly and the first shot put him on his haunches. . . . It took seven shots to put him out of harm's way. Mr. Richardson estimated there were over a hundred bear and lion in the ravine. As we passed into the Tennessee Valley, the hillside was white with bones of elk, deer, and wild cattle killed from time to time for their hides.

– Charles Lauff. *Reminiscences.* 1847.

THE JOURNAL EXCERPT quoted above, in reference to Mill Valley, gives us a notion of the abundance of animal life in the Bay Area just prior to the wave of humanity that flooded into California with the Gold Rush of 1849. The changes that resulted from this mass influx altered the landscape dramatically. The magnitude of that change has been gauged by Ray Dasmann as follows: "Throughout California, in the sixty years from 1850 to 1910, a massive faunal change, matched only by the postglacial extinctions, took place. The fauna that survived and finally regained lost ground was different from what had been . . . before."[35]

When the Coast Miwok were the sole human inhabitants of the area, wildlife was much more abundant than it is today. Fox and bobcat were seen daily, huge herds of tule elk roamed through Olema Valley and grazed peacefully on the bunchgrass that covered outer Point Reyes. Grizzly bear undoubtedly dominated the landscape, wandering between habitats as seasonal food sources became available – elk calves in spring, salmonberries in summer, acorns in fall, and salmon as the first rains of winter swelled the creeks.

It is hard for us to envision several grizzlies gorging on a whale carcass at Limantour Beach or the October sky darkened with migrant waterfowl. Today we are left with a remnant of diversity, a shard of the former abundance. Yet after more than a century of civilized colonization, Point Reyes still displays an abundance of mammalian life compared with most areas of central California. The solitary hiker has a reasonable chance of seeing a bobcat stalk a brush rabbit, a gray fox skitter across a trail, or even a mountain lion disappear in the shadows of a rocky outcrop.

The following accounts summarize what is known about the land mammals of Point Reyes. Some are recently extirpated, others have recently arrived; most have been here since the Miwok shared the oak woodlands at Bear Valley, the abalone beds at Arch Rock, and the salmon runs in Lagunitas Creek with their kindred spirits.

Table 5. Historic Changes in Populations of Selected Species of Land Mammals at Point Reyes from before 1860 to the Present.

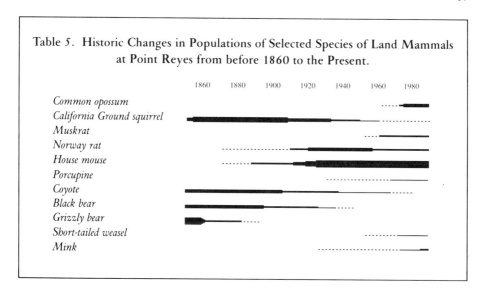

MARSUPIALS: Common Opossum

THE **COMMON OPOSSUM,** the only marsupial native to North America, is not native to Point Reyes or to the Pacific Coast. After the first known introduction into California at San Jose about 1900 (for meat, delicious with sweet potatoes), opossums spread rapidly southward; by 1931 they were common on the coastal slope from San Francisco Bay south to the Mexican border. Point Reyes avoided the onslaught until about 1968 when an adult with young was described from Muddy Hollow, near Limantour Beach. Subsequently, there were few records until 1983. One opossum seen just south of Inverness in January 1983 was the first in a series of sightings that began passing along the natural history grapevine. By the summer of 1983, opossums were becoming common casualties on the roads of east and north Marin, and since early 1984 they have been equally common at Point Reyes.[19, 47]

The sudden invasion is not easily explained. The obvious natural precedent was the record rainfall in the winters of 1981 through 1983. Perhaps those historic storms precipitated an explosion of productivity within the insect community that in turn encouraged proliferation by opossums? Interestingly, the opossum population boom paralleled an increase in reports of coyotes in the area.

INSECTIVORES: Shrews and Moles

S HREWS ARE VERY SMALL, active, mouse-like animals with voracious appetites. Their
high metabolism requires them to eat as much as twice their weight in insects, earth-
worms, lizards, and even mice each day. Because of their small size, speed, and mostly
nocturnal habits, they are seldom seen by people. Their runways pass under the litter on
the forest floor or through the dank grasses of wet fields and marshes. Skulls of shrews
can be found occasionally in the regurgitated pellets of owls, kestrels, and kites.

Trowbridge's shrew and vagrant shrew (in its various forms) are both distributed
widely throughout the peninsula; the former is probably the most common species of
shrew at Point Reyes. Trowbridge's shrew tends to occur in drier environments than the
vagrant shrew. A shrew encountered in coastal scrub or dry Douglas fir forest is likely to
be Trowbridge's; one seen in the salt marsh or damp swale is likely to be a vagrant shrew.
A third species, the Pacific shrew, is nocturnal, occurs in moist habitats, but is rather
rare here.[11, 27, 61]

Although also members of the insectivore order of mammals, moles are not as
active as shrews, but they are as seldomly seen. These are burrowing animals whose
tunnels serve to till the soil. Their stout bodies with powerful, shovel-like forelimbs are
well adapted to their burrowing habit; researchers have estimated that moles burrow
through 10 to 15 feet of soil per hour.[16]

Two species, the shrew-mole and the broadhanded mole, occur at Point Reyes.
Both are limited in distribution according to soil characteristics and each is fairly common in appropriate moist or soft soil habitats. Because these animals are so rarely seen
we must depend on museum specimens to judge their distributions. Most of the specimens of both species are from the moist, forested slopes of Inverness Ridge, especially in
the vicinity of Palomarin, Bolinas, and Inverness. This may reflect the favored collecting
stations of scientists rather than any distributional pattern of the moles, but these locations, with moist, loose soils, are also where we might expect moles to accomplish their
fossorial missions.[4, 47, 61]

LAGOMORPHS: Rabbits and Hares

T WO SPECIES OF RABBITS are a familiar sight at Point Reyes. Although each belongs to
the taxonomic order *Lagomorpha* (hare form), they are members of different families with differing ecological requirements.

The local coastal race of black-tailed hare is darker than interior races. (This pattern of variation in pigmentation, also shared by other species such as the Sonoma chipmunk, black-tailed deer and mountain lion, is known as "Gloger's rule," which states that "races in warm and humid areas are more heavily pigmented [darker] than those in cool and dry areas.") Black-tailed hares are large "jackrabbits" of open brushland. Elongated hind limbs enable black-tails to spring long distances and make sharp turns. To avoid predation, the black-tail uses an element of surprise and escape that works well. When a potential predator is detected, the hare will usually take shelter in the shade of a convenient clump of vegetation or behind a rock and freeze, motionless. If the predator approaches very closely, the hare leaps into stride, zig-zagging across open country until it finds shelter. The effect on the startled predator is momentary confusion, which may afford the hare the advantage it needs to escape. This strategy for surviving in open territory results from various morphological specializations that serve to increase the length and rate of the stride — powerful, elongated, hind limbs and a reduced clavicle that frees the limbs from the sternum. These adaptations are also found in other open country mammals like the cheetah and the antelope.[24, 63]

In contrast, the smaller **brush rabbit** or "cottontail," with relatively poor running ability, is limited to habitats with low, dense vegetative cover, primarily coastal scrub and chaparral. Brush rabbits rarely venture far from bushes, to which they retreat for safety when danger approaches. Nevertheless, this species frequently falls prey to foxes, bobcats, weasels, hawks, and owls. In a study of Muddy Hollow, brush rabbits were found to comprise 12 percent of the mammalian portion of the diet of gray foxes. Brush rabbits are often seen crouched at the edge of the trail or along the roadside, especially in the coyote brush-covered slopes on the west flank of Inverness Ridge.[52]

RODENTS: Aplodontia to Zapus

A S ABUNDANT AND PRIMITIVE land mammals, rodents provide us with a window into the evolution of our climate and landscape through their biogeographical histories. This is illustrated particularly well by two species at Point Reyes: the Point Reyes jumping mouse (*Zapus*) and the Point Reyes mountain beaver (*Aplodontia*). Indeed, these two species are probably among the earliest of the living mammalian inhabitants of the Bay Area. Although once common and widespread throughout the Pacific states, each species is now relatively rare and patchily distributed, a combination of conditions that suggests they are relicts — refugees from an era when the environment was wetter, when the boreal forests were continuous from central California northward, and when each species was more widely distributed.[26, 51]

Mountain Beaver

> This animal, like the redwood tree and the wrentit, is peculiar to the west coast of North
> America, where it occurs scatteringly in the Sierras and northern coast ranges.
> —Joseph Grinnell and Tracy I. Storer. *Animal Life in Yosemite.* 1924.

The mountain beaver is of interest at Point Reyes because of its secretive nature, its isolated distribution, and the fact that Marin County is the southernmost extent of its coastal range.

The name "mountain beaver" is a misnomer for a primitive, short-tailed, muskrat-sized, burrowing (fossorial) rodent that looks something like an overgrown gopher. Also known by its genus name of *Aplodontia* (simple tooth), it belongs to a monotypic family (Aplodontidae) containing only a single species, the mountain beaver, which appears to be the most primitive rodent still living.[51]

The local race, the Point Reyes mountain beaver, which is restricted to "favorable situations within an area of approximately 110 square miles," is isolated, separated from the nearest known population (subspecies *nigra*) in southern Mendocino County by about 70 miles of unsuitable habitat. Geographical isolation has allowed the local race to develop clear racial characteristics; the Point Reyes population is the smallest and grayest race of the species.[41, 57]

Favorable habitat includes moist, sloped soils with dense clumps of sword fern growing in easily excavated, humus-rich soil. A year-round water supply is an essential requirement, resulting from the mountain beaver's inability to concentrate urine and its subsequent high rate of water consumption.[3, 45]

At Point Reyes, Aplodontia is found

Mountain beaver, Aplodontia rufa

along the moist, fern-covered slopes from Tomales Point south along the northeast-facing slopes of Inverness Ridge to Arroyo Hondo at Palomarin. Known colonies are particularly dense around Mount Vision, Point Reyes Hill, Laguna Canyon, and Chute Gulch.

The Arroyo Hondo burrow system is the southernmost known locality in the species' coastal distribution, but it is possible that undiscovered populations exist in the steep canyons on Mount Tamalpais' western slopes south to Muir Woods. Incidental observations include several individuals within the Ledum Swamp drainage system, at Spring Valley, and on the northeast slope of Point Reyes Hill. An extensive colony in Devil's Canyon is nearly continuous with the Home Ranch colony along Home Ranch

Creek. Interestingly, this colony was discovered when the workcrew building the ponds unearthed a burrow system with a backhoe. The driver took an adult mountain beaver home and put it in his bathroom for the night; apparently, the rodent "destroyed" the bathroom. There is no record of the animal's fate. Because the Mount Vision site typifies the species' preferred habitat, a description follows. The colony is on a shaded slope which faces north-northeast with a dip of 30 degrees. The soft soil is riddled with six- to eight-inch diameter holes. These round openings are numerous; many open at the base of a clump of ferns. The dominant overstory is bishop pine with a dense understory of salal and sword fern providing abundant cover. Interspersed with these two ground covers are bracken fern, huckleberry, salmonberry, and various grasses.[47]

Although often associated with what appear to be colonial burrow systems, mountain beavers are not generally regarded as a colonial species. The aggregation in colonies is probably obligatory, based on limited availability of habitat.

Squirrels and Chipmunks

Although it is rather common in grasslands to the north and east, at Point Reyes **Beechey** (or California) **ground squirrels** are few and localized. A small colony is now established at Five Brooks, but as recently as the mid-1970s ground squirrels were absent from Point Reyes. Apparently, a small colony of Beechey ground squirrels was seen at the Palomarin lakes from about 1969 to 1971 but has subsequently become extinct.[47]

Because ground squirrels are a favored prey of coyotes, it has been suggested that coyote distribution shadows ground squirrel distribution. The general absence of ground squirrels may partially account for the lack of coyotes on the peninsula. Although naturalist Ed Heller did not mention ground squirrels on the outer Point in 1899, he did note that coyotes were "common." Perhaps ground squirrels and coyotes have been exterminated by ranchers over the last 85 years.[23, 47]

Ground squirrels tend to occur in dry grasslands where there are slopes or hillsides available for their burrow systems. Their habitat preference for heavily grazed grasslands has been favored by the agricultural trends in California over the last century. Indeed, controlled studies indicate that ground squirrels disappear from grasslands that are free of grazing when the annual grasses are allowed to mature for three consecutive years. However, this fact does not explain the absence of ground squirrels at Point Reyes, where cattle and deer graze most open areas.[32]

The only species of chipmunk that occurs on the peninsula is the **Sonoma chipmunk.** At Point Reyes, chipmunks seem most common in bishop pine and Douglas fir forests with dense understory, but also occur in mixed broadleaf forest and in coastal scrub near streams and arroyos. There are no records of chipmunks for the grasslands of the outer peninsula.

The range of the local population (subspecies *alleni*) of the Sonoma chipmunk extends southward to Muir Woods, north to Nicasio, and northwest on Point Reyes to five miles west of Inverness, near the head of Schooner Bay. It is separated from another population (subspecies *sonomae*) to the north by the Marin-Sonoma grasslands and from another species (Merriam's chipmunk) to the south by San Francisco Bay and the adjacent grasslands. Sonoma chipmunk displays Gloger's rule by being darkest in the westernmost (humid) localities and palest at inland (dry) localities. The individuals at Point Reyes are smaller, shorter tailed, darker, and more reddish in color than populations inland and northward.[5, 26]

The **western gray squirrel,** likewise, is fairly common in forested areas, but seems to prefer mixed broadleaf and oak woodlands where acorns are the favored food. In the bishop pine forest, gray squirrels gnaw diligently on the tightly closed cones and may be important agents for the dispersal of seeds. The chattering "threat" call is often heard from the upper canopy of the forest and they can be heard calling actively before dawn.

The **Douglas squirrel** or "Chickaree," a common resident of the coastal forest to the north, is restricted in its southward distribution by the Sonoma-Marin grasslands, and is therefore absent from the seemingly appropriate habitat on Inverness Ridge and Mount Tamalpais to the east.[26]

Cricitids: Mouse-like Rodents

The three most abundant rodents at Point Reyes are the California meadow vole, the deer mouse, and the valley pocket gopher. Of the three, the gopher is the most familiar. Gopher burrows riddle open pastures and meadows throughout the peninsula. The work of these prodigious diggers is most obvious beneath the firs and oaks around Bear Valley, where the animals, emboldened by their familiarity with people, dare to emerge almost entirely out of their holes. The **deer mouse** is one of the most common mammals throughout the Pacific states, ranging into nearly every habitat. Its hidden runways are most easily discovered beneath deadfall at the forest's edge.

The **California meadow vole** is probably the most abundant mammal at Point Reyes in some years. This species is in the same genus (*Microtus*) as the lemmings of northern latitudes, and like lemmings, goes through cyclical population explosions every three or four years followed by sharp declines. The causes of these microtine outbreaks are poorly understood but are thought to be related to productivity patterns of food plants. There is also evidence from research in the San Francisco Bay Area that following a population peak, meadow vole populations decline because of predation. Years of vole abundance host large numbers of rodent-eating raptors. At Point Reyes, the winter of 1979–80 was such a year; sizable roosts of short-eared and long-eared owls and unusual numbers of red-tailed, rough-legged, ferruginous hawks and black-shouldered kites indicated an abundance of available food. *Microtus* is the primary food item of the black-shouldered kite, and concentrations of these birds may be the clearest indication of vole abundance. Mammalian predators — fox, bobcat, coyote, weasel — undoubtedly benefit from boom years as well. The years of abundance are not well documented, but 1923 was recorded as such a year at Point Reyes, where "people . . . complained of depredations among their flower beds, of begonias being cut into bits during the night."[27, 30, 34, 46]

The distribution of the **western harvest mouse** is apparently concentrated on the marine terraces of the Drake's Estero drainage west of Inverness Ridge, although there are also records from Tomales Point, Abbott's Lagoon, Inverness, Palomarin, and salt marshes on Tomales Bay. The closely related, partially sympatric (occupying the same territory without interbreeding), and federally endangered salt marsh harvest mouse is absent from Point Reyes.[13]

At night, while walking a trail through a wooded thicket, one will occasionally hear the **dusky-footed woodrat's** threat display, a rapid patter of its tail vibrating against the leaves and limbs. Spotted owls, fairly common in old-growth Douglas fir and bishop pine forests at Point Reyes, depend almost entirely on woodrats for food. Indeed, predation by gopher snakes, hawks, owls, foxes, bobcats, ringtails, and probably raccoons poses a constant threat to woodrats.[6, 16]

Dusky-footed woodrats are common in a variety of coastal habitats. Their "lodges" — large (to about six feet tall), conical piles of sticks — are most obvious beneath alders and willows in riparian habitats along Coast Trail, Muddy Hollow Trail, and Olema Creek. They also occur amidst the coyote bush-dominated chaparral and into the dense Douglas fir and oak-bay forests — any place where vegetation provides sufficient food and cover. They mostly eat plant materials, including hazelnut, thimbleberry, and bay laurel flowers.[6]

Although a woodrat's lifespan is only two to three years, the houses are maintained for many years by a succession of tenants. Each house is occupied by a solitary individual, and naturalists have long thought that these animals are asocial. However, studies of 34 lodges from the colony at Laguna Ranch, near Limantour, found recognition between individuals to be indicative of a more complex social organization. Evidence of the formation of a temporary pair-bond further indicates sociability.[6, 33, 64]

Little is known regarding the population cycles of woodrats; however, a great increase in numbers coinciding with an abundance of voles was noted in the Point Reyes area in 1923. Undoubtedly the population fluctuates from year to year; that the peaks and valleys correspond to those of the microtine mice is likely, but is still an open question.[34]

The **red tree mouse** is curious because of its *absence* at Point Reyes. Like the mountain beaver and jumping mouse, this species is generally associated with the "Oregonian" biome – the moist, coniferous forests of the Pacific slope of Oregon and California. Although textbook maps show the range extending from the Columbia River south to San Francisco Bay, there are no known records or specimens from the vicinity of Point Reyes; indeed, its distribution seems to extend southward only to the Russian River in Sonoma County. Those populations to the north, unable to cross the vast Sonoma-Marin grasslands, are isolated from the Douglas fir forest at Point Reyes, which is an island of seemingly appropriate habitat surrounded by effective geographical barriers: water and grassland. The tree mouse is an arboreal species that lives high in the forest canopy; is it possible that its presence here has been overlooked? Curious naturalists have searched through the pellets of spotted owls, a likely predator, for the bones of tree mice. None has been found. Whether the red tree mouse ever occurred at Point Reyes is an open question, but the evidence indicates that it has not in recent years.[4, 26, 61]

Muskrats are most often noticed swimming across open water in still, freshwater ponds bordered by cattail or sedge, such as those at Muddy Hollow, Laguna Ranch, Palomarin, or Olema Marsh. Often mistaken for a beaver (not present at Point Reyes), muskrats are generally smaller than beavers, and have much thinner tails and a light-colored area around the mouth. Although native to California along the Colorado River and in the northeastern counties, the populations in the Central Valley and the San Francisco Bay Area were introduced for fur. Arrival at Point Reyes was first noted in 1974 and numbers have increased subsequently. Now, every leveed freshwater pond seems to have been colonized by this adaptable animal.[5, 27, 47]

The introduction of non-native (exotic) animals into any environment is likely to have deleterious effects, but the effects of muskrats at Point Reyes may be minimal. Freshwater habitat is scarce here; most of the ponds are man-made impoundments associated with cattle ranching. Many of these ponds have naturalized and attracted their own complement of breeding species (red-legged frogs, aquatic garter snakes, yellow-throats, Virginia rails). One can speculate that the muskrats may maintain these ponds by checking the encroachment of cattails. Perhaps the presence of muskrats will encourage an increase in their primary predator, the mink, and thereby increase the threat of an additional predator on ground-nesting birds like rail and quail. Indeed, there is some evidence that minks are increasing.

Another threat posed by muskrats is their tendency to burrow in streambanks and destabilize the floodplain. However, at Point Reyes this may be precluded by the seasonal nature of most of the creeks and arroyos. To date, there is no evidence that muskrats have colonized streambanks.

Point Reyes Jumping Mouse

The extremely long tail and well-developed hind legs of the jumping mouse suggest a cross between a deer mouse and a kangaroo rat. The preferred habitats are wet, grassy meadows adjacent to coniferous forests, marshlands with high growth of sedges or rushes, or low-growing chaparral. Unlike the common deer mouse or vole, the jumping mouse does not use runways but leaps over the dense vegetation, an adaptation that must serve it well in its marshy habitat. This is primarily a nocturnal species.[11, 26, 27]

Like Aplodontia, distribution of the Point Reyes jumping mouse is patchy and the local population is isolated, a combination of conditions suggesting that these are relict populations. Point Reyes is the southernmost extent of this species' distribution, which ranges north along the coastal slope to British Columbia. Specimens at the Museum of Vertebrate Zoology, Berkeley, indicate the jumping mouse occurs at Point Reyes at Ledum Swamp, three miles west of Inverness and at the Drake's Beach turnoff, five miles north-northeast of the Point Reyes Lighthouse. However, little work has been done on this species and it is probably distributed throughout the swales of the outer peninsula.

Porcupine

Prior to 1985 there were only a few sight records or specimens of porcupine from Point Reyes. Three reports in the summer of 1985 may have been indicative of a recent population increase. Each report was from Inverness Ridge. One porcupine was sighted foraging under an apple tree in the Haggerty Gulch drainage on the east slope of Inverness Ridge, another was on the west slope two miles northeast of Limantour Beach, and a third made its presence known by embedding some quills in the nose of a curious horse above the town of Inverness.[47, 61]

The origin of these animals is unknown. Three possibilities present themselves: (1) a small number were here already but were only rarely detected; (2) they are natural immigrants, having arrived here on their own from the more extensive forests of Mount Tamalpais or southern Sonoma County; (3) they were inadvertently imported, perhaps in a truckload of lumber or firewood. The first explanation seems unlikely, given the extensive coverage of the area by hikers and rangers and the absence of visible tree damage. Second, since porcupines are slow-moving and fairly sedentary, immigration seems unlikely. Perhaps inadvertent introduction is the most likely explanation. Whatever the cause of their arrival, if a population becomes established, the effect of their presence on the forests of Inverness Ridge should be closely monitored.

CARNIVORES: Canids, Ursids, Mustelids, Felids

THE LAND-LIVING MEMBERS of the order Carnivora (flesh-eaters) are known as the fissipeds (divided foot), as distinguished from the marine-living pinnipeds (feather foot). A few species are commonly seen (raccoon, striped skunk); several are fairly common but seldom seen (gray fox, bobcat, spotted skunk, long-tailed weasel); others are quite rare (coyote, mountain lion, ringtail); others were once common but are now extinct (black and grizzly bears); the status of others (short-tailed weasel, mink) is not well known.

> Coyotes are as thick as thieves. On Point Reyes ranches it is said they fraternize with the dogs and may be seen romping amicably within pistol shot of peoples back doors. The supervisors [of Marin County] put a five dollar bounty on coyotes in 1891.
> — Jack Mason. *Point Reyes: The Solemn Land.* 1970.

Canids: Foxes and Coyotes

At Point Reyes, the **gray fox** is most frequently found in coastal scrub, chaparral, grasslands, and riparian habitats. The coat is gray on the animal's back, but a reddish cast to the flanks and forelegs may cause confusion with red fox. The black-tipped tail is an unmistakable field mark. Those unfamiliar with this species are often surprised by its small size and cat-like movement. The scat is a familiar sight along fireroads and footpaths; careful examination reveals a diverse diet of rodents, insects, berries, and vegetation — blades of grass often wrap the tight bundle. Although rodents, grasses, and Jerusalem crickets are the fox's favored foods, its diet is supplemented seasonally with fruits (blackberries in summer, coffeeberries in fall and winter) and various arthropods in fall, winter, and spring. Foxes at Point Reyes have smaller home ranges (about 138 acres) than those found in other California studies, indicating a richness in the local habitat.[52]

Red fox does occur at Point Reyes, but the few individuals are almost certainly human-assisted escapees. It is curious, however, that their presence was noted as early as 1899. Their natural distribution in California is restricted to the high Sierra-Cascade; however, a population of unknown origin is now established in the Sacramento Valley and is apparently spreading its range; the possibility that individuals from that population could disperse to Point Reyes cannot be overlooked. Recent sightings indicate that red foxes are increasing at Point Reyes as well as in the greater San Francisco Bay area. The increase in the population of this efficient predator is having a devastating effect on ground nesting birds, like the Clapper Rail, in San Francisco Bay and is a potential threat to nesting seabirds at Point Reyes. It is also likely that the smaller gray fox will suffer from the intrusion of its more aggressive cousin.

The **coyote** is of interest because of its relative rarity at Point Reyes. There are few reliable records between 1900 and the mid-1980s and the possibility of confusion with wild dogs clouds the issue. Beginning in the 1980s, coyotes increased dramatically in agricultural grassland just north and east of Point Reyes, probably in response to the increasing availability of sheep. Shortly thereafter they began appearing on the peninsula. Most sightings are of single animals from the vicinity of Palomarin, Coast Camp, or Abbott's

Gray fox

Lagoon, but on occasion small packs are reported, like the three seen eating a deer carcass at Abalone Flat. Based on the paucity of sightings, rangers estimate that there are probably less than a dozen individuals in the park. The historical record is also vague, but it seems likely that coyotes were formerly common at Point Reyes. In 1846, a Lt. Revere mentioned seeing coyotes in the Olema Valley. In the late 1880s, the Marin County supervisors placed a bounty on coyotes, which were said to be "thick as thieves." During a brief visit in 1899, Ed Heller noted coyotes "common out near the Point." Upon returning to San

Francisco in 1860, 24 years after his first visit (recounted in the classic *Two Years Before the Mast*), Richard Dana, distraught over the vast changes in the area, proclaimed, "the coyotes still bark in the woods, for they belong to no man, and are not touched by his changes." Actually, they were touched by changes even greater than those Dana witnessed; however, given the coyote's tenacious spirit, it seems likely it will return one day. Interestingly, the word "Olema" is derived from the Coast Miwok word "o le" or "o ye," meaning Coyote, the creator and trickster. The village of Olema-loke ("coyote-valley") was apparently located near the present reconstructed Miwok village, Kule Loklo. [21, 36, 48, 70, 71]

There is no substantive evidence that **wolves** have occurred in lowland California in historic times, despite a specific reference to sightings near Olema in 1846 and popular contemporary lore to the contrary. [18, 35]

Ursids: Bears and Raccoons

> In the olden days, when bears were as common in California as cows are now, men used to take advantage of this fear [of fire] and kindle pine-quill fires in and around his haunts in the heads of canyons to drive him out and down and into ambush.
> —Joaquin Miller. *True Bear Stories*. 1900.

Perhaps no other animal is as symbolic of the changes that have scoured the central California landscape as the **grizzly bear**. *Ursus horribilis* dominated this area prior to the

"Mexican period" of the 1800s, during which time bears were destroyed as a threat to livestock or captured for the festive "bear and bull fights" that were a popular entertainment adapted from Spanish tradition. Earlier, the Spanish killed grizzlies to win favor with the natives. The aboriginal peoples tried to avoid the fierce grizzly, although this must have been difficult, since both depended on the seasonal abundance of berries, acorns, and salmon for sustenance. One can imagine a confrontation at the small grove of live oaks on the knoll near Park Headquarters at "Bear" Valley.[48, 58]

Although it belongs to the mammalian order Carnivora, the grizzly bear is an omnivorous predator, an opportunistic nomad who wanders from one seasonal food source to another. As well as visiting oak woodlands in the fall when the ground was littered with acorns, grizzlies in central California roamed through the chaparral rooting rodents and eating berries, and converged on the shores of streams during the salmon spawn. Manzanita was probably a favorite food, and undoubtedly huckleberry and salmonberry brambles were visited. Several accounts indicate that grizzlies were also scavengers. The vaqueros used to bait the bear with a slaughtered bullock, and Spanish explorers reported large numbers visiting the shore at Monterey to feed on beached whales![58, 67]

There are few specific references to grizzlies at Point Reyes, but their former abundance in coastal California leaves little doubt that they occurred here. The first written account was in 1811 when two crewmen of the Yankee sealing ship *The Albatross* put ashore to hunt, possibly near Limantour; they shot a grizzly only after one of them had been mauled. The crewman lived; the bear "proved good eating." In the 1850s a vaquero named Thomas Wood surprised a grizzly in a clover field "on the sand dunes of Tomales Bay" (possibly at Sand Point) and roped it with a riata. After a dramatic tug-of-war, both the bear and the man escaped with their respective lives. The most recent reliable sighting was along Papermill Creek at Tocaloma (less than three miles east of Olema) in about 1884. The last report of a grizzly in Marin County was in 1888, but the description and habitat suggests that this was a black bear.[14, 18, 43, 58, 62]

The extinction of grizzlies from the Bay Area coincided with the Gold Rush and the ensuing invasion of humanity. This new breed of predator had neither the tolerance nor the inclination to coexist with such a formidable beast as the grizzly. The central California newspapers recount over 50 attacks of bears on humans from 1851 to 1860. Retaliation by the settlers was swift and sure; the grizzly was attacked with the same vehemence afforded most Native Americans. In populated areas grizzlies were rare by 1870. In remote areas, a few survived into the twentieth century; the last known grizzly in California was killed in Tulare County in 1922. This unfortunate confrontation might be invoked to illustrate the ecological concept of competitive exclusion (Gause's principle), in which two species are sufficiently similar that one of the two becomes extinct.[27, 31, 37]

Bears were easier [than lions] to come by. . . . [As] late as August 1890, the Bourne boys of Bolinas killed a large black bear in the hills near their home. Bear trapping was common. A cinnamon bear dragged his trap a mile before blacksmith Frank Miller administered the coup de grace, adding one more to his record of 99 bears.
— Jack Mason. *Point Reyes: The Solemn Land.* 1970.

As with humans and grizzlies, the distribution of the grizzly seldom overlaps with the **black bear.** While grizzlies are animals of open brushland or grassland, black bears prefer the forest. An article in the *Marin County Journal* for May 9, 1863 mentions that "brown bears are becoming quite bold and annoying to the people about Olema and Punta Reyes." This and other references to mischievous behavior by "brown bears" suggests that these were black bears of the brown color phase. The black bears that roamed the forested slopes of Inverness Ridge and Mount Tamalpais were probably the southernmost members of the race *altifrontalis* that ranged through the northwest coastal forest from Oregon south to the north shore of San Francisco Bay. It is possible that as the grizzlies were exterminated black bears became more abundant, a phenomenon that occurred in other areas of California. Their presence here was not well documented, and the population was probably extinct by the turn of the century. A 1971 sighting in the Olema Valley near Hagmaier's Pond is equivocal. The isolation of Marin's forests from those of the northern coastal counties by the open grasslands of the Sonoma-Marin borderland are likely to impede recolonization of Point Reyes by this gentler cousin of the grizzly.[5, 18, 23, 62]

The **ringtail** is much rarer at Point Reyes than its common cousin, the familiar **raccoon.** A pair of ringtails nested in the cabin rafters at Palomarin for several years in the late 1960s. Other incidental sightings were at the following locations: Estero Trail, Bass Lake, Coast Guard Station near Palomarin, Olema Creek south of Dogtown, and at Bolinas Lagoon. A specimen was collected near Point Reyes Beach North in 1967. Most of these sightings were in coastal scrub habitat.[47]

Mustelids: Weasels, Badgers, Skunks, and Otters

At Point Reyes, the **long-tailed weasel** is occasionally seen protruding from a gopher hole, frantically sniffing the air; suddenly it will disappear and resurface from another hole some distance away. Although rarely seen, this handsome ferret is quite common, especially in agricultural pastureland and lupine-covered coastal scrub where gopher burrows riddle the ground. The smaller **short-tailed weasel,** or ermine, also occurs here, though it is much rarer than its larger relative. Short-tailed weasels are rarely seen; we only know of their occurrence here through specimens. The first specimen was collected in a salt marsh near Inverness in 1948. Subsequently, individuals were collected at Bear Valley in 1975 and near Tomales Point in 1980. In 1985 through 1987 five specimens of ermines were found killed by domestic cats on the east slope of Inverness Ridge. The locations of the specimens suggest that short-tailed weasels occur in riparian thickets or moist bottomlands with dense vegetative cover. Point Reyes is near the southern extent of the coastal range of the short-tailed weasel.[47, 61]

The status of the **mink** at Point Reyes is difficult to assess. Like the short-tailed weasel, the range of the mink has been shown to extend south along the coast to the north shore of San Francisco Bay; however, records for Marin County and Point Reyes, specifically, are few. A probable sighting at Bear Valley about 1980 was the solitary record until May 1985 when a lactating adult female was found dead on Bear Valley Road, suggesting that a small population is present in the vicinity. Subsequently, several sightings have been reported from the shores of Tomales Bay. Cattail marshes are a preferred habitat, where rodents, muskrats, and waterbirds are favorite foods. A recent increase in the local muskrat population may account for the presence of mink.[27]

Pine martin and **fisher** are mentioned as occurring rarely, according to an old trapper named Martinelli. No other evidence is available. The known distribution of the martin extends southward in the coastal belt only to Sonoma County, but the fisher was reported from Marin historically. It is not likely that either species has occurred here in recent history.[5, 20, 22, 56]

The **badger** is a wary animal restricted to open grasslands and sparse coastal scrub at Point Reyes. The characteristic wide, oblong burrows are easily found: at Tomales Point; from the vicinity of McClure's Ranch and Abbott's Lagoon, south to North Beach on the outer Point; in the high meadows along the southwest slope of Inverness Ridge; and in the meadows along Olema Creek from Five Brooks, south.

Two other mustelid species, **spotted skunk** and **striped skunk**, are sympatric at Point Reyes and throughout much of their

Spotted skunk

range in the western states. The spotted is less well known than the striped because of its strictly nocturnal nature, its small size, and probably its less common status. Here spotted skunks are most frequently seen running across the road in coyote bush-dominated coastal scrub, as near Limantour Beach, Mesa Road at Palomarin, and Sir Francis Drake Boulevard between North Beach and South Beach. It is likely that they are excluded from the wetter riparian forests preferred by striped skunks (and other larger predators) by competition and/or predation. It is interesting to note that each year toward the end of the rainy season (February–March), the number of road-killed skunks of both species increases dramatically, indicating an early spring dispersal pattern.

River otter formerly occurred at Point Reyes where "the southernmost . . . point of occurrence in the coast belt [of California] is a creek flowing into one of the heads of Drake's Bay, near Point Reyes." As recently as 1959, river otter was reported occurring at Drake's Bay; however, they were apparently absent from 1960 until the mid-1980s, probably due to a combination of trapping and degradation of streams by agricultural diking and grazing. A 1975 survey by the California Department of Fish and Game shows the nearest occurrences along the Russian River to the north and Suisun Marsh to the east. A 1987 sighting in Walker Creek by local naturalist Rich Stallcup, followed by another in 1989 at Cypress Grove by John Kelly, and another in Lagunitas Creek in 1991 by myself suggest that otters are beginning to recolonize the Tomales Bay watershed, an encouraging sign.[17, 22, 28]

Felids: Cats

> Bear traps were built in the canyon behind the clubhouse [at Bear Valley], and for the member surfeited with deer hunting there were coyote aplenty, and not a few California lion.
>
> —Jack Mason. *Point Reyes: The Solemn Land.* 1970.

It is a testament to the wilderness of Point Reyes that two native cats still find refuge in the valleys, cliffs, and canyons. Indeed, **bobcats** are quite common in the coastal arroyos, riparian lowlands, and along the edges of meadows bordered by forest. Rodents and rabbits are their primary food items, and both abound. In three years of residence at Laguna Ranch, I came to appreciate the common status of this species; I encountered them more frequently than gray fox, and just as every coastal canyon seemed to have one pair of great horned owls, each also seemed to host a pair of bobcats. There may be a correlation between the abundance of bobcats and the dearth of coyotes, a situation that is reversed in the Santa Cruz area.[5, 27]

In March 1978, I saw a bobcat sitting erect on a branch 40 feet up in a bishop pine; it stood, then climbed higher in pursuit of a western gray squirrel. The agile squirrel escaped out onto the smallest branches, then the bobcat returned to its perch and began grooming its forepaws with its tongue, undaunted by the raucous scolding of the Steller's jays above.

Less common than the bobcat, and rarely seen, is the spirit of wilderness, the **mountain lion,** also known as cougar or puma. This graceful stalker of deer comes in two color phases—one grayish-tan, one reddish-brown. In keeping with "Gloger's rule" (see "Sonoma chipmunk"), the reddish phase is found at Point Reyes. The number of

Feral Cats

Since the first Europeans settled on the peninsula, or perhaps earlier, house cats have strayed freely through field and thicket, perpetually preying on rodents and birds. There is no estimate available on the abundance of these feral cats within the Seashore, but the number must be high. It could be argued that after cattle, feral house cats are the most commonly seen mammals at Point Reyes.

House cats are well adapted to surviving in the wild, and there are few checks on the growth of their population. While great horned owls and automobiles may occasionally kill an individual, this reduction probably puts only a small dent in the overall population. The impact of this introduced predator on the populations of smaller animals is incalculable, but predation pressure must be intense, especially in the vicinity of barns and houses where the pouncers abound. Of course, the problem of feral cats is not restricted to Point Reyes but is widespread throughout rural areas of North America where they have been introduced as pets or to control rodents. Unfortunately, these voracious tabbies do not confine their depredations to undesirable species, but prey also on songbirds and jumping mice.

There have been efforts to control introduced animals on many public lands, but it is curious that feral cats are almost always excluded from these control programs. This is an unfortunate oversight, for as well as eating untold numbers of birds and small mammals, feral cats are competing with native wildlife (such as bobcats, weasels, and foxes) for limited resources.

lions present is not known; however, more than 90 sightings are listed in the files of the National Park Service from 1969 to 1978 and are distributed throughout the year, indicating a resident population rather than occasional wanderers. Sightings are concentrated around Mount Wittenberg and along Coast Trail. There is a single specimen, a cat shot near Bear Valley in 1931. Given their required home range of about 100 square miles, the number must be small; one pair seems a likely estimate. However, a large midden of scat found near Muddy Hollow in 1981 suggests two territorial lions in the area. Cougars mark fecal mounds with scents deposited by anal glands as territorial signals in any situation in which they do not tolerate to other members of their species.[49, 63, 69]

The carcass of a fallow deer, apparently killed by a lion, was found at Muddy Hollow. One wonders what the impact will be on the status of lions if the Park implements a program to reduce the exotic deer populations. Presently, it seems that the black-tailed population is sufficient to support such a predator, which is supposed to take at least one large deer per week. Although primarily a predator of deer, mountain lions will also take skunk, raccoon, bobcat, or even porcupine.[20, 39]

UNGULATES: Pigs, Deer, Cattle, Elk

THE INFLUENCE OF WILD (feral) domesticated ungulates on the environment and native plants and animals is impossible to measure; that the net result is detrimental is
unquestionable. By the mid-1800s the area around Petaluma and other parts of Sonoma
County "abounded" with "immense herds" of wild cattle and horses, according to several
contemporary records. Although there are few specific references to Marin, rampant
herds undoubtedly wandered freely over the unfenced grasslands. The cumulative effect
on the pristine environment was profound; the hooved locusts selected against the perennial grasslands and tilted the balance toward dominance by exotic, annual European
grasses. (See "Coastal Rangeland" in Chapter 3.)[29, 38, 59]

Wild Pig

Wild pigs, hybrids probably arising from crosses between introduced European
boars and escaped domestic pigs, have been rooting the watershed of Mount Tamalpais
and endangering rare populations of orchids for the past decade. By 1984 their range extended into the southern Point Reyes peninsula. Their prolific nature, coupled with a
diverse diet and a tendency to wander, ensures their continued spread unless they are
controlled. In 1965 there were only four California counties in which feral pigs occurred;
by 1985 they were recorded in at least 28. Although opportunistic omnivores, pigs rely
on acorns as a food staple in fall and in lean years may be forced into competition with
the native deer. Additional problems stem from the pig's habit of rooting, which disturbs
the soil, promotes erosion, and pollutes watercourses.[25, 27]

Axis Deer

Native to India, the axis deer has naturalized at Point Reyes since the introduction
of eight individuals in 1947–48. One calculation predicts an annual population growth of
16 percent. The estimate of the minimum population size in 1973 was 401 animals. Until
the Park Service placed a closure on hunting within the Park in 1971, approximately 80
deer per year were killed. Controlled hunting from 1977 to 1983 culled 227 deer from the
herd; the estimated size of the population in 1984 was 350 to 500 animals.[8, 47]

These graceful animals are quite wary compared to the bold fallow deer and even
the native black-tailed deer. Occasionally mixed herds contain axis and fallow deer, or
even axis and black-tails; however, there is no evidence of interbreeding. Males have
antlers that are shed and regrown annually; most individuals go into velvet in spring,
shed in summer, regrow in fall. Yearlings have simple spike antlers, whereas older bucks
carry forked racks with an eye guard (brow tine) near the base. This species, with its

regular series of estrus cycles, can breed throughout the year, as is evidenced by the presence of young fawns during every month.[1,8]

The axis deer diet consists of approximately half grasses, half forbs (weeds). Their preference for grazing puts the axis deer in direct competition with the cattle and fallow deer; the native black-tails are primarily browsers.

During the 1970s, the distribution of axis deer was limited to eight square miles bounded by Limantour Estero to the south, Drake's Estero to the west, and Pierce Point Road to the north. The herd then expanded onto agricultural land north of Pierce Point Road and onto open fields around Bear Valley. Since the late 1980s the herd has declined due to culling, and possibly drought. Now, two reliable places to view the species are: (1) west of Pierce Point Road near the entrance to Tomales Bay State Park and (2) in the vicinity of Home Ranch, near the rocky outcrops northwest of the Estero Trail.

Fallow Deer

A native of the Mediterranean regions of Europe and Asia Minor, the Point Reyes population of fallow deer was established by the introduction of 28 animals in the vicinity of Laguna Ranch between 1942 and 1954. The bulk of the population is presently concentrated on the western slope of Inverness Ridge from Drake's Estero south to Bear Valley. Small numbers range as far south as Palomarin, north to Abbott's Lagoon, and east to Highway 1 in the Olema Valley. A recent culling policy instituted by the National Park Service has reduced the population considerably. From 1977 to 1983 an estimated 576 animals were culled from the herd, leaving between 372 and 950 fallow deer in the area. Censusing techniques have not yet proved successful for monitoring either fallow or axis deer. It is still common to see herds of fallow deer in the vicinity of Bear Valley and between Laguna Ranch and Home Ranch. Individuals have been sighted beyond their usual boundaries, in Samuel P. Taylor State Park (1973); in Tomales Bay State Park; and at Kehoe Ranch, one third of a mile north of Abbott's Lagoon.[47, 60, 68]

The coloration of fallow deer is genetically polymorphic; that is, several color "morphs" occur within the population. An individual animal retains its color type throughout its lifespan. Although ten color types have been differentiated within the species, four types occur at Point Reyes: common, black, white, and menil. There is some individual variability within these generic color types, and seasonal variability results from semi-annual (fall and spring) molting patterns. For example, the "common" type is a brown ground color with white spots in summer, but in winter the spots disappear and the overall color becomes grayer. The menil form has a reddish-brown coat overlain with white spots, which it retains year-round. Both the common and the menil morphs have white rumps; however, the common's rump is bordered by black and the menil's is not.

The pelage of these two types might be easily confused with the similarly spotted axis deer; however, the smaller axis has a dark line down the center of the back and bright white underparts that begin at the throat and extend down the legs and onto the belly. The black form of fallow deer is darkest in summer, fading to grey brown in winter; there is no spotting and no white on the rump. The white form is entirely white. The white form is reported to be the most abundant at Point Reyes, followed by the common, black, and menil varieties, respectively. The predominance of white in the population may reflect the fact that 75 percent of the

Black-tailed deer

introduced animals were white. There may be a slight selective disadvantage to whiteness stemming from increased visibility and resulting in increased vulnerability to predation by mountain lions or human hunters. Also, the visibility of the white deer may bias the census data; the darker animals may have been undercounted.

Unlike the axis deer, mating of fallow deer is strictly seasonal. The males have shed their velvet by the end of August, doing considerable damage to the willow and alder thickets during the shedding period as they rub their racks free of velvet. Males begin rutting in late September and continue into early November. With the loud clacking of their large racks, males spar with one another in open fields along the edges of forests and alder thickets. The rut can become ferocious, and the dawn ruckus – snorting, belching, and clashing – can be disconcerting to the unsuspecting camper. Interestingly, one researcher found the right antler was most frequently broken, perhaps the result of a counterclockwise head rotation during rut sparring. Antlers are shed each spring. The first fawns are born in mid-May.

Black-tailed Deer

Black-tailed, or "mule" deer is the only native deer present at Point Reyes. Hunting pressure was intense during the late 1800s and early 1900s, and competition for food has increased since the introduction of the two exotic deer species in the 1940s. At Tomales Point, the black-tails now compete with tule elk and competition will probably increase as the elk population increases. Elk are usually favored when there is a dietary overlap. An estimated pastoral zone density of 25 black-tails per square mile in 1971 increased to 34 per square mile in 1981, a 38 percent increase since hunting was banned in 1971.[15, 60, 68]

Black-tails are primarily browsers with a diet containing a high percentage of shrubbery, but forbs, grasses, and trees are also eaten, with considerable seasonal shifts between forage species. At Tomales Point, in coastal prairie and scrub, bush lupine is the most common food in fall and winter. Grasses are consumed in winter and forbs in spring and summer. The use of forbs at this season provides necessary nourishment at the onset of calving, molt, and antler growth. The European plantain is the most commonly taken forb, especially in spring and summer, but miner's lettuce is preferred when it is available in spring. Yarrow is taken the year around, while sorrel and curley dock are taken only in summer.[9, 15, 55]

Cattle

> At Point Reyes about 3,000 cows are milked daily. This place is considered the greatest dairy region in the state.
>
> — "Al Barney's Trip to the Country." *Marin County Journal.* 1865.

The narrow-gauge railroad that ran through Point Reyes from Sausalito in the late 1800s carried one million pounds of butter annually and large quantities of milk to the markets of San Francisco Bay. The dairy industry continues to be important at Point Reyes; indeed, the effects of continued intense grazing are especially evident in the grasslands on the outer Point. Apparently the number of cows on the peninsula increased over the century between Al Barney's visit and the creation of Point Reyes National Seashore. In 1960 there were 10,000 head of cattle (7,000 dairy and 3,000 beef); in 1987 about 5,100 head (3,400 dairy, 1,700 beef) graze over 20,659 acres of land on the Point Reyes peninsula. The cumulative effects of such grazing pressure have profoundly altered the plant communities and the face of the landscape.(See "Coastal Rangeland" and "Marshlands" in Chapter 3 for further discussion.)[2, 42, 50]

Tule Elk

The elk herds reminded early European visitors to California of the Old World red deer with which they were familiar; many of the references in the historical literature to "deer" were probably elk. Indeed, the first Europeans to lay eyes on tule elk may have been members of Sir Francis Drake's famous crew when they landed at Point Reyes, as a journal entry attests: "The inland we found to be far different from the shoare, a goodly country and fruitful soil, stored with many blessings fit for the use of man: infinite was the company of very large and fat Deer, which we saw by thousands as we supposed in herd."[38]

Other less ambiguous accounts make it clear that tule elk were at one time abundant at Point Reyes. In December 1595, the Spanish vessel *San Agustin* sank in Drake's Bay and the crew "saw deer walking about, the largest ever found, as could be seen by their antlers. There were a great quantity of horns, one of which . . . showed sixteen palms from point to point."[65]

A bull Tule Elk posed against the backdrop of Tomales Point. The log from the Spanish ship
San Agustin *(shipwrecked in Drake's Bay in December 1595) must have been describing this*
species when it reported ". . . deer walking about, the largest ever found, as could be seen by
their antlers [which] showed sixteen palms from point to point."

In an overland journey from San Rafael to Fort Ross in 1824, Russian sea captain
Otto Von Kotzebue described what were probably elks: "as large as a horse, with
branching antlers . . . ; these generally graze on hills, from whence they can see round
them on all sides, and appear much more cautious than the small [black-tailed] deer." Lt.
Joseph Warren Revere, grandson of Paul Revere and a commissioned officer in the U.S.
Navy during the war with Mexico, came to the Olema Valley in July of 1846 to hunt elk;
in his book *Naval Duty in California* he describes riding into a herd numbering over 400.
Again, in 1880, a reference to Marin County described animals that were probably elk as
having "appeared to have limited their range to the open lands along the coast."[10, 59]

The tule elk that was native to Point Reyes was the same race (*nannodes*) as the great
Central Valley herds; their habitat preference was grassland, with the north coast population occupying oak-grassland and chaparral in areas subject to periodic drought. The
regal Roosevelt elk of Humboldt and Del Norte counties is confined to timber-bordered
grassland with high annual rainfall.[38]

Undoubtedly the change from perennial bunch grasses to annual grasses that
accompanied European colonization was detrimental to the elk herds. An additional
though probably less profound pressure on the population was hunting, especially for
the hide and tallow trade, which was concentrated in the areas around Monterey and
San Francisco bays, and probably had an impact on the Point Reyes herd as well.[7, 38]

While the Sacramento Valley population of elk was virtually exterminated by the time of the Gold Rush, accounts by Revere and Evermann indicate that the population in the Point Reyes-Tomales Bay area was still strong during the years 1846 to 1852. However, two market hunting posts were established in Petaluma in 1850 and it did not take long for the hunters to decimate what remained. One historian estimates that by 1855 most elk were gone from the region.[38]

The reintroduction of 13 adult tule elk (2 males, 11 females) to 2,500 acres at Tomales Point in 1978 and 1979 ended an absence of more than a century. After some initial adult mortality and low reproductive success due to dietary deficiencies and an outbreak of paratuberculosis probably caught from beef cattle, by 1988 the population had grown to 92 individuals. In 1991 the herd reached 130 to 150 animals, the estimated carrying capacity of the reservation.[15, 50]

> Elk and black-tailed deer on Tomales Point may be classified as forb-grass and forb scrub feeders, respectively. Both utilize forbs extensively in the spring and summer months when herbaceous standing crop is at a maximum, and resort to other plant types when they are probably more nutritious in fall and winter. . . . Both herbivores make extensive use of English plantain, an exotic perennial forb that remains green for much of the dry season.[15]

Competition for forage between elk and deer normally favors elk. Elk researcher Peter Gogan estimates that Tomales Point could eventually support about 140 tule elk. He also suggests some management goals to help maintain a self-regulating environment; a perusal of these recommendations is illustrative of the changes that have occurred in the environment since pristine conditions prevailed, and the lengths we must go to approximate those conditions. The recommendations are: (1) establishment of a viable coyote population to exert some control on growth of deer and elk populations; (2) prescribed fire to maintain grasslands in early successional stages with plantain and retard the encroachment of coyote bush; (3) maintenance of stock ponds to encourage even distribution of the elk within their range; (4) introduction of elk from other populations to maintain genetic diversity; (5) culling of females to favor an equal sex ratio; and (6) reduction of the population of the two exotic deer species.[15]

Pronghorn

Like the tule elk with which it shared its range, the pronghorn (antelope) was an abundant resident of the perennial grasslands that once carpeted central California. Whether or not antelope occurred at Point Reyes is uncertain. Evidence includes possible bones excavated from an aboriginal midden on the peninsula and sightings near Olema mentioned by Revere in 1846. However, one authority showed the original range confined to the Central Valley, extending west to the north shore of San Francisco Bay and ending at about the Petaluma River.[5, 11, 36, 40]

REFERENCES

1. Asdell, S. A. 1964. *Patterns of Mammalian Reproduction.* Ithica, N.Y.: Comstock Publications.

2. Barney, A. 1865. Al Barney's Trip to the Country. *Marin County Journal,* May 1865. Reprinted in *Old Marin with Love,* by Marin County American Revolution Bicentennial Commission. San Rafael: Cal Central Press.

3. Camp, C. L. 1918. *Excavations of Burrows of the Rodent Aplodontia; with Observations on Habits of the Animal.* University of California Publications in Zoology 17.

4. California Academy of Sciences. 1986. *Museum catalog for Department of Ornithology and Mammalogy.*

5. Clark, K. E. 1979. *A Preliminary Study of the History and Present Status of the Mammals at Point Reyes National Seashore (Excluding Orders Chiroptera, Pinnepedia, and Cetacea).* Master's thesis, University of California, Santa Cruz.

6. Cranford, J. 1977. Home range and habitat utilization by Neotoma fuscipes as determined by radio-activity. *Journal of Mammalogy 58.*

7. Dana, Richard Henry. *Two Years Before the Mast.* Republished in 1927. New York: International Collector's Library.

8. Elliot, H. W. III. 1973. *A field survey of the exotic axis deer at Point Reyes National Seashore.* Master's thesis, University of California, Davis.

9. Elliot, H. W. III., and R. H. Barrett. 1985. Dietary overlap among axis, fallow, and black-tailed deer and cattle. *Journal of Range Management 38.*

10. Evermann, B. W. 1915. An attempt to save California elk. California Fish & Game 1: 85–96.

11. Fellers, G. M., and J. Dell'Osso. 1986. *An Annotated Checklist of Mammals: Point Reyes National Seashore.* Coastal Parks Association.

12. Finley, J. S. 1955. *Speciation of the Wandering Shrew.* University of Kansas, Museum of Natural History 9.

13. Fisler, G. F. 1965. *Adaptations and Speciation in Harvest Mice of the marshes of San Francisco Bay.* University of California Publication in Zoology 77.

14. Gale, W. A. 1811. Albatross Log Book. In *Solid Men of Boston,* by W. D. Phelps. Master's thesis, University of California, Berkeley.

15. Gogan, P. J. P. 1986. *Ecology of the Tule Elk Range, Point Reyes National Seashore.* Ph.D. dissertation, University of California, Berkeley.

16. Grater, R. K. 1978. *Discovering Sierra Mammals.* Yosemite and Sequoia Natural History Associations.

17. Grinnell, J. 1914. *Distribution of the River Otter in California, with Descriptions of a New Subspecies.* University of California Publications in Zoology 12.

18. Grinnell, J. 1933. *Review of the Recent Mammal Fauna of California.* University of California Publication in Zoology 40.

19. Grinnell, J., and T. I. Storer. 1924. *Animal Life in the Yosemite.* Berkeley: University of California Press.

20. Grinnell, J., J. S. Dixon, and J. M. Linsdale. 1937. *Fur-bearing Mammals of California: Their Natural History, Systematic Status, and Relations to Man.* 2 Vols. Berkeley: University of California Press.

21. Gudde, E. G. 1969. *California Place Names: the Origin and Etymology of Current Geographical Names,* 3d ed. Berkeley: University of California Press.

22. Hall, E. R., and K. R. Kelson. 1959. *Mammals of North America.* 2 vols. New York: Ronald.

23. Heller, E. 1899–1901. *Field notes: California to Oregon.* Mimeo. Point Reyes National Seashore Library.

24. Hildebrand, M. 1960. How animals run. *Scientific American* 202(5).

25. Hoffman, E. 1985. Wild hog in the woods. *Pacific Discovery* 38(3).

26. Hooper, E. 1944. *San Francisco Bay as a Factor Influencing Speciation in Rodents*. Museum of Zoology, University of Michigan, Miscellaneous Publications 59.

27. Ingles, L. G. 1965. *Mammals of the Pacific States*. Stanford, Calif.: Stanford University Press.

28. Kirk, D. 1975. *River Otter Survey Progress Report*. California Department of Fish and Game, Nongame Wildlife Investigations, Job II-1.1.

29. Lauff, C. 1847. Reminiscences. In *Old Marin with Love*, by Marin County American Revolution Bicentennial Commission. San Rafael: Cal Central Press.

30. Laymon, S. A., and W. D. Shuford. 1980. Middle Pacific Coast Region. *American Birds* 34:302-305.

31. LeBoeuf, B. J., and S. Kaza. 1981. *The Natural History of Año Nuevo*. Pacific Grove: Boxwood Press.

32. Linsdale, J. M. 1946. *The California Ground Squirrel*. Berkeley: University of California Press.

33. Linsdale, J. M. and L. P. Tevis. 1951. *The Dusky-footed Woodrat*. Berkeley: University of California Press.

34. Mailliard, J. 1925. Notes on the numerical status of rodent populations in parts of California. *Journal of Mammalogy* 6.

35. Margolin, M. 1978. *The Ohlone Way*. Berkeley: Heyday Books.

36. Mason, J. 1972. *Point Reyes: the Solemn Land*, 2d ed. Inverness, Calif.: North Shore Books.

37. Mayr, E. 1963. *Animal Species and Evolution*. Cambridge, Mass.: Belknap Press.

38. McCullough, D. R. 1969. *The Tule Elk: Its History, Behavior and Ecology*. University of California Publications in Zoology 88.

39. McLean, D. D. 1940. The deer of California, with particular reference to the Rocky Mountain mule deer. California Department of Fish and Game 26: 139-166.

40. McLean, D. D. 1944. The prong-horned antelope in California. *California Fish and Game* 30:221-241.

41. Miller, G. S. 1923. *List of North American Recent Mammals*. Smithsonian U.S. National Museum Bulletin 128.

42. Moore, S. T. 1976. Transportation played a colorful role in Marin history. In *Old Marin with Love*, by Marin County American Revolution Bicentennial Commission. San Rafael: Cal Central Press.

43. Munroe-Fraser, J. P., ed. 1880. *History of Marin County, California*. San Rafael: Alley, Bowen and Co.

44. National Park Service. 1984. *Hunting of Exotic Deer at Point Reyes National Seashore*. Mimeo. Point Reyes National Seashore Library.

45. Nungesser, W. C., and E. W. Pfeiffer. 1965. Water balance and maximum concentrating capacity in the primitive rodent, *Aplodontia rufa*. *Comp. Biochemistry and Physiology* 14.

46. Pearson, O. 1963. *Carnivore-mouse predation*. Paper presented to Society of Mammalogists, Albuquerque, N.M.

47. Point Reyes National Seashore. Records of specimens and sightings of mammals. Typescript.

48. Quinn, A. 1981. *Broken Shore: The Marin Peninsula*. Salt Lake City: Peregrine-Smith.

49. Ralls, K. 1971. Mammalian scent marking. *Science* 171.

50. Ray, D. T. 1981. *Post-release Activity of the Tule Elk at Point Reyes National Seashore*. Master's thesis, University of Michigan, Ann Arbor.

51. Rensberger, J. M. 1975. *Haplomys* and its bearing on the origin of the Aplodontid rodents. *Journal of Mammalogy* 56: 1-14.

52. Rymills, E. M. 1979. *Movements and food habits of gray fox, Urocyon cineoargenteus, in Point Reyes National Seashore*. Master's thesis, San Francisco State University, San Francisco.

53. Storer, T. I. 1932. Factors influencing wildlife in California, past and present. *Ecology* 13: 315-327.

54. Storer, T. I., and L. P. Tevis. 1955. *The California Grizzly.* Berkeley: University of California Press.

55. Taber, R. D., and Dasmann, R. F. 1958. The dynamics of three natural populations of the deer *Odocoileus hemionus columbianus. Ecology* 38: 233-246.

56. Taylor, W. P. 1913. Field notes. University of California, Berkeley. Photocopy.

57. Taylor, W. P. 1918. *Revision of the Rodent Genus Aplodontia.* University of California Publications in Zoology 17.

58. Tevis, L. P. Jr., and T. I. Storer. 1955. *The California Grizzly.* Berkeley: University of California Press.

59. Thompson, R. A. 1896. *The Russian Settlement in California Known as Fort Ross.* Santa Rosa, Calif.: Sonoma Democrat Publishing Company.

60. Thompson, S. 1981. *The Transect Census of Deer in the Pastoral Zone of Point Reyes National Seashore.* Mimeo. Point Reyes National Seashore Library.

61. University of California, Berkeley. 1986. *Museum of Vertebrate Zoology Catalog of Specimens.*

62. Van Atta, C. E. 1946. Notes on the former presence of grizzly and black bears in Marin County, California. *California Fish and Game* 32: 27-29.

63. Vaughn, T. A. 1972. *Mammalogy.* Philadelphia: W. B. Saunders Co.

64. Wallen, K. 1982. Social organization in the dusky-footed woodrat (*Neotoma fuscipes*): a field and laboratory study. *Animal Behavior* 30: 1171-1182.

65. Wagner, H. E. 1924. The voyage to California of Sebastian Rodriguez Cermeno in 1595. *California Historical Society Quarterly* 3: 3-24.

66. Wagner, H. E. 1929. *Spanish Voyages to the Northwest Coast of America in the Sixteenth Century.* San Francisco: California Historical Society.

67. Wagner, H. E. 1931. The last Spanish exploration of the Northwest Coast and the attempt to colonize Bodega Bay. *California Historical Society Quarterly* 10.

68. Wehausen, J. D. 1973. *Some Aspects of the Natural History and Ecology of the Fallow Deer on Point Reyes Peninsula.* Ph.D. thesis, University of California, Davis.

69. Young, S. P. 1946. *The Puma: Mysterious American Cat, Part 1.* New York: Dover Press.

70. Kroeber, A. L. 1925. Handbook of the Indians of California. Bureau of Indian Ethnology Bulletin 78. Washington.

71. Thalman, S. 1990. Personal comment regarding Miwok history.

CHAPTER SEVEN

MARINE MAMMALS
Survivors of the Harvest

The continental shelf in the Gulf of the Farallones is wider (26 nautical miles) than the continental shelf along the entire west coast of the United States. This provides for large, relatively shallow (60 meters) pelagic and benthic habitats for marine mammals, fish and sea birds and their forage items. . . . Land runoff from San Francisco Bay creates raised nutrient levels and ensures high primary productivity (phytoplankton). High productivity resulting from upwelling nearshore and offshore in this basin supports high abundances and diversities of species . . . making this basin one of the most productive and unique areas along the entire coast of California.

— National Coastal Ecosystems Team. *Ecological Characterization of the Central and Northern California Coastal Region.* 1981.

THE PACIFIC OCEAN embraces Point Reyes; her perennial swells sculpt the shoreline, her winter surges lend an unrelenting wildness to the seashore. The area considered in this chapter extends out into the Gulf of the Farallones, from Tomales Point, west to the Cordell Banks and the Farallon Islands, south to the Golden Gate — one of the richest marine environments in the eastern Pacific. Upwelling waters of the Cordell Banks and the Farallon Islands (see Figure 1.) attract herds and pods of a great variety of marine mammals; most species that occur in these waters wander, occasionally or regularly, inshore. The beaches, reefs, and rocks of Point Reyes serve as safe haulout sites and breeding grounds for several species of seals and sea lions, and an array of whales complements the nearshore waters.

It is difficult for us to imagine what Drake's Bay looked like 200 or more years ago. From the few accounts — notebooks of the early explorers and, later, those of sealing and whaling vessels — it must have been quite different than it is today. Kelp beds blanketing Drake's Bay provided anchor to a healthy population of sea otters. Elephant seals crowded the beaches and coves; in season, pods of blue whales and humpbacks wandered nearshore, unafraid of the harpoon. Perhaps attracted to an abundance of plump flesh, killer whales and great white sharks patrolled nearshore, sending seals to the beach and causing the assembled whales to seek refuge in the kelp. This innocent bounty was to end with the arrival of the human orcas — Boston whalers and Russian sealers — here to harvest the sea for resources that were ripe for the taking. In the first half of the nineteenth century, elephant seals were rendered for oil, and sea otters and fur seals were pelted for fur. The second half of the century saw the establishment of commercial whaling along the California coast, and a shore-whaling station with several killer boats started in Bolinas Bay in 1857. Such enterprises continued well into the twentieth century, increasing the efficiency of their operations and decimating the whale populations of the North Pacific. After the Bolinas stations closed, the waters off Point Reyes

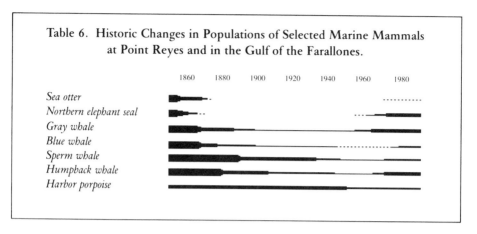

Table 6. Historic Changes in Populations of Selected Marine Mammals at Point Reyes and in the Gulf of the Farallones.

still did not escape the harvest. Two stations were opened near Richmond in San Francisco Bay in 1956. They sent boats out into the Gulf of the Farallones from April through November for 13 years and took about 3,400 whales of 8 species.[16, 48]

As a group, marine mammals have suffered greater predation by humans than any other "resource." Indeed, by the end of the nineteenth century several species formerly abundant in California's coastal waters — most notably, sea otter, fur seal, elephant seal — had been hunted to the brink of extinction. Unlike some of the large terrestrial mammals that never recovered, several of the seals and whales have repopulated our shores, and, especially in recent years, their numbers are increasing dramatically (see elephant seal and blue whale, below). This is an encouraging testament to the ability of humans to correct their transgressions as well as to the remarkable resilience of nature.[10, 11, 49]

SEA OTTER: Shadows in the Shallows

SEA OTTERS FORMERLY BRED at Point Reyes, on the Farallon Islands, and throughout California in nearshore waters. Aboriginal peoples used sea otter pelts for clothing and arrow quivers, but the level of harvest must have been small. Then, in 1786, the Spaniards began trading otter pelts from lower California with China for quicksilver. By the early 1800s, American, English, and Russian vessels, attracted to the commercial potential of these abundant fur bearers, arrived in coastal California, including Point Reyes and the Gulf of the Farallones, and effectively decimated the "sea beavers." The luxuriant pelts were highly prized by Chinese Mandarins for their warmth and beauty. In 1790 an otter pelt brought a market price of $80 to $120 in Canton; by 1834, the price had dwindled to only $30.[20, 38]

In the spring of 1811 three Boston vessels – the *Albatross*, *O'Cain*, and *Isabella* – used Drake's Bay as a base for their ottering activities. These boats supplied Aleut hunters in 130 canoes (*baidarkas*), which went forth to harvest pelts. So intense was the hunting pressure that, as one historian has noted, "no otter had a chance along the coast from Bodega Bay to Pillar Point." Nearly 10,000 pelts were taken in 1811, the year of greatest harvest. In 1812, the Russians established an ottering station at Fort Ross in Sonoma County and continued the exploitation, but the bounty was soon depleted and the station folded in 1841. By 1846 otters had become so hard to find that the merchants abandoned their efforts. After the outbreak of the Mexican War, only two expeditions are known to have hunted otters in the Gulf of the Farallones. "About a dozen" otters were shot in Bolinas Bay in the spring of 1847, and "a few" were taken in Drake's Bay in 1848, but these were the last historic references from these shores.[38]

Sea otters were thought to be extinct in California in the early 1900s until a small population was discovered in an isolated cove just south of Monterey. Since being protected by an international treaty in 1911 (agreed to by the United States, Canada, Japan, Russia, and Great Britain), and a belated California law in 1913, otters have repopulated California from just south of Pismo Beach to just north of Santa Cruz. Although this population of about 1,300 animals has been protected since 1977, their numbers have not grown for more than a decade and may have declined in recent years. The cause of this recent threat is gill and trammel nets that entangle and drown the otters.[11, 14, 52]

Sea otters, when present in California waters, participate as members of a triangular community of organisms: otters, urchins, and kelp. One of the otter's primary food sources is the purple sea urchin, which grazes on young kelp plants. By containing the urchin population, the otter is allowing the kelps to reproduce and develop into large beds, essential areas for the otters to anchor themselves and bear young. The kelp beds in nearshore waters of the Gulf of the Farallones were probably much more extensive when otters were abundant. With the depletion of otters, the balance was tilted in favor of the urchin. With one of their primary predators eliminated, the urchin population increased and overgrazed the young kelp. Over time, the kelp failed to reproduce and the beds disappeared. The otters managed to repopulate the Monterey coast in the 1930s, but at Point Reyes few kelp beds remain and it is difficult to imagine an otter population reestablishing itself successfully.[11, 18, 47, 52]

Occasionally, sea otters are reported from Point Reyes. If these sight records are accurate, they represent wandering individuals, probably from the Santa Cruz area, where the closest population survives. Sightings on file with the Park were: near the Fish Docks, early 1970s; at Kelham Beach, 1974; and near Double Point, 1975. Otters are known to disperse during the warm-water phase of fall, so sightings might be anticipated during those months. Indeed, in October 1986 a sea otter was seen around the Farallon Islands, where it remained for four days; apparently the animal was wounded and Point Reyes Bird Observatory biologists speculated that it was the victim of a shark attack. The only other recent specimens from Point Reyes include: one found in Drake's Bay in October 1970; one sick individual found at Kehoe Beach in 1972; and one at North Beach in May 1981.[42, 54]

There has been some consideration by the Park Service of reintroducing sea otters into the kelp beds off Drake's Beach, but that idea has not been pursued. In recent years the population has been shifting slowly northward, recently reinhabiting Point Año Nuevo. It is possible, given time and protection from persecution by humans, that otters will recolonize these shores of their own accord. At Sculptured Beach beds of bull kelp and California kelp may await the otters' return. The possibility lends some excitement to a walk along Drake's Beach, as we scan the bobbing kelp bladders in the hope of spotting a head with long whiskers and a curious gaze.[28]

PINNIPEDS: Seals and Sea Lions

THIS TERM (literally "feathered feet") refers to seals and sea lions. Five of the six species of pinnipeds found in California visit Point Reyes. The exception, the southern fur seal, ranges only about as far north as Point Conception; however, even this species may once have occurred here.[39]

SEALS

Harbor Seal

Our counts of over 2,500 animals confirm that this small section of shoreline [the Point Reyes peninsula] supports the largest concentration of harbor seals in California.
— Sarah Allen. *Harbor Seals at Point Reyes.* 1985.

Harbor seals, though gregarious by nature, are very shy and wary of humans. This caution must serve them well, for they manage to survive and flourish in close proximity to people in coastal estuaries and beaches all along the Pacific coast. At Point Reyes, concentrations are found at the mouth of Tomales Bay, the mouth of Drake's Estero, Double Point, Duxbury Reef, and Bolinas Lagoon, but numbers shift between sites seasonally, reflecting differing uses of each area. In Tomales Bay, numbers are usually stable throughout spring and summer, then increase in winter during the herring spawn. In contrast, at breeding locations including Drake's Estero, Double Point, and Tomales Point, numbers increase during the breeding season (May–July), then decrease rapidly in the fall. The seals also tend to abandon areas on the outer coast after the breeding season, while in estuaries, buffered from the effects of winter storms and high tides, numbers remain relatively stable through winter.[7]

Point Reyes, with a breeding population upwards to 2,500 animals, supports about 20 percent of the California population and produces up to 25 percent of the pups born in the state. The Point Reyes population seems to be maintaining stable numbers; however, on the nearby Farallones numbers have increased dramatically since the first pup was born in 1974.[2,7]

The seals tend to forage at night and during high tides, then at mid-day or on lower tides they haul out on sandspits and offshore rocks in large pods. At the first sign of danger – approaching dogs or people – the entire herd retreats to the safety of the water; the seals usually rehaul after about one-half hour. Disturbance lowers breeding success because the mothers may be separated from the pups before they have bonded. In a study of disturbance, seals were flushed from haulout sites 25 percent of the time, except near the mouth of Tomales Bay where the disturbance was inflated to 41 percent, primarily as the result of activity by clam diggers. Human disturbances include clam diggers, low-flying aircraft, hikers and dogs, and boats that approach too closely. Unavoidable disturbances also occur: landslides, deer, and gulls. (Gulls descend soon after a pupping to devour the afterbirth.) Harbor seals, like murres and otters, also drown in gill nets; a survey from 1982 to 1984 estimated 200 harbor seals killed in each of 3 years along the Sonoma to San Mateo coast.[5,21]

Many of the fish eaten by harbor seals (perch, flounder, eelpout, greenling) are bottom-feeders that occur in shallow water, but herring and other open-water schooling species are also taken, and weaned pups like shrimp.[5,29]

Harbor seals, like all "earless" seals (such as the elephant seal), cannot bend the hind flippers forward under the body and therefore is awkward on land. They shimmy across the beach on their bellies. As a result, haulout areas are usually quite close to the water's edge. However, unlike elephant seals, harbor seals are small, usually 5 or 6 feet long, weighing about 150 to 200 pounds. Their small size has protected them inadvertently; they have never suffered the hunting pressure that so decimated the elephant seal and fur seal populations.

Northern Elephant Seal

One of the most remarkable and encouraging biological stories of the Pacific Basin involves the abundance, decimation, and subsequent recovery of the elephant seal.

According to the earliest accounts, this species was abundantly distributed from Cabo San Lorenzo in Baja California north to the Point Reyes peninsula. However, during the first half of the nineteenth century, Russian, British, and American sealers slaughtered the species to the edge of extinction for the oil rendered from its blubber. The elephant seal was second only to the much-sought sperm whale as a source of oil. By 1868, the scientific community thought the species was extinct, but in 1892 a small population was discovered on Isla de Guadalupe, 150 miles west of Baja. At its nadir, the population had dwindled below 100 individuals. Subsequently, given the eventual protection of the Mexican and United States governments, the population began to increase and reinhabit former breeding grounds. By the 1930s, some of the islands of Southern California were recolonized; Año Nuevo was visited in 1955 and breeding began in 1961; the Farallones were visited as early as 1959 and breeding began in 1972. The Farallon group has increased dramatically since; the number of pups born each year continued to grow through 1983, when it peaked at 475; then, following the El Niño years, numbers dropped a little. The winter of 1985–1986 produced 434 pups, but 35 percent (about normal) died before being weaned. Survival of pups is expected to increase as the breeding cows gain age and experience.[8, 11, 27, 31, 45]

Point Reyes is the northernmost site in the breeding range of the elephant seal. Although they were abundant in the nineteenth century, elephant seals began to visit some of the more remote beaches of Point Reyes for the first time in this century in 1972. The first pup was born in 1976 at Drake's Beach, but did not survive. A small colony (six animals) established itself at a small cove, inaccessible to humans, below the Point Reyes Headlands in 1981; in 1983 a bull arrived and the colony grew to 11 animals; in 1984, the first pup survived to weaning and the colony has grown steadily since. By the end of the 1986 breeding season, the colony consisted of one bull, his harem of 19 females, 6 subadult males, and 19 pups. Five of those 1986 pups died, possibly in a landslide that filled their small cove after heavy winter rains. As at other colonies, catastrophic events — landslides, large swells associated with severe storms, limited prey associated with unusually warm water — are likely to exact a high toll on pups.[8, 45]

Elephant seals have also been seen at Point Reyes Beach, Drake's Beach, and near Chimney Rock, but because these locations are accessible to humans and dogs, it is not likely that colonies will establish themselves at any of them. The rapid growth of the Point Reyes Headland colony mirrors the pattern at Año Nuevo and the Farallones. Assuming the animals can find refuge on beaches free from human disturbance, and that the breeding sites provide appropriate protection for small pups from extreme tides, it is reasonable to predict that Point Reyes will be seal-wealthy before the millenium.

An increasing elephant seal population at Point Reyes may be accompanied by an increase in seal predators, most predictably great white shark and killer whale. An

Mature adult elephant seals – bulls – raise their heads and face off in a characteristic battle pose. Males fight for the right to dominate a select territory and a harem of females. The demands on an alpha bull are intense; few alphas last more than two consecutive seasons before a younger, stronger male arrives to challenge and displace the former alpha.

When the breeding season is over, the adult males disperse and the females and juvenile males congregate in large herds to molt.

increase in shark predation on pinnipeds, particularly elephant seals, has been documented at the Farallones.[3]

Elephant seals vary greatly in size according to sex; the females weigh about 2,000 pounds and are about 10 feet long; males may weigh up to 8,000 pounds and grow to 22 feet in length.[39, 46]

Males and females differ in behavior as well as size. Juveniles (subadults), adult females, and adult males segregate themselves from one another. In late November the first breeding bulls arrive on the breeding grounds; as the large males arrive, the smaller juveniles (of both sexes) who were hauled out during the fall begin to leave. By early January the breeding cows who were inseminated 11 months earlier begin to give birth; only a few subadult males remain. In February the cows leave, with the last bull leaving several days after the last cow. As the breeding animals leave, juveniles begin to return to molt in mid-April, leaving before the bulls return to molt in mid-June. If you have ever witnessed the testosterone-induced belligerence of a bull elephant seal in full rut, it's easy to understand why all other members of the colony tend to avoid him.

Limited information available on diet suggests that elephant seals rely on open-water schooling fishes and it is likely that the United States ban on foreign commercial fishing within the 200-mile limit benefited this species by reducing competition for prey species.[4, 29]

SEA LIONS

TWO SPECIES OF SEA LIONS occur at Point Reyes, the California sea lion and the northern sea lion, each near the edge of its breeding range. The coast of central California, from Point Conception to Point Reyes, is the only area where the two breeding populations overlap. California sea lions breed from Point Reyes south to Baja California; northern sea lions breed from the Channel Islands north to the Bering Sea. When two closely related species share the same area (sympatry), there is usually a difference in the prey being taken (resource partitioning). California sea lions eat mostly schooling fishes while northern sea lions rely more on bottom fishes; both species also take squid and octopus.[29]

The abundance and distribution of each species has been changing in recent years: Californias have been increasing, northerns have been decreasing. Despite long-term trends, these populations respond relatively quickly to changes in the environment (fluctuations in water temperature, availability of food, etc.) and the trends witnessed to date may accelerate or even reverse in the future. For example, no one knows why sea lions of both species were nearly absent from the Farallones in the fall of 1986.

California Sea Lion

One can sometimes see the bear-like California sea lions from Limantour or Great Beach as they "porpoise" through the water, traveling in herds, probably in search of schools of fish. More often, they are lying on the rocks below the "Sea Lion Overlook," basking in the sun or barking in the fog. When the winter herring run is on, they enter Tomales Bay; on a still January night the barking carries through the moist air and sometimes can be heard in Inverness.

Although individuals wander as far north as British Columbia, the birth of two pups at Southeast Farallon Island on May 31, 1974 established the northernmost breeding record. Numbers on the Farallones, and probably at Point Reyes, have been increasing dramatically since the early 1970s when researchers began keeping track. Indeed, the species has been increasing in number throughout its range over the last 50 years. At the Farallones the numbers increased rapidly from high counts of 500 animals in the early 1970s up to 1,300 to 1,400 by 1974; by the summer of 1984 nearly 6,000 individuals were counted! A threefold increase in numbers between 1978 and 1982 represents an increase in the number of immature sea lions migrating north; prior to 1978, only adult and subadult males moved northward.[1,2,3,7,42]

Why are California sea lions increasing? Three phenomena have each probably had an influence: 1) changing ocean temperatures, 2) the collapse of the sardine population, and 3) the 200-mile limit on foreign fishing. With the decline of the sardine fishery in the 1940s, several species that fed on sardines declined as well, including the northern sea lion. Perhaps the reduction of northern sea lions and a reduced competition for resources allowed California sea lions to increase and expand northward.[1]

In 1977 the federal government imposed a 200-mile fishing limit on the foreign harvest of Pacific whiting. It has been suggested that this fishery competed with the sea lions and the subsequent increase reflects the increased availability of whiting in the Gulf of the Farallones. However, numbers have declined radically since 1984; in 1985 the peak count was less than 1,000. It is likely that the high numbers in 1984 were associated with El Niño warm waters and subsequent declines reflect decreasing water temperatures.[4,42]

On Point Reyes, thorough surveys from 1982 to early 1984 found a maximum of 763 animals. Seasonal peaks in numbers in 1983 seemed to coincide with southward migration in March, northward migration in September, and the herring run in Tomales Bay in late December. In 1984, when unusually high numbers visited the Seashore, the high numbers lasted from May through August, but then peaked again during the winter herring run.[7]

Northern Sea Lion

Scanning the sea lion herd through binoculars, amidst the dark roan Californias, we notice some very blonde individuals, with larger pectoral fins and shorter noses that give their faces a puggish expression. These are the northern sea lions, the rarer species that shares the haulout with its southern cousins.

Concurrent with an increase in California sea lions, northern sea lions have declined in California over the last 50 or more years, a pattern that has been mirrored at the Farallones and Point Reyes. At the Farallones, a population of 700 to 900 animals present in the 1920s and 1930s had declined to 100 to 200 by the 1970s. On the mainland, at Point Reyes, the population is smaller still; fewer than twenty animals have been counted in recent years. This small herd is composed mostly of females and young males that stay year round; adult males visit only during the breeding season. Although there have been reports

Northern sea lion

of pups at Point Reyes in the past (1979), it appears that the Headlands now serve only as a haulout site.[2,7]

The reasons for the decline in the local northern sea lion population are not well understood. The Farallones population has many premature births, high pup mortality, and low pregnancy rates, conditions that may be related to bacterial or viral infections. Shootings of northern sea lions by fishermen have also been noted. Other factors contributing to the decline may include competition with the increasing California sea lion population, environmental contamination (organochlorine residues), changing ocean temperatures, and the collapse of the sardine population.[2,27]

Northern Fur Seal

Although seldom seen from shore, fur seals are fairly common visitors to the Gulf of the Farallones. Numbers have apparently increased since the early 1970s when sightings were rare. Most of these individuals are adult females and juveniles.

Historically, fur seals were abundant; in the 3 years of 1810 to 1812, over 70,000 skins were taken from the Farallon Islands. Many authors assign the pristine Farallon population to the southern fur seals; however, the establishment of a breeding colony of northern fur seals south of the Farallones at San Miguel Island in 1965 suggests that this species may have been the original inhabitants of the Farallones. Sightings of tagged animals at

Cordell Banks and the Farallones indicate that the local fur seals are from San Miguel Island rather than wanderers from Alaska. Although most of the animals seen at the Farallones are females and juveniles, adult males are often seen at Cordell Banks. Occasional visits to the Farallones by adult males in early summer lend hope to the establishment of a future breeding population in the Gulf of the Farallones.[39, 40, 46, 49]

WHALES: Baleen and Toothed

At the Point Reyes Lighthouse, after a winter rain in mid-January, the ocean air can be brilliantly clear, the Farallones stand crisply on the horizon, and the water's surface is calm, an almost tropical blue. People stand on the overlook scanning the sea with binoculars or naked eyes; quiet, expectant, hopeful. Then, after long silence, someone shouts "there" and points to a cloudy mist about 100 yards off the Lighthouse. Everyone turns and sees a gray back with knuckled vertebrae arc through the water. Soon another gray whale blows and arcs, but this one raises its flukes, eliciting a series of "ahhs" from the assembled folk. As the whale dives, a calm slick is left on the surface of the sea, a whale "footprint." Soon the ocean is alive with blows, flukes, and even breaching bodies of gray whales. Everyone is shouting "there" and "wow" together; a large pod is rounding the Point en route to Baja.

BALEEN WHALES

Gray Whale

Point Reyes, jutting westward into the roiling Pacific, is one of the best sites in California to experience the gray whale on its long journey from the nutrient-rich feeding grounds in the Gulf of Alaska to the breeding bays in Baja and western Mexico. The gray whale is the symbolic animal of Point Reyes. Perhaps no other sight is as evocative of Point Reyes as a crowd of sweatered strangers, huddled shoulder to shoulder behind a granodiorite conglomerite windbreak, pointing and cheering as the brow of a gray whale breaks the surface and its vapor spout vanishes in the spray above the surging ocean swells.

Of all the great whales, the California gray whale occurs in the shallowest water. This primitive, barnacled bottom-feeder hugs the shoreline on its southward migration toward Baja. By late November we see the first spouts; these early migrants are mostly pregnant females traveling alone. They will be followed in December and January by pods of two or more adult males, nonpregnant females and immatures. The peak of migration is usually within a week of New Year's Day, but this varies considerably from year to year. During peak movement, up to 100 whales a day are counted from the Lighthouse, and up to 60 a day from the Farallones. Undoubtedly, many individuals go by undetected. Most of the population has passed by late January and stragglers are spotted irregularly into February.[27]

Northward-moving animals seem to pass our coast in two pulses. The early pulse (February–March) includes mostly whales that are not accompanied by calves, presumably adult males, pregnant females, and juveniles. Most of these animals may be well offshore, several miles out, though some come in quite close, just below the coastal headlands. In early March 1977, we watched a pair mating very nearshore just below the Lighthouse. We could see the phallus as the male floated alongside his mate; they joined quietly, breathing on the surface, planting the seed that would take 11 months to grow to its 1-ton birth weight. The mother would travel into the Gulf of Alaska and back to Baja (nearly 10,000 miles) before giving birth to the calf conceived at Point Reyes.

Gray whale and calf

The second northward migratory pulse (April–May) is composed mostly of females with newborn calves. Although cow/calf pairs are seen at the Farallon Islands, most of these pairs usually move very close to shore. In April 1980, I saw a large mother with her smaller calf (one-third the size of the mother) surfacing and blowing together within the breakers at Limantour, moving languidly northward along the edge of Drake's Bay. The inshore movement of the vulnerable cow/calf pairs may serve to afford some protection from predators. Cows and calves may head into the breakers to avoid attacks by killer whales.[2, 34, 43]

Scammon reported that, originally, northward migration of cows with newborn calves was very close to shore, but that they shifted their path farther offshore to avoid the threat of coastal whaling stations. From the late 1800s until the early 1970s, a period that encompasses commercial whaling along the California coast, it was commonly believed that the northward migration occurred farther offshore. As recently as 1971, mammalogists claimed that "the route taken by females with calves during spring migration is unknown" but that they "apparently travel offshore." Recent studies show that cow/calf pairs are again hugging the coast.[9, 43, 44, 45]

Since 1970, small numbers of gray whales (two or three) have been spending spring and summer around the Farallones. Interestingly, these are often recognized as the same individuals in successive years. Indeed, grays have been recorded in the Gulf of the Farallones during every month of the year, though they are exceedingly rare in the fall period of warm water, especially October.[2, 27]

The original size of the eastern Pacific gray whale population is estimated at about 30,000 animals, but by 1900 it was considered near extinction. The gray whale population has been increasing since it received international protection in 1947. Recent estimates place the population at 12,000 to 17,000 individuals. With an increase in the Pacific population, there has been a concurrent increase in sightings from Point Reyes, since virtually the entire population passes these shores in migration.[33]

Blue Whale

Like the grizzly bear and tule elk, blue whales symbolize the abundance of life that graced coastal California in the early days. As recently as 1874, it seems that blue whales occurred "at all seasons on the coasts of California. During the months of May to September they are often found in large numbers close to shore, at times playing about the ships at anchor, near capes, or islands."[45] Blues were hunted to near extinction in the last half of the nineteenth and the first half of the twentieth centuries. By the mid-1960s the world population was thought to be reduced to less than 1,000 individuals, making it one of the most critically endangered cetaceans in the world. Blues killed off the coast in the 1950s and 1960s (mostly in September and October) were probably southward migrants. Their near-absence from the Gulf of the Farallones during the 1970s ended with a sighting near the North Farallones in October 1977. None was seen again until late July 1981, an observation that was followed by four others that fall. Increasing numbers have been seen in each subsequent year. In the summer and fall of 1986, boat and aerial surveys estimated at least 20 to 25 blue whales in the Gulf of the Farallones, with highest concentrations directly off Point Reyes (near Cordell Banks) and just west of the Farallones. In early October 1986, 40 blues were spotted at the Southeast Farallon Island. In September 1986, up to six were seen clearly from the Point Reyes Lighthouse. Although most sightings occur in the months from July to October, beginning in 1986 spring and summer records began accumulating. This dramatic increase in blue whale sightings may foreshadow an ongoing increase in the blue whale population in the Gulf of the Farallones. The possibility of seeing the blow of the largest mammal ever to grace the earth will increase tenfold the excitement of gazing out over the Pacific from the Point Reyes Lighthouse.[15, 23, 27, 42, 51]

Fin Whale

Although rarely encountered at Point Reyes, the fin whale uses central California as a major summering ground. Historically it is the most abundant baleen whale off the California coast in spring and summer. (The wintering grounds reportedly extend south

Whale Bones

In our discussion of geology (Chapter 2) we invoke the metaphor of the Point Reyes peninsula as a granitic whale. Ironically, this metaphor becomes personified not in the peninsula's granite but in the more recent Miocene formations in the coastal cliffs at Bolinas and at Drake's Estero.

In 1976, College of Marin students and teachers discovered fossil whale bones in the Bolinas Headlands. By 1984, a nearly complete fossil whale had been excavated from the site. Preliminary work identified the bones as those of a baleen whale about six million years old. Subsequent searches in Drake's Estero came across "a plethora of additional fossil whale bones."[13]

These findings are significant because in general few fossil remains are found on the west coast. The whale graveyard at Drake's Estero suggests that during the late Miocene and early Pliocene epochs, when the rocks of Point Reyes might have been 80 miles to the south and the sea temperatures warmer, they were the site of the birth and death of whales in some shallow lagoon. As these bones are examined and classified they will contribute to our sparse knowledge of cetacean evolution and taxonomy, as well as provide insight into the marine environment of the Late Tertiary period.

of Point Reyes, from Big Sur south to Cabo San Lucas.) Whaling records from the Golden Gate Fishing Company show that "finbacks" were the most frequently taken species: 1,054 were killed in the Gulf of the Farallones from 1956 through 1969. Fins still occur in large numbers far offshore, especially from May through July. An occasional coastal stray is reported from the Point Reyes Lighthouse. Recent sightings from the Farallon Islands are scattered from early April to early September, with pods of up to six animals counted.[2, 33, 42]

Sei Whale

Similar to the more common finback, the sei whale was also taken in by the killer boats of the Golden Gate Fishing Company, with 379 recorded. These are the fastest swimmers of the great whales and their oil content is relatively small, two factors that delayed the pressures of commercial whaling but failed to protect the population from a dangerous decline. In these waters, seis feed on surface plankton and small schooling fish such as anchovies and sardines. The distribution is similar to the fin whale, breeding farther south in winter and shifting northward in summer. Recent sightings are few, with only two records from the Farallones: June 29, 1972 and June 10, 1974.[2, 16, 33, 42]

Minke Whale

A small whale of immense beauty and spiritual power (a cetacean Merlin), the minke whale is rare in these waters. In temperate waters it may occur in any season. Although minkes may approach shore and even enter bays and estuaries, the only local records are of individuals from the Farallones: June 19, 1976; June 23, 1984; September 17, 1983; September 19, 1976; September 25, 1984; November 1, 1984; February 4, 1976; and one at the Cordell Banks on August 5, 1982.[27,42,54]

Humpback Whale

Our boat rocks in the Pacific swell, within sight of the Point Reyes Headlands; the drone of the fog horn is muffled by the mist and the motor's hum. Having seen a whale spout 200 feet off starboard a few minutes earlier, we stand on the prow, hands on our binoculars, eyes squinting, expectant. Then, surprisingly close, a huge bulk (45 feet long, perhaps 18 tons) propels itself nearly out of the water, vertically, seeming to defy all physical laws, spins and splashes on the surface, flooding the deck and the delighted whalewatchers with spray. Suddenly, two more giants emerge, mimicking the first and causing a boatload of enchanted naturalists to cheer in spontaneous unison. This is the humpback, with its long wide pectoral fins, the most acrobatic of the great whales.

*   *   *

Of all the species occurring in the Gulf of the Farallones, humpbacks are perhaps the most seasonal. Their occurrence corresponds to the "Oceanic phase" of warm water in the fall. Interestingly, this is the season when gray whales are least likely to be seen. Although less coastal than the gray, humpbacks are occasionally seen from land. They are an acrobatic species, sometimes propelling their great hulks well out of the water under the power of their long pectoral fins. A whale seen from the shore of Point Reyes in September or October is most likely a humpback. However, the dates of fall occurrence vary annually, extending from early August through late November.[2,23,24,26,27]

Scammon's description of humpbacks as "scattered over the sea as far as the eye can discern from the masthead," compared with the meager pods encountered in recent years, if accurate, gives an indication of the depredation the population suffered during the first half of the twentieth century. Because of its habit of moving fairly nearshore, humpbacks were one of the most heavily harvested species by the shore stations. The Golden Gate Fishing Company took 841 humpbacks during their 13 years of operation, the second most commonly killed species.[16,48]

In recent years, humpbacks have been fairly common during fall (August through September), but rare in spring. Encouragingly, spring sightings at the Farallon Islands have been increasing since the first reports in 1977. Humpbacks were seen fairly commonly in June 1986. Fall surveys in the Gulf of the Farallones in 1986 estimated about 100 animals, with most in the region between Point Reyes and Fanny Shoal.[15, 42, 51]

Beaked Whales

Beaked whales belong to a poorly known family (Ziphidae) that apparently ranges far out to sea, beyond the continental shelf. Three species have occurred at Point Reyes when they washed up on the beach: Stejneger's beaked whale, one found dead at Limantour, June 13, 1974; Hubb's beaked whale at Drake's Bay, 1950; and Cuvier's beaked whale, one found dead at Stinson Beach, August 26, 1983, another at Limantour, November 24, 1981, and a skull recovered at Santa Maria Creek, January 18, 1986.[16, 54]

TOOTHED WHALES

Sperm Whale

Sperm whales occur in deep waters beyond the continental shelf. Large numbers were taken by commercial whalers off this coast until 1969. There are a few recent records from the Farallones, as follows: two, a cow with calf, on May 15, 1970; one on June 25, 1982. A calf washed ashore on South Beach at Point Reyes in June 1991.[2, 42]

Pygmy Sperm Whale

This little-known species probably occurs beyond the continental shelf; therefore, beached individuals are the only occurrences likely here. One washed up on the beach at Point Reyes in late December, 1968; its stomach contained many squid beaks, indicative of deep-water habitat. Another washed up on Stinson Beach, October 12, 1986, and died shortly thereafter.[54]

Harbor Porpoise

Occasionally, when standing on shore and studying the calm waters of Drake's or Bolinas bays, the observer will glimpse a blunt, triangular fin and a small, brownish back arch slowly through the water's surface. With patience, one may spot the animal again as it slowly resurfaces farther along the shoreline. Unlike other porpoises and dolphins, this small, secretive species never leaps from the water or bow-rides ships. It is the shyest of the breed.

Despite its cautious behavior, the harbor porpoise has suffered extreme depredation at the hands of humans, particularly in recent years. Harbor porpoise suffer high mortality as the result of drowning in gill nets, long curtains of eight-inch mesh monofilament (nylon), hung vertically in nearshore waters to catch halibut (and other fish), but indiscriminately responsible for the death of many species of marine birds and mammals. Since monitoring of the beaches of San Mateo, San Francisco, and Marin counties began in 1983, annual mortality has ranged from 23 to 43 harbor porpoise per year with 200 to 300 per year taken along the central California coast. Interestingly, mortality increases in September and October; whether that reflects an increase in the local population or increased use of gill nets during those months is, as yet, unknown. Nor do we know what proportion of gill net-related mortality is detected or what percentage of the population is falling prey to this method of fishery. Various agencies are currently trying to work out an equitable solution to the problem.[21]

Harbor porpoise

The most frequently sighted ocean cetacean in the Gulf of the Farallones is usually seen singly or in pairs, though occasionally family groups or pods of up to 30 animals have been reported. Harbor porpoise is a cold-water, inshore species, occurring in the shallow water mostly within the 30-fathom contour. Observers on the Farallones patrol report most sightings between April and August, the period of cold water upwelling. Sightings of large groups (25 to 35 animals) apparently feeding at the Cordell Banks in mid-September are of interest. Perhaps they herd there during the warm-water months. I saw two full-sized harbor porpoise with a very small individual in Bolinas Bay in August 1975, indicating that they calf in the inshore waters at Point Reyes.[25, 30, 51]

Dietary studies show that although many species of fish are taken, most are open-water or inshore schooling species, with rockfish and anchovy being favored, at least in spring and early summer.[29]

North Pacific Pilot Whale

A pod of 10 pilot whales was observed from the Point Reyes Lighthouse on January 19, 1985. Interestingly, this gregarious species is known to congregate near shore during winter months when squid are spawning. The similarity between the pilot whale and false killer whale casts doubt on any sight record. Pilot whales commonly range to 40°N latitude and false killers commonly range only to about 30°N; therefore, one is probably more likely to encounter the former at Point Reyes, which is at 38°N.[33, 37, 50]

Orca (Killer whale)

Orcas occur rarely in these waters, but it is likely that numbers will increase as numbers of pinnipeds, the favored food of the orca, increase. In addition to seals and sea lions, orcas prey on cetaceans; baby gray whales are particular targets along the Pacific coast. On Point Reyes Bird Observatory's cruises from the Golden Gate to Southeast Farallon Island, orcas were sighted on only 2 of 263 censuses. Most sightings occur from mid-May to early December with a cluster of October records. A pod of 50 orcas at the Cordell Banks on November 2, 1986 was the largest group seen south of Puget Sound in recent memory and is suspected of being from that population. Records outside this time period include: 3 or 4 seen on February 11, 1980, about 10 miles due northwest of Point Reyes; 10 heading south past the Farallones on February 12, 1980; 6 on April 16, 1977; and a family group of 7 on May 7, 1976. To generalize, although there seems to be some seasonal shift in distribution, orcas, though rare in the waters of Point Reyes, may occur at any time of year.[2, 9, 25, 34]

Northern Right Whale Dolphin

This sleek, thin-bodied, gregarious species, with no dorsal fin, tends to associate with white-sided dolphin, though the latter is much more likely to be encountered in the Gulf of the Farallones. Although most likely to ride a ship's bow, it has been reported riding the pressure waves of gray whales! Most sightings of this dolphin off the central California coast are from May to September, and most are in very deep water. The few records from the Gulf of the Farallones include: "summer 1963" at Farallon Islands; some associating with Risso's dolphins west of the Farallones on June 17, 1986; 7 on October 24, 1982 at Cordell Banks; 20 in deep water northwest of Point Reyes on November 14, 1985 and 4 on November 20, 1985.[16, 33, 42, 51]

Pacific White-sided Dolphin

The Pacific white-sided dolphin, an animal of temperate latitudes, might occur in the Gulf of the Farallones at any time of year. Numbers tend to diminish in southern California by the end of May, when it is assumed they disperse northward for the summer. Traveling in large herds, they frequent waters from the edge of the continental shelf landward, often associating with sea lions. To see a large herd of white-sideds moving swiftly through the water, surfacing and blowing in perfect unison, is an awesome experience. The movement is perfectly synchronized to the human eye, rivaled only by the shimmering aerial display of a flock of shorebirds over a winter shore.[33]

The few sightings indicate that white-sideds are rather uncommon in the Gulf of the Farallones; but, after harbor porpoise and Dall's porpoise, it is the third most likely to be seen of the small cetaceans. It was seen only once (a pod of 6 on June 9, 1974, 30 kilometers west of the Golden Gate) by Point Reyes Bird Observatory observers out of 263 census trips to Southeast Farallon Island. Seasonal occurrence is difficult to assess; a winter record on February 9, 1970 suggests they occur during cold-water months; however, more than 150 seen near Cordell Banks on September 23, 1982 and 30 in deep water just north of Point Reyes on November 14, 1985 were probably warm-water occurrences.[25, 42, 51, 54]

Dall's Porpoise

Out of nowhere, a group of six or eight Dall's will appear on the prow of a fast-moving boat, crisscrossing the wake, weaving over and under one another in a fluid braid, then vanishing as quickly as they arrived into the ocean's charcoal swells. This is a small, stout animal, about six feet long, with a striking black-and-white pattern and a blunt, triangular dorsal fin. Dall's is a cold-water species that reportedly feeds primarily on squid; however, stomach contents from north-central California showed open-water schooling fish (Pacific hake and Pacific tomcod) as favored items. Sometimes they are encountered quite near shore and there seems to be a shoreward movement in autumn. Point Reyes lies near the southern edge of their range (though seasonally some will wander south to Baja), which extends north to the Bering Strait. Records indicate that it is a year-round resident in the vicinity of the Farallones, and during the 1970s Point Reyes Bird Observatory found it to be the second most common cetacean (after harbor porpoise) between San Francisco and Southeast Farallon Islands. It is the most frequently seen porpoise or dolphin around the Cordell Banks.[17, 29, 53]

Risso's Dolphin

Risso's dolphin, which probably feeds almost entirely on squid, is considered a pelagic (deep-water) species, and is most often encountered in warmer waters. The only record at Point Reyes is of a carcass found dead on the mudflat at the south end of Tomales Bay, October 26, 1978. Its occurrence here will most likely coincide with warm-water temperatures from late spring through fall. Most observations from the Gulf of the Farallones are clustered in May and June. Occasionally it is sighted from the Farallones, as when a chorus line of 50 Rissos cavorted on May 3, 1986. Another was found dead there on May 20, 1973. On June 17, 1986, hundreds were seen west of the islands. There is also a cluster of fall records between late October and mid-November from the Farallones and at the Cordell Banks where 80 to 100 Rissos, some consorting with humpback whales, were observed on October 24, 1982.[17, 30, 42, 54]

Common Dolphin

The common dolphin is a gregarious, warm-water species that takes a seasonal variety of prey, but often associates with schooling tuna. Point Reyes is at the northern boundary of its usual distribution, but most sightings are south of Point Conception. According to one source, they ranged northward to central California "until the turn of the century."[39] Whether their subsequent rarity reflects a southward shift of the population, decreasing seawater temperatures, or a decrease in the size of the population are moot points. Common dolphins still occur in these waters occasionally. Most encounters are during periods of warm water from late August to early November. Most impressive was a herd of 150 at Southeast Farallon Island on September 26, 1985.[42]

REFERENCES

1. Ainley, D. G., and T. J. Lewis. 1974. The history of the Farallon Island marine bird populations, 1854–1972. *Condor* 76: 432-446.

2. Ainley, D. G., H. R. Huber, R. P. Henderson, and T. James Lewis. 1977. Studies of marine mammals at the Farallon Islands, California, 1970–1975. *Final Report to U.S. Marine Mammal Commission.* Bolinas, Calif.: Point Reyes Bird Observatory.

3. Ainley, D. G., C. S. Strong, H. R. Huber, T. J. Lewis, and S. H. Morrell. 1981. *Predation by Sharks on Pinnipeds at the Farallon Islands.* California Department of Fish and Game Fishery Bulletin 78.

4. Ainley, D. G., H. R. Huber, and K. M. Bailey. 1982. *Population Fluctuations of California Sea Lion and the Pacific Whiting Fishery off Central California.* California Department of Fish and Game Fishery Bulletin 80(2).

5. Allen, S. G. 1985. Harbor seals at Point Reyes. *Point Reyes Bird Observatory Newsletter* 68.

6. Allen, S. G. 1987. Harbor seals and northern elephant seals in Point Reyes. *Proceedings of the Symposium on Current Research Topics in the Marine Environment.*

7. Allen, S. G., and H. R. Huber. 1984. Pinniped assessment in Point Reyes, California, 1983–1984. *Final Report to Point Reyes–Farallon Islands National Marine Sanctuary.* Bolinas, Calif.: Point Reyes Bird Observatory.

8. Allen, S. G., S. C. Peaslee, and H. R. Huber. 1986. A colony of elephant seals on Point Reyes peninsula, California. *Final Report to the Point Reyes–Farallon Islands National Marine Sanctuary.* Bolinas, Calif.: Point Reyes Bird Observatory.

9. Baldridge, A. 1974. *Migrant Gray Whales with Calves and Sexual Behavior of Gray Whales in the Monterey Area of Central California, 1967–1973.* California Department of Fish and Game Fishery Bulletin 72.

10. Bartholomew, G. A., and C. L. Hubbs. 1960. Population growth and seasonal movements of the northern elephant seal, *Mirounga augustirostris. Mammalia* 24: 313-324.

11. Bolin, R. L. 1938. Reappearance of the southern sea otter along the California coast. Journal of Mammalogy 19: 301-306.

12. Bonnot, P. 1951. The sea lions, seals, and sea otter of the California coast. *California Fish and Game* 37: 371-388.

13. Chan, G. L. 1985. Preliminary investigation of fossil whales in the Point Reyes peninsula, Marin County, California. *Proposal to National Park Service.* Point Reyes, Calif.: Point Reyes National Seashore.

14. Chapman, D. G. 1981. Can marine mammals survive man? In *Coast Alert: Scientists Speak Out*, edited by T. C. Jackson and D. Reische. San Francisco: Friends of the Earth.

15. Cubbage, J. C., J. Calambokidis, K. C. Balcomb, and G. H. Steiger. 1987. Humpback whales in the Gulf of the Farallones National Marine Sanctuary: report of ongoing research. *Proceedings of the Symposium on Current Research Topics in the Marine Environment.*

16. Daugherty, A. E. 1972. *Marine Mammals of California.* California Department of Fish and Game.

17. Dohl, T. P., M. L. Bonnell, R. C. Guess, K. I. Briggs. 1982. *Marine Mammal and Seabird Study, Central and Northern California.* Santa Cruz, Calif.: Santa Cruz Center for Coastal Marine Studies.

18. Faurot, E. R., J. A. Ames, and D. P. Costa. 1986. Analysis of Sea Otter, *Enhydra lutris,* scats collected from a California haulout site. *Marine Mammal Science 2.*

19. Fellers, G. M., and J. Dell'Osso. 1986. *An Annotated Checklist of Mammals: Point Reyes National Seashore.* Point Reyes: Coastal Parks Association.

20. Heizer, R. F., and A. B. Elsasser. 1980. *The Natural World of the California Indians.* California Natural History Guides 46. Berkeley: University of California Press.

21. Heneman, B. 1984. Gill net news. *Point Reyes Bird Observatory Newsletter 66.*

22. Heneman, B. 1987. Gill nets: the search for solutions. *Point Reyes Bird Observatory Newsletter 75.*

23. Huber, H. R., D. G. Ainley, R. J. Boekelheide, R. P. Henderson, and B. Bainbridge. 1981. Studies of marine mammals at the Farallon Islands, California, 1979–1980. *Report to Marine Mammal Commission 79/06.* Bolinas, Calif.: Point Reyes Bird Observatory.

24. Huber, H. R., R. J. Boekelheide, T. McElroy, R. P. Henderson, C. Strong, D. G. Ainley. 1982. Studies of marine mammals at the Farallon Islands, California, 1980–1981. *Report to National Marine Fisheries Service.* Bolinas, Calif.: Point Reyes Bird Observatory.

25. Huber, H. R., D. G. Ainley, and S. H. Morrell. 1982. Sightings of cetaceans in the Gulf of the Farallones, California, 1971–1979. *California Fish and Game* 68(3).

26. Huber, H. R., C. Beckham, J. Nisbet, A. Rovetta, and J. Nusbaum. 1985. Studies of marine mammals at the Farallon Islands, 1982–1983. *Report to National Marine Fisheries Service.* Bolinas, Calif.: Point Reyes Bird Observatory.

27. Huber, H. R., L. Fry, A. Rovetta, S. Johnson, and J. Nusbaum. 1985. Studies of marine mammals at the Farallon Islands, 1983–1985. *Final Report to National Marine Fisheries Service,* Southwest Fisheries Center. Bolinas, Calif.: Point Reyes Bird Observatory.

28. Inman, A. E. 1969. Reintroduction of sea otters at Point Reyes. *Memorandum to Superintendent.* Point Reyes National Seashore, Point Reyes, Calif.

29. Jones, R. E. 1981. Food habits of smaller marine mammals from northern California. *Proceedings of the California Academy of Sciences.*

30. LaBarr, M. S., and D. G. Ainley. 1985. Depth distribution of harbor porpoise off central California. *Report to National Marine Fisheries Service.* Bolinas, Calif.: Point Reyes Bird Observatory.

31. LeBoeuf, B. J. 1981. Mammals. In *The Natural History of Año Nuevo,* edited by LeBoeuf and Kaza. Pacific Grove: Boxwood Press.

32. LeBoeuf, B. J., D. G. Ainley, and T. J. Lewis. 1974. Elephant seals on the Farallones: population structure of an incipient colony. *Journal of Mammalogy* 55: 370-385.

33. Leatherwood, S., R. R. Reeves, W. F. Perrin, and W. E. Evans. 1982. *Whales, Dolphins, and Porpoises of the Eastern Pacific and Adjacent Arctic Waters: A Guide to Their Identification.* National Oceanic and Atmospheric Administration Technical Report, NMFS Circular 444.

34. Morejohn, G. V. 1968. A killer whale–gray whale encounter. *Journal of Mammalogy* 49: 327-328.

35. Miller, T. 1975. *The World of the California Gray Whale*. Santa Ana: Baja Trail Publication.

36. National Coastal Ecosystem Team. 1981. *Ecological Characterization of the Central and Northern California Coastal Region. Vol. 4*. U.S. Fish and Wildlife Service.

37. Norris, K. S., and J. H. Prescott. 1961. *Observations on Pacific Cetaceans in California and Mexican Waters*. University of California Publications in Zoology 63.

38. Ogden, A. 1941. *The California Sea Otter Trade: 1784–1848*. Berkeley: University of California Press.

39. Orr, R. T. 1972. *Marine Mammals of California*. California Natural History Guides 29. Berkeley: University of California Press.

40. Peterson, R. S., B. J. LeBoeuf, and R. L. DeLong. 1968. Fur seals from the Bering Sea breeding in California. *Nature* 219: 899–901.

41. Point Reyes Bird Observatory. 1985. *The Impacts of the T/V Puerto Rican Oil Spill on Marine Bird and Mammal Populations in the Gulf of the Farallones, 6–19 November 1984*. Special Scientific Report.

42. Point Reyes Bird Observatory. 1967–1987. Field notes and journal entries. Typescript.

43. Poole, M. M. 1984. Migration corridors of gray whales along the central California Coast, 1980–1982. In *The Gray Whale*, by McJones and S. L. Swartz. New York: Academic Press.

44. Rice, D. W., and A. A. Wolman, 1971. *The Life History and Ecology of the Gray Whale (Eschrichtius robustus)*. Special Publication No. 3, American Society of Mammalogists.

45. Scammon, C. M. 1874. *The Marine Mammals of the Northwestern Coast of North America*. San Francisco: John Carmany and Sons.

46. Scheffer, V. 1958. *Seals, Sea Lions, and Walruses: A Review of the Pinnipedia*. Stanford, Calif.: Stanford University Press.

47. Scofield, W. L. 1941. The sea otters of California did not reappear. *California Fish and Game* 27 (1).

48. Scofield, W. L. 1954. *California Fishing Ports*. California Department of Fish and Game Fishery Bulletin 96.

49. Starks, E. C. 1922. Records and capture of fur seals on land in California. *California Fish and Game* 8.

50. Timossi, I. 1985. Personal communication.

51. Webber, M. A., and S. M. Cooper. 1983. *Autumn Sightings of Marine Mammals and Birds near Cordell Banks, California 1981–82*. Walnut Creek, Calif.: Cordell Banks Expeditions.

52. Wilson, S. 1984. California's surviving sea otters: still threatened. *Pacific Discovery* 37 (3).

53. Yocom, C. F. 1946. Notes on Dall's porpoise off California. *Journal of Mammalogy* 27.

54. Zoological museum specimens at Museum of Vertebrate Zoology, University of California, Berkeley and at California Academy of Sciences, San Francisco.

Tomales Bay looking west toward Inverness Ridge.

SPECIES LIST 1.
Selected Native Plants of the Point Reyes Peninsula.

More than 800 species of plants occur on the peninsula, but about 30% of those, including common species like *Eucalyptus*, Monterey pine, poison hemlock, and ice plant were "introduced" subsequent to European colonization. For a comprehensive list of the plants, both native and alien, refer to *Point Reyes National Seashore Plant Checklist*. 1990. Gary Fellers, Virginia Norris, and Wilma Follette. Point Reyes National Seashore Association. A list of selected native plant species is given below. After the common name, some species are modified by letter codes that indicate local status, as follows: r = rare or restricted in distribution; * = Point Reyes is the only locale of occurrence in Marin County; e = endemic; known only from Point Reyes; s = southernmost station in distributional range; ? = status uncertain (occurrence reported, but not confirmed).

Common Name	Latin Name
Ferns and fern allies	
California maidenhair	*Adiantum jordanii*
Western five-finger	*Adiantum pedatum*
Coastal lady fern	*Athyrium filix-femina*
Deer fern	*Blechnum spicant*
Coastal wood fern	*Dryopteris arguta*
Spreading wood fern	*Dryopteris austriaca*
Goldenback fern	*Pityrogramma triangularis*
California polypody	*Polypodium californicum*
Leather fern	*Polypodium scouleri*
Western sword fern	*Polystichum munitum* (two varieties)
Western bracken fern	*Pteridium aquilinum*
Western chain fern	*Woodwardia fimbriata*
American water fern	*Azolla filiculoides*
Common horsetail	*Equisetum arvense*
Giant horsetail	*Equisetum telmateia* var. *braunii*
Wetland monocots: cat-tails, sedges, tules, rushes, etc.	
Common cat-tail	*Typha latifolia*
Bur-reed	*Sparganium eurycarpum*
Seep pondweed	*Potamogeton pectinatus*
Leafy pondweed	*Potamogeton foliosus*
Wigeon grass	*Ruppia maritima*
Eelgrass	*Zostera marina*
Surfgrass	*Phyllospadix torreyi*
Flowering quillwort	*Lilea scillioides*
Tall papyrus	*Cyperus eragrostris*
Three-square	*Scirpus americanus*
California bulrush	*Scirpus californicus*
Common tule	*Scirpus acutus*
Alkali bulrush	*Scirpus robustus*
California beaked-rush (r)	*Rhynchospora californica*
Sedges	*Carex* species (several rare species)
Duckweed	*Lemna minor*
Rushes	*Juncus* species
Wood-rush	*Luzula comosa*
Seaside arrowgrass	*Triglochin maritima*
Slender arrowgrass	*Triglochin concinna*

Grasses

Seaside bromegrass	*Bromus maritimus*
Large mountain bromegrass	*Bromus marginatus*
California bromegrass	*Bromus carinatus*
Narrow-flowered bromegrass	*Bromus vulgaris*
California fescue	*Festuca californica*
Red fescue	*Festuca rubra*
Idaho fescue	*Festuca idahoensis*
Pacific alkali grass	*Puccinellia grandis*
Mannagrass	*Glyceria* species
Nodding semaphore grass (r)	*Pleuropogan refractus*
Howell bluegrass	*Poa howellii*
Douglas bluegrass	*Poa douglasii*
Poa	*Poa confinis*
San Francisco bluegrass	*Poa unilateralis*
Saltgrass	*Distichlis spicata* (two varieties)
Oniongrass	*Melica* species
Gould's rye grass	*Elymus pacificus*
Blue wild-rye	*Elymus glaucus* (two varieties)
Wheat-like wildrye	*Elymus triticoides*
Vancouver wildrye	*Elymus vancouverensis*
American dune-grass	*Elymus mollis*
California bottlegrass (r)	*Elymus californicus*
Meadow barley	*Hordeum brachyantherum*
California barley	*Hordeum californicum*
Wall barley	*Hordeum glaucum*
June grass	*Koeleria macrantha*
Tall trisetum	*Trisetum canescens*
Slender hairgrass	*Deschampsia elongata*
Tufted hairgrass	*Deschampsia caespitosa* subsp. *holciformis*
Thurber's reedgrass (s,r)	*Calamagrostris crassiglumis*
Hall's bentgrass	*Agrostris halli*
Leafy bentgrass	*Agrostris diegoensis*
Seashore bentgrass	*Agrostris pallens*
Blasdale's bentgrass (s)	*Agrostris blasdalei*
Western bentgrass	*Agrostris exarata*
California bentgrass	*Agrostris densiflora*
Small-leaved bentgrass	*Agrostris microphylla*
Awned bentgrass (e,r)	*Agrostris clivola* var. *punta-reyensis*
Austral bentgrass	*Agrostris langligula* var. *australis*
Water foxtail (r)	*Aloplecurus aequalis* var. *sonomensis*
Alpine timothy	*Phleum alpinum*
Purple needlegrass	*Stipa pulchra*
Pacific cordgrass	*Spartina foliosa*
California vanilla grass	*Hierochloe occidentalis*
Canarygrass	*Phalaris californica*

Lilies, irises, orchids

Star lily	*Zigadenus fremontii*
Camass (s)	*Camassia quamash*

Soap plant	*Chlorogalum pomeridianum*
Coast onion	*Allium dichlamydeum*
Muilla (*)	*Muilla maritima*
Dwarf brodiaea	*Brodiaea coronaria* var. *macropoda*
Harvest brodiaea	*Brodiaea elegans*
Marsh triteleia	*Triteleia peduncularis*
Triteleia	*Triteleia laxa*
California tiger lily	*Lilium pardalinium*
Western lily (r)	*Lilium occidentale*
Fragrant fritillary (r)	*Fritillaria liliacea*
Mission bells	*Fritillaria affinis*
Hairy star tulip	*Calochortus tolmiei*
Coast trillium	*Trillium ovatum*
Giant wake-robin (?)	*Trillium chloropetalum*
Western Solomon's seal	*Smilacina racemosa* var. *amplexicaulis*
Slim Solomon's seal	*Smilacina stellata* var. *sessilifolia*
Pacific May-lily	*Maianthemum dilatatum*
Fairy bells	*Disporum hookeri*
Fairy lantern	*Disporum smithii*
Blue-eyed grass	*Sisyrinchium bellum*
Yellow-eyed grass	*Sisyrinchium californicum*
Ground iris	*Iris macrosiphon*
Douglas iris	*Iris douglasiana*
Stream orchis	*Epipactis gigantea*
White rein orchis	*Habenaria dilatata* var. *leucostachys*
Rein orchis	*Habenaria elegans* var. *maritima*
Lady's tresses	*Spiranthes romanzoffiana*
Rattlesnake plantain	*Goodyera oblongifolia*
Spotted coralroot (?)	*Corallorhiza maculata*
Striped coralroot	*Corallorhiza striata*

Ginger, nettle, buckwheat and goosefoot

Coast nettle	*Urtica californica*
Wild ginger	*Asarum caudatum*
Western knotweed	*Polygonum bistortoides*
Smartweed	*Polygonum amphibium* var. *emersum*
Marin knotweed (r)	*Polygonum marinense*
Dune knotweed	*Polygonum paronychia*
Water smartweed	*Polygonum punctatum*
Golden dock	*Rumex maritimus*
Western dock	*Rumex occidentalis*
Willow-leaved dock	*Rumex salicifolius*
Wild buckwheat	*Eriogonum latifolium* (two subspecies)
Spine-flower	*Chorizanthe cuspicata*
Sonoma spine-flower (r)	*Chorizanthe valida*
California saltbrush	*Atriplex californica*
Fathen	*Atriplex patula* (two varieties)
Soaproot	*Chenopodium californicum*
Coast goosefoot	*Chenopodium macrospermum*
Pickleweed	*Salicornia virginica*

Four-o'clocks, purslanes, and pinks

Yellow sand verbena	*Abronia latifolia*
Beach sand verbena	*Abronia umbellata*
Red maids	*Calandrinia ciliata* var. *menziesii*
Miner's lettuce	*Claytonia perfoliata*
Water-chickweed	*Montia fontana*
Indian lettuce	*Montia sibirica*
Spring snow	*Cerastium arvense*
Douglas' sandwort	*Minuartia douglasii*
Beach pearlwort	*Sagina crassicaulis*
Western pearlwort	*Sagina occidentalis*
Large campion	*Silene scouleri* subsp. *grandis*
Large-flowered sand spurry	*Spergularia macrotheca*
Chickweed	*Stellaria* (four native species)

Buttercups, larkspurs

California buttercup	*Ranunculus californicus* (two varieties)
Creeping buttercup	*Ranunculus flammula* var. *ovalis*
Aquatic buttercup (r)	*Ranunculus lobbi*
Prickle-fruited buttercup	*Ranunculus muricatus*
Tall buttercup	*Ranunculus orthorhynchus*
Small-flowered buttercup (s)	*Ranunculus uncinatus* var. *parviflorus*
Meadow rue	*Thalictrum polycarpum*
Columbine	*Aquilegia formosa* var. *truncata*
Red larkspur	*Delphinium nudicaule*
Coast larkspur	*Delphinium californicum*
Beautiful larkspur	*Delphinium decorum*
Yellow larkspur	*Delphinium luteum*

Poppies and mustards

Cream cups	*Platystemon californicus*
California meconella	*Meconella californica*
California poppy	*Eschscholzia californica*
Yellow cress	*Rorippa palustris* subsp. *occidentalis*
Milk maids	*Cardamine californica* (two varieties)
Bitter cress	*Cardamine oligosperma*
Coast rock cress (r)	*Arabis blepharophylla*
Tower mustard	*Arabis glabra*
Hairy rock cress	*Arabis hirsuta*
Douglas' wallflower	*Erysimum capitatum*
Coast wallflower	*Erysimum concinnum*
San Francisco wallflower (r)	*Erysimum franciscanum*
Peppergrass	*Lepidium lasiocarpum*
California mustard	*Thelypodium lasiophyllum*

Stonecrops, rockbreakers, and roses

Pacific stone-crop	*Sedum spathulifolium*
Rock lettuce	*Dudleya cymosa*
Sea lettuce	*Dudleya farinosa*
Brook foam	*Boykinia occidentalis*

Alum-root	*Heuchera* (two native species)
Woodland star	*Lithophragma heterophyllum*
Fringe-cups	*Tellima grandiflora*
Silverweed	*Potentilla* (two species)
California horkelia	*Horkelia californica*
Wedge-leaved horkelia (?)	*Horkelia cuneata* var. *sericea*
Point Reyes horkelia (r)	*Horkelia marinensis*
Wild strawberry	*Fragaria californica*
Beach strawberry	*Fragaria chiloensis*
Western lady's mantle	*Alchemilla occidentalis*
Wood rose	*Rosa gymnocarpa*

Peas

Bicolored lupine	*Lupinus bicolor* (three subspecies)
Summer lupine	*Lupinus formosus*
Sky lupine	*Lupinus nanus*
Small-anther lupine	*Lupinus polycarpus*
Succulent lupine	*Lupinus succulentus*
Showy indian clover (r) (?)	*Trifolium amoenum*
Clover	*Trifolium* (fourteen native species)
Lotus	*Lotus* (eight native species)
Hemp	*Psoralea orbicularis*
Rattleweed	*Astragalus nuttallii*
Marsh locoweed	*Astragalus pycnostachyus*
Vetch	*Vicia* (three or four native species)
Sweet pea	*Lathyrus* (four or five native species)

Oxalis, milkwort, starworts, meadowfoam, and sumac

Hairy wood sorrel	*Oxalis pilosa*
Milkwort	*Polygala californica*
Water starwort	*Callitriche heterophylla*
California water starwort	*Callitriche marginata*
Common meadowfoam	*Limnanthes douglasii* var. *douglasii*
Point Reyes meadowfoam (e,r)	*Limnanthes douglasii* var. *sulphurea*
Snow white meadowfoam	*Limnanthes douglasii* var. *nivea*
Poison oak	*Toxicodendron diversilobum*

Mallows, St. John's worts, rockroses, and loosestrife

Point Reyes checkerbloom (e)	*Sidalcea rhizomata*
Checkerbloom	*Sidalcea malvaeflora*
Tinker's penny	*Hypericum anagalloides*
Alkali heath	*Frankenia grandiflora*
Broom rose	*Helianthemum scoparium*
Blue violet	*Viola adunca*
Redwood violet	*Viola sempervirens*
Loose strife	*Lythrum hyssopifolia*

Evening primrose, elk clover, and parsley

Marsh willow herb	*Epilobium watsonii* var. *franciscanum*
Lovely clarkia	*Clarkia concinna*

Maritime godetia	*Clarkia davyi*
Farewell-to-spring	*Clarkia amoena* subsp. *amoena*
Evening primrose	*Oenothera hookeri*
Contorted sun cup	*Camissonia contorta* var. *stringulosa*
Small primrose	*Camissonia micrantha*
Beach evening primrose	*Camissonia cheiranthifolia*
Sun cups	*Camissonia ovata*
Elk clover	*Aralia californica*
Pennywort	*Hydrocotyle verticillata* var. *triradiata*
Marsh pennywort	*Hydrocotyle ranunculoides*
Footsteps-of-spring	*Sanicula arctopoides*
Pacific sanicle	*Sanicula crassicaulis*
Sweet cicily	*Osmorhiza chilensis*
Rattlesnake weed	*Daucus pusillus*
Squaw potato (r)	*Perideridia gairdneri*
Lovage	*Ligusticum apiifolium*
Water hemlock	*Cicuta bolanderi*
Water parsley	*Oenanthe sarmentosa*
Lileopsis	*Lilaeopsis occidentalis*

Primroses, thrifts, gentians, morning-glories, and phloxes

Wood angelica	*Angelica tomentosa*
Coast angelica	*Angelica hendersonii*
Cow parsnip	*Heracleum maximum*
Coyote thistle	*Eryngium armatum*
Chaffweed	*Centunculus minimus*
Star flower	*Trientalis latifolia*
Shooting star	*Dodecatheon hendersonii*
Sea thrift	*Armeria maritima*
Marsh rosemary	*Limonium californicum*
Gentian	*Gentian oregana*
Microcala	*Microcala quadrangularis*
Monterey centaury	*Centaurium muhlenbergii*
Beach morning glory	*Calystegia soldanella*
Western morning glory	*Calystegia occidentalis*
Dodder	*Cuscata salina*
Collomia	*Collomia heterophylla*
Phlox	*Phlox gracilis*
Blue coast gilia	*Gilia chamissonis*
Gilia (s)	*Gilia millefoliata*
Large-flowered linanthus (s)	*Linanthus grandiflorus*
Small-flowered linanthus (*)	*Linanthus parviflorus* var. *roseaceus*
Common linanthus	*Linanthus androsaceus*
Skunkweed	*Navarretia squarrosa*

Waterleafs and borages

Baby blue-eyes	*Nemophila manziensii* var. *menziesii*
Northcoast phacelia (r)	*Phacelia insularis* var. *continentis*
Fern phacelia	*Phacelia distans*
Stinging phacelia	*Phacelia malvifolia*
Yerba santa	*Eriodictyon californicum*

Heliotrope	*Heliotropium currassavicum*
Cryptantha	*Cryptantha* spp. (several species)
Forget-me-not	*Allocarya californica*
Fiddleneck	*Amsinckia intermedia*
Coast fiddleneck	*Amsinckia spectabilis*

Mints

Selfheal	*Prunella vulgaris* var. *atropurpurea*
Coast hedge nettle	*Stachys chamissonis*
Ridge hedge nettle	*Stachys rigida* var. *quercetorum*
Yerba buena	*Satureja douglasii*
Marsh mint	*Mentha arvensis*
Western pennyroyal (*)	*Mondarella villosa* var. *francisciana*
Curley-leaved mondarella (r)	*Mondarella undulata* var. *undulata*

Nightshades

Purple nightshade	*Solanum xanti*
Black nightshade	*Solanum americanum*

Figworts ("Scrophs")

Toad flax	*Linaria canadensis* var. *texana*
Chinese houses	*Collinsia heterophylla*
California bee plant	*Scrophularia californica*
Marsh monkeyflower	*Mimulus guttatus*
Musk flower	*Mimulus moschatus* var. *sessifolius*
Marsh speedwell	*Veronica scutellata*
American brooklime	*Veronica americana*
Wight's indian paintbrush	*Castilleja wightii*
Franciscan paintbrush	*Castilleja franciscana*
Point Reyes paintbrush (e,r)	*Castilleja leschkeana*
San Francisco owl's clover (r)	*Orthocarpus floribundus*
Owl's clover	*Orthocarpus* (eight other native species)
Point Reyes bird's beak (e,r)	*Cordylanthus maritimus* subsp. *palustris*

Plantains

Pacific seaside plantain	*Plantago maritima* ssp. *juncoides*
Mexican plantain	*Plantago hirtella* var. *galeottiana*
Annual coast plantain	*Plantago bigelovii*

Madder and gourds

Bedstraw	*Galium* spp. (four native species)
Wild cucumber	*Marah fabaceus*
Coast manroot	*Marah organus*

Bellflower and Sunflowers

Swamp harebell (*,r)	*Campanula californica*
Golden chrysopsis	*Chrysopsis villosa* var. *bolanderi*
Goldenrod	*Solidago* (four native species)
Beach aster	*Corethogyne californica* var. *obovata*
Common California aster	*Aster chilensis*
Seaside daisy	*Erigeron glaucus*

Supple daisy (r)	*Erigeron supplex*
California rayless daisy	*Erigeron inornatus* var. *viscidulus*
Narrow-leaved cudweed	*Filago gallica*
Erect evax	*Evax sparsiflora*
Cudweed	*Gnaphalium* (several species)
Pearly everlasting	*Anaphalis margaritacea*
Spiny cocklebur	*Xanthium spinosum*
Silver beachweed	*Franseria chamissonis*
Narrow-leaved mule's ears	*Wyethia angustifolia*
Bur marigold	*Bidens laevis*
Coast tarweed	*Hemizonia corymbosa*
Hayfield tarweed	*Hemizonia lutescens*
Tarweed (r)	*Hemizonia multicaulis*
Beach layia (r)	*Layia carnosa*
Tidy tips	*Layia platyglossa*
Goldfields	*Lasthenia* (five species)
Wooly sunflower	*Eriophylum lanatum* var. *arachnoideum*
Lizard tail	*Eriophylum staechadifolium* var. *artemisiaefolium*
Sneezeweed	*Helenium puberulum*
Point Reyes blennosperma (e,r)	*Blennosperma nanum* var. *robustum*
Mayweed	*Anthemis cotula*
Yarrow	*Achillea millefolium*
Common soliva	*Soliva sessilis*
California mugwort	*Artemesia douglasiana*
Groundsel	*Senecio aronicoides*
Franciscan thistle (r)	*Circium andrewsii*
Cobweb thistle	*Circium occidentale*
Chickory	*Cichorium intybus*
Marsh scorzonella	*Microseris paludosa*
Coast microseris	*Microseris bigelovii*
Narrow-leaved microseris	*Microseris linearifolia*
Tall milk aster	*Stephanomeria virgata*
Sow thistle (*)	*Sonchus oleraceus*
Western dandelion	*Agroseris* (three species)
Hawkweed	*(Hieracium albiflorum*

Native shrubs and trees

Western yew	*Taxus brevifolia*
Coast redwood (r)	*Sequoia sempervirens*
Bishop pine	*Pinus muricata*
Douglas fir	*Pseudotsuga menziesii*
Coulter willow	*Salix sitchensis*
Arroyo willow	*Salix lasiolepis*
Yellow willow	*Salix lucida* var. *lasiandra*
Sandbar willow	*Salix exigua*
Red willow	*Salix bonplandiana*
Red alder	*Alnus rubra*
California hazelnut	*Corylus californica*
Golden chinquapin	*Castanopsis chrysophylla*
Tanbark oak	*Lithocarpus densiflorus*

Coast live oak	*Quercus agrifolia* var. *frutescens*
Canyon live oak	*Quercus chrysolepus*
California wax-myrtle	*Myrica californica*
California bay	*Umbellaria californica*
Flowering currant	*Ribes sanguineum* var. *glutinosum*
Canyon gooseberry (s)	*Ribes menziesii*
Ocean spray	*Holodiscus discolor*
Toyon	*Heteromeles arbutifolia*
Service berry	*Amelanchier pallida*
Chamise	*Adenostoma fasciculatum*
Oso berry	*Osmaronia cerasiformis*
Bog lupine	*Lupinus polyphyllus* var. *grandifolius*
Coastal bush lupine	*Lupinus arboreus*
Point Reyes lupine (r)	*Lupinus tidestromii* var. *layneae*
Chamisso bush lupine (*)	*Lupinus chammissonis*
Big-leaf maple	*Acer macrophyllum*
California box elder	*Acer negrundo* var. *californicum*
California buckeye	*Aesculus californicus*
Coffee berry	*Rhamnus californica*
Sticky laurel	*Ceonothus velutinus* ssp. *hookeri*
Ceonothus or blue-blossom	*Ceonothus thyrsiflorus*
Glory mat	*Ceonothus gloriosus* var. *gloriosus*
Mount Vision ceonothus (e)	*Ceonothus gloriosus* var. *porrectus*
Blue gum	*Eucalyptus globulus*
Creek dogwood	*Cornus californica*
Silk-tassel bush	*Garrya elliptica*
Madrone	*Arbutus menziesii*
Kinnikinnick or Mt. Vision manzanita (s,*)	*Arctostaphylos uva-ursi*
Marin manzanita	*Arctostaphylos virgata*
Huckleberry manzanita (e)	*Arctostaphylos cushingiana*
Labrador tea	*Ledum glandulosum*
Salal	*Gaultheria shallon*
Huckleberry	*Vaccinium ovatum*
Bush monkeyflower	*Mimulus aurantiacus*
Red elderberry	*Sambucus callicarpa*
Blue elderberry	*Sambucus coerulea*
Snowberry	*Symphoricarpos rivularis*
Twinberry	*Lonicera involucrata*
California honeysuckle	*Lonicera hispidula* var. *vacillans*
Pacific gumplant	*Grindelia strica*
Gumweed	*Grindelia rubricaulis*
Gumplant (*)	*Grindelia arenicola*
Salt-marsh baccharis	*Baccharis douglasii*
Prostrate coyote bush	*Baccharis pilularis* var. *pilularis*
Coyote bush	*Baccharis pilularis* var. *consanguinea*
Mock heather	*Haplopappus ericoides*
Jaumea	*Jaumea carnosa*
Coast sagebrush	*Artemesia californica*
Artemesia	*Artemesia pycnocephala*

SPECIES LIST 2.
Major Marine Invertebrates of the Point Reyes Peninsula.

PORIFERA: sea sponges.

Common Name	Latin Name
Cork sponge	*Prosuberites* species
Calcareous sponge	*Leucosolenia eleanor*
Little white sponge	*Leucilla nuttingi*
Karatose sponge	*Aplysilla glacialis*
Skunk sponge	*Lissodendoryx* species
Red star sponge	*Ophlitaspongia pennata*
Purple haliclona	*Haliclona* species
Sharp-spined leuconia	*Leuconia heathi*
Yellow-boring sponge	*Cliona celata*
Red encrusting sponge	*Plocamia karykina*
Yellow nipple sponge	*Hymeniacidon* species
Polymastia	*Polymastia pachymastia*

CNIDERIANS: sea anemone and allies.

Tubularia hydroid	*Tubularia marina*
Orange-colored hydroid	*Garveia annulata*
Obelia	*Obelia* species
Sertularia	*Sertularia* species
Green's bushy hydroid	*Abientinaria greenii*
Giant ostrich-plume hydroid	*Aglaophenia struthionides*
Dainty ostrich-plume hydroid	*Aglaophenia latirostris*
Plumularia	*Plumularia* species
Cat's eye	*Pleurobrachia bachei*
Bell-shaped jellyfish	*Polyorchis* species
Striped jellyfish	*Chrysaora melanaster*
By-the-wind-sailor	*Velella velella*
Moon jelly	*Aurelia aurita*
Proliferating anemone	*Epiactus prolifera*
Giant green anemone	*Anthopleura xanthogrammica*
Aggregating anemone	*Anthopleura elegantissima*
Burrowing anemone	*Anthopleura artemisia*
Big red anemone	*Tealia lofotensis*
Plumose anemone	*Metridium senile*
Small red anemone	*Corynactus californica*
Solitary coral anemone	*Balanophyllia elegans*

BRYZOANS: the moss animals.

Several genera are common in the intertidal.

ECHINODERMS: sea stars, sea cucumbers, brittle stars, sea urchins.

Leather star	*Dermasterias imbricata*
Bat star	*Patiria miniata*
Red seastar	*Henricia leviuscula*

Dawson's sunstar	*Solaster dawsoni*
Six-rayed star	*Leptasterias hexactis*
Little six-rayed star	*Leptasterias pusilla*
Purple seastar	*Pisaster ochraceous*
Short-rayed seastar	*Pisaster brevispinus*
Common seastar	*Pisaster giganteus*
Twenty-rayed star	*Pycnopodia helianthoides*
Red sea cucumber	*Cucumaria miniata*
White sea cucumber	*Eupentacta quinquesemita*
Large sea cucumber	*Parastichopus californicus*
Synaptid sea cucumber	*Leptosynapta albicans*
Daisy brittle star	*Ophiopholis aculeata*
Little brittle star	*Amphipholis pugetana*
Western brittle star	*Amphiodia occidentalis*
Spiny brittle star	*Ophiothrix spiculata*
Purple sea urchin	*Stongylocentrotus pupuratus*
Red sea urchin	*Strongylocentrotus franciscanus*
Sand dollar	*Dendraster excentricus*

UROCHORDATES: the tunicates.

The tunicates, also known as sea squirts, though unknown to most people are one of the most common animals in the intertidal zone. Sea squirts occur most commonly in cold-water areas free from wave shock. Vast colonies grow in bays and harbors on pilings and docks. As filter feeders, they siphon detritus and help to clean the water. Commonly encountered genera are *Ascidia, Clavelina, Ciona* and *Styela.*

CRUSTACEANS: barnacles, shrimp, crabs, and allies.

Leaf barnacle	*Pollicipes polymerus*
Acorn barnacle	*Balanus glandula*
Subtidal acorn barnacle	*Balanus crenatus*
Thatched barnacle	*Balanus cariosus*
Great barnacle	*Balanus nubilus*
Rock louse	*Ligia occidentalis*
Isopod	*Idothea resecata*
Beach hopper	*Orchestoidea californiana*
Skeleton shrimp	*Caprella* species
Skeleton shrimp	*Metacaprella kennerlyi*
Eye-shaded shrimp	*Betaeus* species
Hairy crab	*Hapalogaster cavicauda*
Pebble crab	*Paraxanthias taylori*
Red copepod	*Tigriopus californicus*
Red copepod	*Clausidium vancouverense*
Parasitic copepod	*Mytilicola orientalis*
Broken-back shrimp	*Spirontocarius prionota*
Bay shrimp	*Crangon* species
Blue ghost shrimp	*Upogebia pugettensis*
Bay ghost shrimp	*Callianassa californiensis*
Mole crab	*Emerita analoga*

Spiny mole crab	*Blepharipoda occidentalis*
Stone crab	*Hapalogaster cavicauda*
Turtle crab	*Cryptolithodes sitchensis*
Hermit crab	*Pagurus* species
Pelagic red crab	*Pleuroncodes planipes*
Flat porcelain crab	*Petrolisthes cinctipes*
Porcelain crab	*Pachycheles pubescens*
Thick-clawed porcelain crab	*Pachycheles rudis*
Kelp crabs	*Pugettia* species
Encrusting crab	*Mimulus foliatus*
Sharp-nosed crab	*Scyra acutifrons*
Masking crab	*Loxorhynchus crispatus*
Rock crab	*Cancer antennarius*
Dungeness crab	*Cancer magister*
Red crab	*Cancer productus*
Pea crab	*Fabia subquadrata*
Pea crabs	*Pinnixa* species
Pea crab	*Scleroplax granulata*
Lined shore crab	*Pachygrapsus crassipes*
Purple shore crab	*Hemigrapsus nudus*
Sea spider	*Pycnogonum stearnsi*

MOLLUSKS: abalones, limpets, snails, clams, nudibranchs, chitons, and octopi.

Red abalone	*Haliotis rufescens*
Black abalone	*Haliotis cracherodii*
Flat abalone	*Haliotis walallensis*
Pinto abalone	*Haliotis kamtschatkana*
Keyhole limpet	*Fissurella volcano*
Two-spotted keyhole limpet	*Megatebennus bimaculatus*
Keyhole limpet	*Diodora arnoldi*
Rough keyhole limpet	*Diodora aspera*
Dunce cap limpet	*Acmaea mitra*
Chaffy limpet	*Acmaea paleacea*
Ribbed limpet	*Collisella digitalis*
Rough limpet	*Collisella scabra*
File limpet	*Collisella limatula*
Shield limpet	*Collisella pelta*
Seaweed limpet	*Notoacmea insessa*
Surfgrass limpet	*Notoacmea paleacea*
Plate limpet	*Notoacmea scutum*
Owl limpet	*Lottia gigantea*
Top snails	*Calliostoma* species
Brown turban snail	*Tegula brunnea*
Black turban snail	*Tegula funebralis*
Periwinkles	*Littorina* species
Eroded periwinkle	*Littorina planaxis*
California horn snail	*Cerithidea californica*
Horn snail	*Batillaria zonalis*
Hooked slipper snail	*Crepidula adunca*
Giant moon snail	*Polinices lewisii*

Leafy hornmouth	*Ceratostoma foliatum*
Atlantic oyster drill	*Urosalpinx cinerea*
Japanese oyster drill	*Ocenebra japonica*
Unicorn whelk	*Acanthina spirata*
Channeled dog whelk	*Nucella canaliculata*
Emarginated dog whelk	*Nucella emarginata*
Wrinkled dog whelk	*Nucella lamellosa*
Dire whelk	*Searlesia dira*
Wrinkled dove snail	*Amphissa columbiana*
Dog whelk	*Nassarius obsoletus*
Channeled nassa	*Nassarius fossatus*
Cooper's lean nassa	*Nassarius cooperi*
Purple olive	*Olivella biplicata*
Brown sea hare	*Aplysia californica*
Taylor's sea hare	*Phyllaplysia taylori*
Pleurobranchaea	*Pleurobranchaea bachei*
Cadlina	*Cadlina* species
Chan's nudibranch	*Hallaxa chani*
Scarlet nudibranch	*Rostanga pulchra*
Monterey dorid	*Archidoris montereyensis*
Sea lemon	*Anisodoris nobilis*
Ring-spotted dorid	*Diaulula sandiegensis*
Hopkin's rose	*Hopkinsia rosacea*
Wine-plume dorid	*Acanthodoris nanaimoensis*
Spotted triopha	*Triopha maculata*
Sea clown nudibranch	*Triopha catalinae*
Melibe	*Melibe leonina*
Cockscomb nudibranch	*Antiopella barbarensis*
Chalk-lined nudibranch	*Dirona albolineata*
Spotted dirona	*Dirona picta*
Three-lined nudibranch	*Coryphella trilineata*
Fighting phidiana	*Phidiana pugnax*
Hermissenda	*Hermissenda crassicornis*
Shag-rug nudibranch	*Aeolidia papillosa*
Reticulate button snail	*Trimusculus reticulatus*
Horse mussel	*Volsella senhousii*
California mussel	*Mytilus californianus*
Bay mussel	*Mytilus edulis*
Olympia oyster	*Ostrea lurida*
Japanese oyster	*Crassostrea gigas*
Eastern oyster	*Crassostrea virginica*
Abalone jingle	*Pododesmus cepio*
Rock scallop	*Hinnites giganteus*
Heart cockle	*Clinocardium nuttallii*
Gem clam	*Gemma gemma*
Washington clam	*Saxidomus nuttalli*
Littleneck clam	*Protothaca staminea*
Japanese littleneck	*Protothaca semidecussata*
Horseneck clam	*Tresus nuttallii*
Bent-nosed clam	*Macoma nasuta*

White sand clam	*Macoma secta*
Purple clam	*Nuttallia nuttallii*
Pacific razor clam	*Siliqua patula*
Little gaper	*Hiatella arctica*
Geoduck clam	*Panopea generosa*
Flat-tipped piddock	*Penitella penita*
Merten's chiton	*Lepidozona mertensii*
Lined chiton	*Tonicella lineata*
Nuttall's chiton	*Nuttallina californica*
Mossy chiton	*Mopalia muscosa*
Mossy chiton	*Mopalia ciliata*
Mossy chiton	*Mopalia lignosa*
Veiled chiton	*Placiphorella velata*
Leather chiton	*Katharina tunicata*
Gumboot chiton	*Cryptochiton stelleri*
Common squid	*Loligo opalescens*
Red octopus	*Octopus rubescens*
Giant octopus	*Octopus dofleini*

MARINE WORMS: flatworms, ribbon worms, peanut worms, segmented worms.

Scale worm	*Arctonoe fragilis*
Arabella	*Arabella semimaculata*
Red joint worm	*Axiothella rubrocinta*
Cirratulid worm	*Dodecaceria* species
Red blood worm	*Euzonius mucronata*
Plume worm	*Eudistylia polymorpha*
Glycerid worm	*Glycera americana*
Scale worm	*Halosydna brevisetosa*
Scale worm	*Harmothoe imbricata*
Scale worm	*Hesperonoe complanta*
Flatworm	*Hoploplana californica*
Flatworm	*Leptoplana chloranota*
Ribbon worm	*Micrura verrilli*
Big nereid worm	*Neanthes brandti*
Nephtys	*Nephtys caecoides*
Nereid tube worm	*Nereis* species
Flatworm	*Notoplana* species
Flatworm	*Oregoniplana opisthopora*
Ribbon worm	*Paranemertes peregrina*
Sipunculid worm	*Phascolosoma agassizii*
Green-plumed worm	*Phoronopsis viridis*
Flat nereid worm	*Platynereis agassizi*
Polychaete	*Pista pacifica*
Feather-duster worm	*Sebella media*
Serpulid polchaete	*Serpula vermicularis*
Sipunculid worm	*Sipunculus nudus*
Sipunculid worm	*Themiste pyroides*
Ribbon worm	*Tubulanus polymorphus*
Sand-tube polychaete	*Thelepus crispus*
Fat innkeeper worm	*Urechis caupo*

SPECIES LIST 3.

Amphibians and Reptiles of the Point Reyes Peninsula and the Gulf of the Farallones.

Status categories: C = common; FC = fairly common; U = uncommon; R = rare; X = extremely rare

Common Name	Latin Name	Status
Pacific giant salamander	*Dicamptodon ensatus*	U
Rough-skinned newt	*Taricha granulosa*	FC
California newt	*Tachina torosa*	FC
Ensatina	*Ensatina eschscholtzi*	U
California slender salamander	*Batrachoseps attenuatus*	C
Arboreal salamander	*Aneides lugubris*	R
Western toad	*Bufo boreas*	U
Pacific treefrog	*Hyla regila*	C
Red-legged frog	*Rana aurora*	U
Bullfrog	*Rana catesbeiana*	C
Western fence lizard	*Sceloporus occidentalis*	C
Western skink	*Eumeces skiltonianus*	U
Southern alligator lizard	*Gerrhonotus multicarinatus*	U
Northern alligator lizard	*Gerrhonotus coeruleus*	C
Rubber boa	*Charina bottae*	U
Ringneck snake	*Diadophis punctatus*	U
Sharp-tailed snake	*Contia tenuis*	R
Western yellow-bellied racer	*Coluber constrictor*	U
Pacific gopher snake	*Pituophis melanoleucus*	C
Common kingsnake	*Lempropeltis getulus*	X
Red-sided garter snake	*Thamnophis sirtalis*	FC
Western terrestrial garter snake	*Thamnophis elegans*	C
Western aquatic garter snake	*Thamnophis couchi*	U
Western rattlesnake	*Crotalus viridis*	X
Western pond turtle	*Clemmys marmorata*	C
Green sea turtle	*Chelonia mydas*	X
Loggerhead sea turtle	*Caretta caretta*	R
Pacific Ridley sea turtle	*Lepidochelys olivacea*	X

SPECIES LIST 4.

Birds of the Point Reyes Peninsula and the Gulf of the Farallones.*

Status symbols are as follows: C = common; FC = fairly common; U = uncommon; R = rare; X = extremely rare. An asterisk (*) following the common name indicates a breeding species; double asterisk (**) indicates a species which formerly bred but is now extirpated. Status refers to the season of most regular occurrence.

This list does not include species that have occurred only on S.E. Farallon Island.

Common Name	Latin Name	Status
Red-throated loon	*Gavia stellata*	FC
Pacific loon	*Gavia pacifica*	FC
Common loon	*Gavia immer*	FC
Yellow-billed loon	*Gavia adamsii*	X
Pied-billed grebe*	*Podilymbus podiceps*	FC
Horned grebe	*Podiceps auritus*	FC
Red-necked grebe	*Podiceps grisegena*	U
Eared grebe	*Podiceps nigricollis*	FC
Western grebe	*Aechmophorus occidentalis*	C
Clark's grebe	*Aechmophorus clarkii*	U
Short-tailed albatross	*Diomedea albatrus*	X
Black-footed albatross	*Diomedea nigripes*	U
Laysan albatross	*Diomedea immutabilis*	R
Northern fulmar	*Fulmarus glacialis*	FC
Mottled petrel	*Pterodroma inexpectata*	X
Pink-footed shearwater	*Puffinus creatopus*	U
Flesh-footed shearwater	*Puffinus carneipes*	R
Buller's shearwater	*Puffinus bulleri*	U
Sooty shearwater	*Puffinus griseus*	C
Short-tailed shearwater	*Puffinus tenuirostris*	R
Black-vented shearwater	*Puffinus opisthomelas*	R
Townsend's shearwater	*Puffinus auricularis*	X
Wilson's storm-petrel	*Oceanites oceanicus*	X
Fork-tailed storm-petrel	*Oceanodroma furcata*	R
Leach's storm-petrel	*Oceanodroma leucorhoa*	U
Ashy storm-petrel	*Oceanodroma homochroa*	FC
Black storm-petrel	*Oceanodroma melania*	R
Red-footed booby	*Sula sula*	X
American white pelican	*Pelecanus erythrorhynchos*	FC
Brown pelican	*Pelecanus occidentalis*	C
Double-crested cormorant	*Phalacrocorax auritus*	C
Brandt's cormorant*	*Phalacrocorax penicillatus*	C
Pelagic cormorant*	*Phalacrocorax pelagicus*	FC
Magnificent frigatebird	*Fregata magnificens*	X
American bittern*	*Botaurus lentiginosus*	R
Least bittern	*Ixobrychus exilis*	X
Great blue heron*	*Ardea herodias*	C
Great egret*	*Casmerodius albus*	C
Snowy egret*	*Egretta thula*	FC
Little blue heron	*Egretta caerulea*	X

Cattle egret	*Bubulcus ibis*	R
Green-backed heron*	*Butorides striatus*	R
Black-crowned night-heron	*Nycticorax nycticorax*	FC
White ibis	*Eudocimus albus*	X
White-faced ibis	*Plegadis chihi*	X
Wood stork	*Mycteria americana*	X
Tundra swan	*Cygnus columbianus*	R
Trumpeter swan	*Cygnus buccinator*	X
Greater white-fronted goose	*Anser albifrons*	R
Snow goose	*Chen caerulescens*	R
Ross' goose	*Chen rossii*	R
Emperor goose	*Chen canagica*	X
Brant	*Branta bernicla*	C
Canada goose	*Branta canadensis*	U
Wood duck*	*Aix sponsa*	R
Green-winged teal	*Anas crecca*	C
"Eurasian"	(crecca group)	X
Mallard*	*Anas platyrhynchos*	C
Northern pintail	*Anas acuta*	C
Garganey	*Anas querquedula*	X
Blue-winged teal	*Anas discors*	R
Cinnamon teal*	*Anas cyanoptera*	C
Northern shoveler*	*Anas clypeata*	C
Gadwall*	*Anas strepera*	FC
Eurasian wigeon	*Anas penelope*	R
American wigeon	*Anas americana*	C
Canvasback	*Anas americana*	C
Redhead	*Aythya americana*	U
Ring-necked duck	*Aythya collaris*	FC
Tufted duck	*Aythya fuligula*	X
Greater scaup	*Aythya marila*	C
Lesser scaup	*Aythya affinis*	FC
King eider	*Somateria spectabilis*	X
Harlequin duck	*Histrionicus histrionicus*	R
Oldsquaw	*Clangula hyemalis*	R
Black scoter	*Melanitta nigra*	U
Surf scoter	*Melanitta perspicillata*	C
White-winged scoter	*Melanitta fusca*	C
Common goldeneye	*Bucephala clangula*	FC
Barrow's goldeneye	*Bucephala islandica*	R
Bufflehead	*Bucephala albeola*	C
Hooded merganser	*Lophodytes cucullatus*	R
Common merganser	*Mergus merganser*	R
Red-breasted merganser	*Mergus serrator*	FC
Ruddy duck*	*Oxyura jamaicensis*	C
Turkey vulture	*Cathartes aura*	C
Osprey*	*Pandion haliaetus*	FC
Black-shouldered kite*	*Elanus caeruleus*	U
Bald eagle	*Haliaeetus leucocephalus*	R
Northern harrier*	*Circus cyaneus*	FC

Sharp-shinned hawk	*Accipiter striatus*	FC
Cooper's hawk*	*Accipiter cooperii*	FC
Northern goshawk	*Accipiter gentilis*	X
Red-shouldered hawk	*Buteo lineatus*	FC
Broad-winged hawk	*Buteo platypterus*	R
Swainson's hawk	*Buteo swainsoni*	X
Red-tailed hawk*	*Buteo jamaicensis*	C
Ferruginous hawk	*Buteo regalis*	R
Rough-legged hawk	*Buteo lagopus*	R
Golden eagle	*Aquila chrysaetos*	R
American kestrel*	*Falco sparverius*	C
Merlin	*Falco columbarius*	U
Peregrine falcon**	*Falco peregrinus*	U
Prairie falcon	*Falco mexicanus*	R
Ring-necked pheasant (i)	*Phasianus colchicus*	X
California quail*	*Callipepla californica*	C
Yellow rail	*Coturnicops noveboracensis*	X
Black rail*	*Laterallus jamaicensis*	R
Clapper rail	*Rallus longirostris*	X
Virginia rail*	*Rallus limicola*	FC
Sora*	*Porzana carolina*	U
Common moorhen*	*Gallinula chloropus*	R
American coot*	*Fulica americana*	C
Sandhill crane	*Grus canadensis*	X
Black-bellied plover	*Pluvialis squatarola*	C
Lesser golden plover	*Pluvialis dominica*	
"American"	(*dominica* group)	U
"Pacific"	(*fulva* group)	U
Mongolian plover	*Charadrius mongolus*	X
Snowy plover*	*Charadrius alexandrinus*	FC
Semipalmated plover	*Charadrius semipalmatus*	FC
Killdeer*	*Charadrius vociferus*	C
Mountain plover	*Charadrius montanus*	X
Eurasian dotterel	*Charadrius morinellus*	X
American black oystercatcher	*Haematopus bachmani*	U
Black-necked stilt	*Himantopus mexicanus*	R
American avocet	*Recurvirostra americana*	FC
Greater yellowlegs	*Tringa melanoleuca*	FC
Lesser yellowlegs	*Tringa flavipes*	U
Solitary sandpiper	*Tringa solitaria*	R
Willet	*Catoptrophorus semipalmatus*	C
Wandering tattler	*Heteroscelus incanus*	U
Spotted sandpiper	*Actitis macularia*	U
Whimbrel	*Numenius phaeopus*	U
Long-billed curlew	*Numenius americanus*	FC
Bar-tailed godwit	*Limosa lapponica*	X
Marbled godwit	*Limosa fedoa*	C
Ruddy turnstone	*Arenaria interpres*	U
Black turnstone	*Arenaria melanocephala*	C
Surfbird	*Aphriza virgata*	R

Red knot	*Calidris canutus*	U
Sanderling	*Calidris alba*	C
Semipalmated sandpiper	*Calidris pusilla*	R
Western sandpiper	*Calidris mauri*	C
Little stint	*Calidris minuta*	X
Least sandpiper	*Calidris minutilla*	C
White-rumped sandpiper	*Calidris fuscicollis*	X
Baird's sandpiper	*Calidris bairdii*	U
Pectoral sandpiper	*Calidris melanotos*	U
Sharp-tailed sandpiper	*Calidris acuminata*	X
Rock sandpiper	*Calidris ptilocnemis*	X
Dunlin	*Calidris alpina*	C
Curlew sandpiper	*Calidris ferruginea*	X
Stilt sandpiper	*Calidris himantopus*	X
Buff-breasted sandpiper	*Tryngites subruficollis*	X
Ruff	*Philomachus pugnax*	X
Short-billed dowitcher	*Limnodromus griseus*	C
Long-billed dowitcher	*Limnodromus scolopaceus*	FC
Common snipe	*Gallinago gallinago*	U
Wilson's phalarope	*Phalaropus tricolor*	R
Red-necked phalarope	*Phalaropus lobatus*	FC
Red phalarope	*Phalaropus fulicaria*	FC
Pomarine jaeger	*Sterocarius pomarinus*	U
Parasitic jaeger	*Sterocarius parasiticus*	U
Long-tailed jaeger	*Sterocarius longicaudus*	R
South polar skua	*Catharacta maccormicki*	R
Franklin's gull	*Larus pipixcan*	X
Little gull	*Larus minutus*	X
Common black-headed gull	*Larus ridibundus*	X
Bonaparte's gull	*Larus philadelphia*	FC
Heermann's gull	*Larus heermanni*	C
Mew gull	*Larus canus*	C
Ring-billed gull	*Larus delawarensis*	C
California gull	*Larus californicus*	C
Herring gull	*Larus argentatus*	FC
Thayer's gull	*Larus thayeri*	U
Western gull*	*Larus occidentalis*	C
Glaucous-winged gull	*Larus glaucescens*	C
Glaucous gull	*Larus hyperboreus*	R
Black-legged kittiwake	*Rissa tridactyla*	U
Sabine's gull	*Xema sabini*	R
Caspian tern	*Sterna caspia*	C
Royal tern	*Sterna maxima*	X
Elegant tern	*Sterna elegans*	C
Common tern	*Sterna hirundo*	U
Arctic tern	*Sterna paradisaea*	U
Foster's tern	*Sterna forsteri*	C
Least tern	*Sterna antillarum*	X
Black tern	*Chlidonias niger*	X
Common murre*	*Uria aalge*	C

Pigeon guillemot*	*Cepphus columba*	FC
Marbled murrelet	*Brachyramphus marmoratus*	U
Xantus' murrelet (*scrippsi*)	*Synthliboramphus hypoleucus*	R
Crested auklet	*Aethia cristatella*	X
Ancient murrelet	*Synthliboramphus antiquus*	U
Cassin's auklet	*Ptychoramphus aleuticus*	C
Parakeet auklet	*Cyclorrhynchus psittacula*	X
Rhinocerous auklet	*Cerorhinca monocerata*	U
Tufted puffin*	*Fratercula cirrhata*	R
Horned puffin	*Fratercula corniculata*	X
Rock dove* (i)	*Columba livia*	U
Band-tailed pigeon*	*Columba fasciata*	FC
White-winged dove	*Zenaida asiatica*	X
Mourning dove*	*Zenaida macroura*	FC
Black-billed cuckoo	*Coccyzus erythropthalmus*	X
Yellow-billed cuckoo	*Coccyzus americanus*	X
Common barn owl*	*Tyto alba*	FC
Western screech owl*	*Otus kennicottii*	U
Great horned owl*	*Bubo virginianus*	C
Snowy owl	*Nyctea scandiaca*	X
Northern pygmy-owl	*Glaucidium gnoma*	R
Burrowing owl	*Athene cunicularia*	R
Spotted owl*	*Strix occidentalis*	U
Long-eared owl*	*Asio otus*	R
Short-eared owl*	*Asio flammeus*	R
Northern saw-whet owl*	*Aegolius acadicus*	FC
Lesser nighthawk	*Chrodeiles acutipennis*	X
Common nighthawk	*Chordeiles minor*	X
Common poorwill	*Phalaenoptilus nuttallii*	R
Whip-poor-will	*Caprimulgus vociferus*	X
Black swift	*Cypseloides niger*	R
Chimney swift	*Chaetura pelagica*	X
Vaux's swift	*Chaetura vauxi*	U
White-throated swift	*Aeronautes saxatalis*	R
Black-chinned hummingbird	*Archilochus alexandri*	X
Anna's hummingbird*	*Calypte anna*	C
Costa's hummingbird	*Calypte costae*	X
Calliope hummingbird	*Stellula calliope*	R
Rufous hummingbird	*Selasphorus rufus*	U
Allen's hummingbird*	*Selasphorus sasin*	C
Belted kingfisher*	*Ceryle alcyon*	FC
Lewis' woodpecker	*Melanerpes lewis*	X
Acorn woodpecker*	*Melanerpes formicivorus*	C
Yellow-bellied sapsucker	*Sphyrapicus varius*	X
Red-naped sapsucker	*Sphyrapicus nuchalis*	X
Red-breasted sapsucker*	*Sphyrapicus ruber*	U
Nutall's woodpecker*	*Picoides nuttallii*	U
Downy woodpecker	*Picoides pubescens*	FC
Hairy woodpecker*	*Picoides villosus*	FC
Northern flicker	*Colaptes auratus*	C

"Yellow-shafted"	(*auratus* group)	R
"Red-shafted"	(*cafer* group)	C
Pileated woodpecker*	*Dryocopus pileatus*	R
Olive-sided flycatcher*	*Contopus borealis*	FC
Western wood-pewee*	*Contopus sordidulus*	C
Willow flycatcher	*Empidonax traillii*	R
Least flycatcher	*Empidonax minimus*	X
Hammond's flycatcher	*Empidonax hammondii*	X
Dusky flycatcher	*Empidonax oberholseri*	X
Gray flycatcher	*Empidonax wrightii*	X
Pacific-slope flycatcher*	*Empidonax difficilis*	C
Black phoebe*	*Sayornis nigricans*	C
Eastern phoebe	*Sayornis phoebe*	X
Say's phoebe	*Sayornis saya*	U
Dusky-capped flycatcher	*Myiarchus tuberculifer*	X
Ash-throated flycatcher*	*Myiarchus cinerascens*	FC
Great crested flycatcher	*Myiarchus crinitus*	X
Tropical kingbird	*Tyrannus melancholicus*	R
Cassin's kingbird*	*Tyrannus vociferans*	X
Western kingbird*	*Tyrannus verticalis*	U
Eastern kingbird	*Tyrannus tyrannus*	X
Scissor-tailed flycatcher	*Tyrannus forficatus*	X
Eurasian skylark	*Alauda arvensis*	X
Horned lark*	*Eremophila alpestris*	FC
Purple martin*	*Progne subis*	R
Tree swallow*	*Tachycineta bicolor*	C
Violet-green swallow*	*Tachycineta thalassina*	C
Northern rough-winged swallow*	*Stelgidopteryx serripennis*	FC
Bank swallow	*Riparia riparia*	R
Cliff swallow*	*Hirundo pyrrhonota*	C
Barn swallow*	*Hirundo rustica*	C
Stellar's jay*	*Cyanocitta stelleri*	C
Scrub jay*	*Aphelocoma coerulescens*	C
Pinyon jay	*Gymnorhinus cyanocephalus*	X
Clark's nutcracker	*Nucifraga columbiana*	X
American crow*	*Corvus brachyrhynchos*	FC
Common raven*	*Corvus corax*	FC
Mountain chickadee	*Parus gambeli*	X
Chestnut-backed chickadee*	*Parus rufescens*	C
Plain titmouse*	*Parus inornatus*	U
Bushtit*	*Psaltriparus minimus*	C
Red-breasted nuthatch*	*Sitta canadensis*	U
White-breasted nuthatch	*Sitta carolinensis*	R
Pygmy nuthatch*	*Sitta pygmaea*	C
Brown creeper*	*Certhia americana*	FC
Rock wren*	*Salpinctes obsoletus*	U
Canyon wren	*Catherpes mexicanus*	X
Bewick's wren*	*Thryomanes bewickii*	C
House wren	*Troglodytes aedon*	R

Winter wren*	*Troglodytes troglodytes*	C
Sedge wren	*Cistothorus platensis*	X
Marsh wren*	*Cistothorus palustris*	C
American dipper	*Cinclus mexicanus*	X
Golden-crowned kinglet*	*Regulus satrapa*	FC
Ruby-crowned kinglet	*Regulus calendula*	C
Blue-gray gnatcatcher	*Polioptila caerulea*	R
Western bluebird*	*Sialia mexicana*	FC
Mountain bluebird	*Sialia currucoides*	X
Townsend's solitaire	*Myadestes townsendi*	X
Veery	*Catharus fuscescens*	X
Gray-cheeked thrush	*Catharus minimus*	X
Swainson's thrush*	*Catharus ustulatus*	C
Hermit thrush*	*Catharus guttatus*	C
Wood thrush	*Hylocichla mustelina*	X
American robin*	*Turdus migratorius*	C
Varied thrush	*Ixoreus naevius*	FC
Wrentit*	*Chamaea fasciata*	FC
Gray catbird	*Dumetella carolinensis*	X
Northern mockingbird	*Mimus polyglottos*	U
Sage thrasher	*Oreoscoptes montanus*	X
Brown thrasher	*Toxostoma rufum*	X
Yellow wagtail	*Motacilla cinerea*	X
Red-throated pipit	*Anthus cervinus*	X
American pipit	*Anthus rubescens*	FC
Cedar waxwing (*?)	*Bombycilla cedrorum*	FC
Phainopepla	*Phainopepla nitens*	X
Brown shrike	*Lanius cristatus*	X
Northern shrike	*Lanius excubitor*	X
Loggerhead shrike*	*Lanius ludovicianus*	U
European starling* (i)	*Sturnus vulgaris*	C
White-eyed vireo	*Vireo griseus*	X
Bell's vireo	*Vireo bellii*	X
Solitary vireo	*Vireo solitarius*	
"Cassin's"	*cassinii* group	R
"Eastern"	*solitarius* group	X
"Rocky Mountain"	*plumbeus* group	X
Yellow-throated vireo	*Vireo flavifrons*	X
Hutton's vireo*	*Vireo huttoni*	FC
Warbling vireo*	*Vireo gilvus*	C
Philadelphia vireo	*Vireo philadelphicus*	X
Red-eyed vireo	*Vireo olivaceus*	X
Tennessee warbler	*Vermivora peregrina*	R
Orange-crowned warbler*	*Vermivora celata*	C
Nashville warbler	*Vermivora ruficapilla*	R
Virginia's warbler	*Vermivora virginiae*	X
Lucy's warbler	*Vermivora luciae*	X
Northern parula*	*Parula americana*	R
Yellow warbler*	*Dendroica petechia*	FC
Chestnut-sided warbler	*Dendroica pensylvanica*	R

Magnolia warbler	*Dendroica magnolia*	R
Cape May warbler	*Dendroica tigrina*	R
Black-throated blue warbler	*Dendroica caerulescens*	R
Yellow-rumped warbler	*Dendroica coronata*	
"Audubon's"*	*auduboni* group	C
"Myrtle"	*coronata* group	C
Black-throated gray warbler	*Dendroica nigrescens*	U
Townsend's warbler	*Dendroica townsendi*	FC
Hermit warbler*	*Dendroica occidentalis*	U
Black-throated green warbler	*Dendroica virens*	X
Blackburnian warbler	*Dendroica fusca*	R
Yellow-throated warbler	*Dendroica dominica*	X
Pine warbler	*Dendroica pinus*	X
Prairie warbler	*Dendroica discolor*	R
Palm warbler	*Dendroica palmarum*	R
Bay-breasted warbler	*Dendroica castanea*	R
Blackpoll warbler	*Dendroica striata*	R
Cerulean warbler	*Dendroica cerulea*	X
Black-and-white warbler	*Mniotilta varia*	R
American redstart	*Setophaga ruticilla*	R
Prothonotary warbler	*Protonotaria citrea*	X
Worm-eating warbler	*Helmitheros vermivorus*	X
Ovenbird	*Seiurus aurocapillus*	R
Northern waterthrush	*Seiurus noveboracensis*	R
Kentucky warbler	*Oporornis formosus*	X
Connecticut warbler	*Oporornis agilis*	X
Mourning warbler	*Oporornis philadelphia*	X
MacGillivray's warbler*	*Oporornis tolmiei*	U
Common yellowthroat*	*Geothlypis trichas*	FC
Hooded warbler	*Wilsonia citrina*	X
Wilson's warbler*	*Wilsonia pusilla*	C
Canada warbler	*Wilsonia canadensis*	X
Painted redstart	*Myioborus pictus*	X
Yellow-breasted chat	*Icteria virens*	R
Summer tanager	*Piranga rubra*	X
Scarlet tanager	*Piranga olivacea*	X
Western tanager	*Piranga ludoviciana*	U
Rose-breasted grosbeak	*Pheucticus ludovicianus*	R
Black-headed grosbeak*	*Pheucticus melanocephalus*	FC
Blue grosbeak	*Guiraca caerulea*	X
Lazuli bunting*	*Passerina amoena*	U
Indigo bunting	*Passerina cyanea*	R
Dickcissel	*Spiza americana*	X
Green-tailed towhee	*Pipilo chlorurus*	X
Rufous-sided towhee*	*Pipilo erythrophthalmus*	C
California towhee*	*Pipilo crissalis*	C
Rufous-crowned sparrow*	*Aimophila ruficeps*	R
American tree sparrow	*Spizella arborea*	X
Chipping sparrow*	*Spizella passerina*	U
Clay-colored sparrow	*Spizella pallida*	R

Brewer's sparrow	*Spizella breweri*	X
Black-chinned sparrow	*Spizella atrogularis*	X
Vesper sparrow	*Pooecetes gramineus*	R
Lark sparrow*	*Chondestes grammacus*	R
Black-throated sparrow	*Amphispiza bilineata*	X
Sage sparrow	*Amphispiza belli*	X
Lark bunting	*Calamospiza melanocorys*	X
Savannah sparrow*	*Passerculus sandwichensis*	C
Grasshopper sparrow*	*Ammodramus savannarum*	U
Sharp-tailed sparrow	*Ammodramus caudacutus*	X
Fox sparrow	*Passerella iliaca*	C
Song sparrow*	*Melospiza melodia*	C
Lincoln's sparrow	*Melospiza lincolnii*	U
Swamp sparrow	*Melospiza georgiana*	R
White-throated sparrow	*Zonotrichia albicollis*	R
Golden-crowned sparrow	*Zonotrichia atricapilla*	C
White-crowned sparrow*	*Zonotrichia leucophrys*	C
Harris' sparrow	*Zonotrichia querula*	X
Dark-eyed junco	*Junco hyemalis*	
"Oregon"*	*oreganus* group	C
"Slate-colored"	*hyemalis* group	R
"Gray-headed"	*caniceps* group	X
McCown's longspur	*Calcarius mccownii*	X
Lapland longspur	*Calcarius lapponicus*	R
Chestnut-collared longspur	*Calcarius ornatus*	R
Snow bunting	*Plectrophenax nivalis*	X
Bobolink	*Dolichonyx oryzivorus*	R
Red-winged blackbird*	*Agelaius phoeniceus*	C
Tricolored blackbird*	*Agelaius tricolor*	C
Western meadowlark*	*Sturnella neglecta*	FC
Yellow-headed blackbird	*Xanthocephalus xanthocephalus*	X
Rusty blackbird	*Euphagus carolinus*	X
Brewer's blackbird*	*Euphagus cyanocephalus*	C
Common grackle	*Quiscalus quiscula*	X
Brown-headed cowbird*	*Molothrus ater*	FC
Orchard oriole	*Icterus spurius*	X
Hooded oriole	*Icterus cucullatus*	X
Northern oriole	*Icterus galbula*	
"Bullock's"*	*bullockii* group	U
"Baltimore"	*galbula* group	X
Scott's oriole	*Icterus parisorum*	X
Purple finch*	*Carpodacus purpureus*	C
Cassin's finch	*Carpodacus cassinii*	X
House finch*	*Carpodacus mexicanus*	C
Red crossbill (*?)	*Loxia curvirostra*	U
Pine siskin*	*Carduelis pinus*	C
Lesser goldfinch*	*Carduelis psaltria*	FC
Lawrence's goldfinch*	*Carduelis lawrencei*	X
American goldfinch*	*Carduelis tristis*	C
Evening grosbeak	*Coccothraustes vespertinus*	R
House sparrow* (i)	*Passer domesticus*	C

SPECIES LIST 5.

Mammals of the Point Reyes Peninsula and the Gulf of the Farallones.

Status categories: C = common; FC = fairly common; U = uncommon; R = rare; X = extremely rare; ? = status unknown.

Common Name	Latin Name	Status
Common possum	*Didelphis marsupialis virginiana*	C
Trowbridge's shrew	*Sorex trowbridgii montereyensis*	C
Vagrant shrew	*Sorex vagrans vagrans*	C
Pacific shrew	*Sorex pacificus sonomae*	R
Shrew mole	*Neurotrichus gibbsii hyacinthinus*	FC
Broad-handed mole	*Scapanus latimanus caurinus*	FC
Pallid bat	*Antrozous pallidus pacificus*	C
Silver-haired bat	*Lasionycteris noctivagans*	U
Big brown bat	*Eptesicus fuscus bernardinus*	FC
Red bat	*Lasiurus borealis teliotis*	U
Hoary bat	*Lasiurus cinereus cinereus*	C
Little brown myotis	*Myotis lucifugus alascensis*	U
California myotis	*Myotis californicus caurinus*	FC
Fringed myotis	*Myotis thysanodes thysanodes*	C
Long-legged myotis	*Myotis volans longicrus*	?
Yuma myotis	*Myotis yumanensis saturatus*	C
Long-eared bat	*Plecotus townsendii townsendii*	R
Mexican free-tailed bat	*Tadarida brasiliensis mexicana*	FC
Black-tailed hare	*Lepus californicus californicus*	C
Brush rabbit	*Sylvilagus bachmani ubericolor*	C
Mountain beaver	*Aplodontia rufa phaea*	R
Beechey ground squirrel	*Spermophilus beecheyi douglasi*	R
Western gray squirrel	*Sciurus griseus griseus*	C
Sonoma chipmunk	*Eutamias sonomae alleni*	U
Botta pocket gopher	*Thomomys bottae minor*	C
Western harvest mouse	*Reithrodontomys megalotis longicaudis*	U
Deer mouse	*Peromyscus maniculatus rubidus*	C
Dusky-footed woodrat	*Neotoma fuscipes monochroura*	C
California vole	*Microtus californicus eximus*	C
Muskrat	*Ondatra zibethica*	U
Norway rat	*Rattus norvegicus norvegicus*	C
House mouse	*Mus musculus*	C
Pacific jumping mouse	*Zapus trinotatus orarius*	U
Porcupine	*Erethizon dorsatum epixanthum*	R
Gray whale	*Eschrichtius robustus*	C
Blue whale	*Balaenoptera musculus*	U
Minke whale	*Balaenoptera acutorostrata*	R
Fin-backed whale	*Balaenoptera physalus*	R
Sei whale	*Balaenoptera borealis*	R
Humpback whale	*Megaptera novaeangliae*	FC
Stejneger's beaked whale	*Mesoplodon stejnegeri*	R
Hubb's beaked whale	*Mesoplodon carlhubbsi*	R
Cuvier's beaked whale	*Ziphius cavirostris*	R

Sperm whale	*Physeter catodon*	R
Pygmy sperm whale	*Kogia breviceps*	R
Harbor porpoise	*Phocaena phocaena*	FC
North Pacific pilot whale	*Globicephala scammonii*	R
Killer whale	*Orcinus orca*	U
Northern right whale dolphin	*Lissodelphis borealis*	R
Pacific white-sided dolphin	*Lagenorynchus obliquidens*	FC
Dall's porpoise	*Phocoenoides dalli*	FC
Risso's dolphin	*Grampus griseus*	R
Common dolphin	*Delphinus delphis*	R
Coyote	*Canis latrans ochropus*	R
Red fox	*Vulpes fulva*	R
Gray fox	*Urocyon cinereoargenteus townsendi*	FC
Black bear	*Euarctos americanus altifrontalis*	X
Grizzly bear	*Ursus mendocinsis*	X
Ringtail	*Bassariscus astutus raptor*	R
Raccoon	*Procyon lotor psora*	C
Short-tailed weasel	*Mustela erminea streatori*	R
Long-tailed weasel	*Mustela frenata munda*	FC
Mink	*Mustela vison aestruarina*	R
Badger	*Taxidea taxus neglecta*	U
Spotted skunk	*Spilogale putorius phenax*	U
Striped skunk	*Mephitis mephitis occidentalis*	C
River otter	*Lutra canadensis brevipilosus*	R
Sea otter	*Enhydra lutris nereis*	R
Mountain lion	*Felis concolor californicus*	R
Bobcat	*Lynx rufus californicus*	FC
Feral cat	*Felis domesticus*	C
Northern fur seal	*Callorhinus ursinus*	R
Northern (Steller) sea lion	*Eumetopias jubata*	U
California sea lion	*Zalophus californicus*	C
Harbor seal	*Phoca vitulina*	C
Northern elephant seal	*Mirounga angustirostris*	U
Wild pig	*Sus scrofa*	U
Fallow deer	*Dama dama dama*	U
Axis deer	*Axis axis axis*	U
Tule elk	*Cervus elaphis nannodes*	FC
Black-tailed deer	*Odocoileus hemionus columbianus*	C

Hypothetical — species for which there is anecdotal evidence, none of which is confirmed by a specimen.

Black rat	*Rattus rattus*	[2]
Ribbon seal	*Histriophoca fasciata*	[6]
Fisher	*Martes pennanti*	[2]
Marten	*Martes americana*	[2]
Wolverine	*Gulo luscus*	[2]
Beaver	*Castor canadensis*	[2]
Pronghorn	*Antilocapra americana*	[2]

Sources

1. California Academy of Sciences: Mammal collection as of 10 Feb 1986.
2. Clark, K. E. 1979. *A preliminary study of the history and present status of the mammals at Point Reyes National Seashore (excluding Chiroptera, Pinnepedia, and Cetacea).* Santa Cruz: University of California.
3. Fellers, G. M. and J. Dell'Osso. 1986. *An annotated checklist of mammals of Point Reyes National Seashore.* Coastal Parks Association.
4. Ingles, L. G. 1965. *Mammals of the Pacific States.* Stanford University Press.
5. Museum of Vertebrate Zoology, University of California, Berkeley: Mammal collection as of 27 January 1986.
6. Scammon, C. M. 1874. *The Marine Mammals of the Northwestern Coast of North America.* San Francisco: John Carmany and Sons.

INDEX

For scientific names of species, see Species Lists, pp. 189–217.
Page numbers for subjects of illustrations and photographs are in **bold**.